SIGNS OF THE WALI

NARRATIVES AT THE SACRED SITES IN PAMIJAHAN, WEST JAVA

SIGNS OF THE WALI

NARRATIVES AT THE SACRED SITES IN PAMIJAHAN, WEST JAVA

Tommy Christomy

Published by ANU E Press
The Australian National University
Canberra ACT 0200, Australia
Email: anuepress@anu.edu.au
This title available online at: http://epress.anu.edu.au/wali_citation.html

National Library of Australia
Cataloguing-in-Publication entry

Author: Christomy, Tommy, 1959-
Title: Signs of the wali [electronic resource] : narratives at the sacred sites in Pamijahan, West Java / author, Tommy Christomy.
Publisher: Canberra : ANU E Press, 2008.
ISBN: 9781921313691 (pbk.) 9781921313707 (web)
Notes: Bibliography.
Subjects: Islam and culture--Indonesia--Java.
Muslim saints--Indonesia--Java.
Islamic shrines--Indonesia--Jawa Barat.
Sundanese (Indonesian people)--Rites and ceremonies.
Sundanese literature--History and criticism.
Saints in literature.
Dewey Number: 899.22209

All rights reserved. No part of this publication may be reproduced, stored in a retrieval system or transmitted in any form or by any means, electronic, mechanical, photocopying or otherwise, without the prior permission of the publisher.

Cover design by ANU E Press

This edition © 2008 ANU E Press

Islam in Southeast Asia Series

Theses at The Australian National University are assessed by external examiners and students are expected to take into account the advice of their examiners before they submit to the University Library the final versions of their theses. For this series, this final version of the thesis has been used as the basis for publication, taking into account other changes that the author may have decided to undertake. In some cases, a few minor editorial revisions have made to the work. The acknowledgements in each of these publications provide information on the supervisors of the thesis and those who contributed to its development. For many of the authors in this series, English is a second language and their texts reflect an appropriate fluency.

This publication — based on the thesis originally submitted in January 2003 for the Degree of Doctor of Philosophy at The Australian National University — is a substantially revised volume.

Table of Contents

Foreword	xi
1. Introduction	1
Custom: *Tali Paranti*	1
B. Going to Pamijahan	4
C. Signs	6
D. Narratives	9
E. Research Questions	15
F. Volume Structure	17
2. Signs in the Valley	19
3. Manuscripts in Pamijahan: *Kakantun Karuhun*	25
A. Introduction	25
A Shattariyyah Manuscript (ms. A)	27
A Shattariyyah Manuscript (ms. B)	29
A Shattariyyah Manuscript (ms. C)	30
A Shattariyyah Manuscript (ms. D)	31
Kitab Istiqal Tarekat Qadiriyyah-Naqhsabandiyyah (ms. E)	32
A Shattariyyah Manuscript (ms. F)	35
Babad Pamijahan (Ms. G)	36
Babad Pamijahan (Ms. H)	36
Conclusion	37
4. The *Babad Pamijahan*: Sunda, Java and the Identity of the Pamijahanese	39
A. Introduction	39
B. The *Babad* in Sunda	41
C. The *Babad Pamijahan* (BP)	42
D. Translation of The *Babad Pamijahan* (Ms H)	44
E. The Structure of the *Babad*	47
F. The Narrative of East and West	47
G. The Horizontal Axis	48
H. The Vertical Axis	50
I. *Saur Sepuh* or 'What the Ancestors Say...'	52
J. The References	56
K. Space and Place: Limestone (*Karang*)	57

L. The Interpretant: The East and The West	58
M. Sumedang and Mataram	60
N. Conclusion	62
5. *Karuhun,* Space, Place and Narratives	65
A. Introduction	65
B. *Karuhun*	66
C. The Sacred Landscape of Pamijahan and its Environs	68
D. Four Symbolic Spaces	71
E. *Kokocoran* and the Notion of Proximity	74
F. The Places	77
G. Mystical Paths	81
H. Conclusion: The Growing Signs	85
6. Linking to the Wider Worlds of Sufism	91
A. Introduction	91
B. The Roots of Shattariyyah	92
C. The Shattariyyah Order in the World of Islam	94
D. The Shattariyyah *Silsilah* in Indonesia	95
E. The Shattariyyah *Silsilah* in West Java	99
F. Shaykh Abdul Muhyi	99
G. The Successors	103
H. Conclusion	108
7. Grasping the Wali's Teaching	111
A. Introduction	111
B. Origins of Shattariyyah Teaching	116
C. *Martabat Tujuh* or The Seven Grades	116
D. Conclusion	126
8. Tapping A Blessing in The House of A Young Sufi	129
A. Introduction	129
B. Holding the Line, Grasping the Blessing	129
C. The *Zawiya*	133
D. The Communal Congregation	137
E. The *Baiah* Session	143
F. The Shattariyyah *Dikir*	147
G. Conclusion: Telling Stories, Taking Precedence	149
9. Pilgrimage at Pamijahan: Practice and Narrative	157

A. Introduction	157
Mediation or Approach	159
C. Custodianship	162
D. Pilgrims	169
E. The sequence of rituals	172
F. The Prescribed Sequences	186
10. Conclusion	193
Glossary	195
	203
Bibliography	211
Original Acknowledgments for the Thesis	219

Foreword

Signs of the Wali is a remarkable study. It focuses on a place of pilgrimage (*ziarah*) — Pamijahan in Tasikmalaya — that is of great historical significance for the foundations of Islam on Java. Pamijahan is the burial site of Shakyh Abdul Muhyi, the prominent exponent and noted teacher of Sufi Order, Shattiriyyah. Through its custodians, who oversee the places of visitation for an ever increasing number of pious visitors, Pamijahan retains its links to the past while endeavouring to propagate the message of Islam in a changing contemporary context.

In *Signs of the Wali*, Dr Tommy Christomy charts his personal intellectual journey. A study initially conceived of as a philological exploration of historical manuscripts was transformed into a study of 'living manuscripts' — the contemporary narratives of the custodians (*juru kunci* or *kuncen*) at Pamijahan. In a growing body literature on the study of *ziarah* in Indonesia and elsewhere in the Islamic world, this study is a milestone. It is a study of depth and nuance written with an understanding of the past but with an equal understanding of modern-day Sundanese language and culture. It is sophisticated in its approach to literary and semiotic analysis and incorporates anthropological acumen that provides an essential context.

Signs of the Wali also offers vital insights into the past and present role of Sufi orders (*tarekat*) in West Java. As elsewhere in the Islamic world, *tarekat* and *ziarah* intersect in popular practice at Pamijahan. Dr Christomy explores this intersecting world, explaining the steps of his own research investigations that enfold as a journey of discovery as he proceeds. This investigation involves the search for traces of *Tarekat* Shattiriyyah in Pamijahan, given the pervasive presence of *Tarekat* Qadirriyah-Nashabandiyyah throughout Tasikmalaya. That *Tarekat* Shattiriyyah survives to this day is itself evidence of the tenacity that its historical roots have established in a particular place.

Good research sets directions and opens avenues for more inquiries. Dr Christomy's works suggests a range of possibilities for further research on the sacred sites, oral history and the transmission of Islamic knowledge in specific social contexts in Indonesia generally and in Java in particular. One hopes that this study will prompt more critical investigations that continue these invaluable efforts.

With initial degrees from the Faculty of Letters at the University of Indonesia, Dr Chistomy took up a position as Associate Professor at Hankuk University of Foreign Studies in Seoul shortly after submitting his doctoral dissertation in Southeast Asian Studies at The Australian National University. He has now returned to the University of Indonesia where he holds the position of Senior

Lecturer in the Faculty of Humanities. This appointment gives him an admirable vantage point for conducting further research along the lines he has set forth.

James J. Fox

Chapter 1: Introduction

Custom: *Tali Paranti*

On a Thursday evening in mid-July 1972, close to the time of the *maghrib* or sunset prayers, my grandmother ordered me to go and pick seven different kinds of flower buds from the gardens in people's backyards in our village. She also told me to go to the small shop on the edge of the village to buy a fine cigar, or *surutu*. When I returned with the flower buds and the cigar she led me to a room located in the farthermost back part of our house where our paddy was stored between seasons. She asked me to put the buds in a bowl filled with the spring water that spouted from from a bamboo pipe, or *pancuran,* in the back yard. She then burned incense, *menyan*. For a minute, we remained silent as the smoke and the aroma of the incense wafted out through narrow spaces in the bamboo walls and roof. Meanwhile the call to prayer, the *adzan*, had sounded. The boys of my village, in their checked sarongs and black caps (*pecis*) made their way to a small mosque for the *shalat* prayers. The whole village was enveloped in serenity as we prayed, the women at home and the men and boys at the mosque.

Times moved on. Grandma, who in her daily activities was a small *batik* cloth trader, or *tukang batik,* in the Tasikmalaya market, was faced with financial difficulties. Her partner had asked her to give him a certificate of land title to be deposited in the bank as surety for a loan. Then, instead of acquiring additional capital to develop the business, she experienced the most horrible episode of her life. She was summoned to court by the bank. It turned out that her partner had been unable to return the money he had borrowed and that Grandma, as the guarantor, had to pay it back herself.

All the members of my family were in a panic because the land comprised 90% of their assets. Grandma came to me and asked me to accompany her in her ancient car, a 1948 Morris. We travelled to various sacred sites and visited some prominent clerics, or *kiai,* of West Java. The purpose was clear: to find a way, *neangan tarekah. Tarekah*[1] is a Sundanese word which is close to the term *turuq* or the 'way of the orders' in Sufism. Grandma's *tarekah* was simply to find a way to solve her problem, not to perform any mystical practices. Visiting holy sites, spending a night in vigil in a sacred tomb and in the boarding house nearby were the main items in our itinerary.

We returned home to the village with lists of mystical chants written in Arabic, which were considered to be amulets. We were in a slightly more optimistic mood. Having travelled through the interior of the southern part of West Java, which in the 1970s had not yet been touched by paved hot-mix roads, or even a single concrete path, Grandma returned with her spirit refreshed. Several months later, the court found that Grandma's partner had falsified the lease documents from the bank. After a year of struggling in court, Grandma won the case and got her titles to the family land back.

Ten years after the court case, as a young man, I went to the University of Indonesia in Jakarta to study Indonesian literature. During holidays, I frequently spent my days in the village where Grandma had retired from being a *tukang batik*. Most of her life was now dedicated to reading the Qur'an in study sessions (*pengajian*) in the village. I often asked her about the seven kinds of flower buds, the bowl of water and the cigar in the rice store. Her answers never satisfied me. She replied that she "just followed the *tali paranti*." In Sundanese, *tali* means a rope made from bamboo or the bark of a tree, *paranti* means a device, a tool, or custom. Thus, *tali paranti* is the string or rope taken from culture which is used to tie everything that is scattered: it is custom. I myself had an upbringing in the same culture as my grandmother, the customs of the traditional Sundanese Islam of Tasikmalaya.

Grandma also used to perform an old ritual to purify the rice harvested in a season. Some Sundanese still retain ritual practices related to the myth of Dewi Sri, the female deity who introduced the cultivation of rice to the people of Sunda (Wessing 1974: 207). From the point of view of the anthropology of Islam, as demonstrated by Geertz (1960/1976), Grandma's narratives could be see as examples of the syncretic incorporation of Islam into the local environment. With respect to Sundanese society, Newland (2001) and Muhaimin (Muhaimin 1995:4-7) have taken the discussion further on the consequences of Geertz's concepts (1976). Exploring the three famous cultural categories proposed by Geertz of *priyayi*, *santri*, and *abangan* (Geertz 1976: 121, 227), Newland (2001) sees local Islam in West Java, particularly in the area around Garut, about 70 km from Pamijahan, as mainly syncretic.

However, the term 'syncretism' is in fact not as clear as crystal, at least not for Muhaimin, who studied Islamic practices in Cirebon, about 200 km to the North of Pamijahan (1995). Muhaimin (1995: 109) tries to comprehend the issue from a different angle, that of the concept of *ibadah*, or serving God. Instead of identifying a particular ritual action in Islam as syncretic or as part of *abangan* or *santri* practice, he uses two terms of exegesis: *ibadah* or not *ibadah*. A local custom can be transformed semiotically into a religiously acceptable act of Islamic *ibadah*. Thus various local practices may be identified as heretical and syncretic, but from the devotee's point of view this may not necessarily be the case. Often the devotee's *intention* may be overlooked. In Islam, particularly in the Syafe'i school of jurisprudence, intention (*niat*) should initiate a ritual, and the intention should even be pronounced clearly in the heart and on the lips. There is no *ibadah* without intention.

Introduction

In the case of my story, some parts of Granmda's *tali paranti* were capable of being transformed into *ibadah* when she intended them to serve God. The demarcation of sacred and profane is fine because a particular act may be recognised as *ibadah* in certain circumstances but in others as non-*ibadah*. The contrast between *tali paranti* and 'religion', as stated in my grandmother's narratives then still leaves room for debate. Such narratives are easily found among the Sundanese, and even throughout the islands of Java. This phenomenon reflects the intersection between *tali paranti* and religion, and between these two poles there are people who create and produce narratives in order to comprehend the scattered 'signs' (Parmentier 1994 and 1997) around them.

Throughout this volume, I will discuss the nature and function of narratives at the sacred sites of Pamijahan or Safarwadi near Tasikmalaya in West Java. The *wali* in the title of my study, Shaykh Abdul Muhyi (1640-1715), was a holy man who still today mediates the wishes of the people of Pamijahan, as well as those of the pilgrims who come to the site from other areas. A negotiation occurs there between an ideal and reality, and this perpetuates the existence of Pamijahan as an important sacred site. To a large extent, this significance is found in the narratives relating to the site. By narrative, I mean a mode of communication in which people make an attempt to comprehend their various experiences within a framework of represented time. Narratives, predominantly the narratives of the *wali*, tow the past into the present.

This volume is a study of traditional narratives which are recited and received both by villagers and pilgrims in regard to the local pilgrimage (*ziarah*) tradition in Pamijahan, particularly at Shaykh Abdul Muhyi's sacred site. The narratives will be examined as part of the popular beliefs of Priangan Timur or the eastern part of West Java. Locating them in the wider context of Sundanese oral and written traditions, my investigation will illuminate the nature and function of such traditions in the particular case of Pamijahan.

The research will elucidate the role of the *kuncen*, the custodians of sacred sites, as guides and spiritual brokers who maintain the narratives. It will also be important to investigate the villagers' as well as visitors' view of the *kuncen* in regard to local pilgrimage. The study will also enhance comparative studies concerned with networks of holy men or saints (*wali*) on the island of Java (Pemberton 1994; Fox 1991: 20). I want to argue that people respond to, and participate in, saint veneration on pragmatic grounds. However, these grounds are subject to interpretation and contestation in time and space. In redefining their narratives, various individuals, such as custodians, Sufis, and even to some extent government functionaries, are considered to be authoritative persons by virtue of their capacity to conduct and manipulate narratives. As this argument develops, it will be important to understand the modes of signification in the village.

B. Going to Pamijahan

I was brought up about 70 km from Pamijahan, the site of my fieldwork. The traditions of this village are not totally unfamiliar to me. After the sunset *maghrib* prayers, the leader (*imam*) of the congregation in the small mosque where I lived in Kampung Benda, Tasikmalaya, often recited a ritual *hadiyah*. This is a chant presented as a gift to the Prophet Muhammad, his companions, to a *wali*, or to relatives who have passed away. The name of Shaykh Abdul Muhyi was one of the names recited in this ritual *hadiyah*. My family and neighbours occasionally went on pilgrimages to Pamijahan. I myself went to Pamijahan for the first time when I was an undergraduate student. Subsequently I went there several more times, accompanying colleagues and relatives as they undertook pilgrimages.

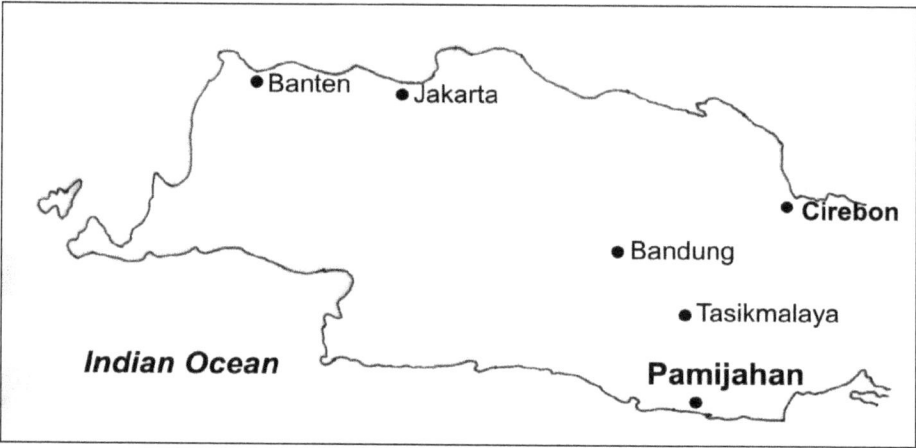

Figure 1. Pamijahan, West Java

I came to Pamijahan for research in August 1996, initially spending almost seven months in the village. For the first three months, I stayed in a house belonging to the younger brother of a site custodian, a *kuncen*. However, in December 1996, I received a personal grant to do library research on Shaykh Abdul Muhyi's manuscripts in Leiden, the Netherlands, for a month, and I left the village. In March 1997 I returned to Pamijahan for another three months. At this time, a young Pamijahan scholar, Kang Undang, a graduate of State Institute of Islamic Studies in Bandung (IAIN Sunan Gunung Jati) and an immediate descendant of Abdul Muhyi, offered me shelter.

The first three months of my fieldwork in Pamijahan were spent getting oriented, undertaking a census, making maps and conducting interviews, both open and structured, with pilgrims. I called my field strategy *makan bubur panas,* or "sipping hot rice porridge". I started eating, as it were, from the edge, beginning with peripheral and marginal issues and proceeding gradually to the crucial, sacred and 'hot' topics in the village. I conducted my first interviews in

Panyalahan, a fringe hamlet in the village complex of Pamijahan, and only later moved on to interviews in Pamijahan proper. In the view of villagers, Panyalahan is a less sacred site than Pamijahan. However, as I will discuss later, Panyalahan often challenges the authority of Pamijahan.

At this stage in my work, I had the opportunity to interview the old *kuncen* of Panyalahan as well as his predecessor. Both have now passed away. I also had access for the first time to Panyalahan's sacred manuscripts. My reason for pursuing the *makan bubur panas* strategy was that I had to obtain a smooth entry to the village by first learning its various modes of signification without intruding into village affairs. For this reason I conducted only open interviews, allowing informants to talk as long as they wanted. I did not interrupt what they had to say unless there were technical reasons to do so.

For the next three months after I had gathered initial data from Panyalahan in the outer areas of Pamijahan, I focused on Pamijahan itself. For several reasons gathering data in Pamijahan was not easy. Some of prominent custodians, the *kuncen* or key bearers, had encountered bad experiences with students and university researchers who had come to the village a year before. They felt scrutinised, spied on, and disturbed by the bombardment of questions regarding the legitimacy of *ziarah* and the relationship of *ziarah* to Islamic doctrines. It is widely known that reformist Islamic organizations such as the Muhammadiyah and Persatuan Islam (Persis) do not agree with local *ziarah* practices in rural areas. Neither the *kuncen* nor the villagers wanted to be subjected to this endless delicate debate. Their reluctance to be drawn into such debates is not because they lack the knowledge to engage in them, but because, according to them, it would be a waste of time and disruptive to their lives. More than that, they later confessed to me that some researchers had removed certain written materials from the village. One *kuncen* asked me to go to Tasikmalaya to find a manuscript 'borrowed' four months before by a lecturer from the university in Tasikmalaya. Slowly I learned what to do and what not to do in the village.

So it was helpful not to ask difficult structured questions in the first stages of my fieldwork but rather to present myself as a student who wanted to know the teachings of the ancestors by allowing the villagers to perform as 'teachers'. I did not make critical field notes in front of them but rather allowed the local people to teach and tell. However, I was learning about iconic, indexical, and symbolical signs through their stories, performances, rituals, and other socially recognised acts. Rather than provoking them with structured questions, I simply joined in their daily schedule.

Informants often invited me to go to chat and smoke with them in a small shelter in the neighbourhood called Batu Ngijing near the Pamijahan river. The villagers of Pamijahan are forbidden to smoke in the inner sacred territory of the village (see Chapter 5) so they move to a less sacred area to gather and relax after a day in the paddy fields or working as guides for pilgrims. This unassuming spot is important in village affairs. It has become an informal place of assembly where people discuss issues in their village. Thanks to my frequent presence in this place, I found myself often invited to the homes of key persons in local Sufi orders and in the guild of site custodians (*pakuncenan*).

The final stage of my fieldwork was quite different from the previous ones. I had to check the validity of some crucial categories. For me, this was the most challenging phase because now I had to provoke the villagers with a host of structured questions. It was at this stage that I asked for permission to attend Sufi rituals and received permission to see inside the tomb of Shaykh Abdul Muhyi. It was also at this stage that issues of precedence and contestation in village society became evident. This was the most difficult phase of my work because I had to understand this contestation without disturbing villagers' daily activities. I also had to study a Sufi manual, a process that could only occur under the guidance of a Sufi master. In March 1997, I returned to Canberra but again in January 2000 went back to Pamijahan, updating my data and gathering new information from the village itself and from government offices in Tasikmalaya.

Essentially my research was an exercise in the implementation of, and testing of, a semiotic approach to the understanding of culture within the scholarly tradition initiated by the American philosopher C.S. Peirce (1839-1914). This meant pursuing the Peircean notion that signs have three key dimensions: representamen, referent and interpretant. I set out to collect data on the properties of representamens in Pamijahan. I then strove to comprehend their references based on the assumptions of the villagers. Finally, I tried to reach an understanding of the relationship between representamens and their reference within the complex discourse and interpretation of the interpretants there. This is the framework which informs the structure of the volume.

C. Signs

Following the penetration of cultural studies and the humanities by the legacy of Saussure, Peirce has now been 're-invented' by a diverse group of scholars but not exclusively associated with the university of Chicago (cf. Sebeok 1997). Semiotics has become widely known as the 'science of signs' or, if not a science, it is a method of unveiling signification in the production of signs (Eco 1979: 32, 1999: 12). Saussure and Peirce, the two founders of semiotics, were interested in the nature of signs in our lives, but they developed different theoretical frameworks. Saussure is better known as a structuralist while Peirce is, according to his followers, a proponent of pragmatics (Parmentier 1987, 1994 and 1997).

Saussurean structuralist semiotics focuses on the binary relation within signs between a 'signifier' and a 'signified', though there is no compulsory relation between the form of the signifier and its signified reference. The meaning of signs is derived from 'differences' or contrasts within a wider, total, synchronic, or timeless system. The Saussurean view has provided researchers in various areas with an explicit theoretical framework and the results, in many instances, have been marvellous. In the study of culture, Lévi-Strauss (Levi-Strauss 1968-1977) is the most prominent descendant of Saussurean semiotics. The utility of binary logic is seen most clearly in his famous essay on "The Story of *Asdiwal*". Lévi-Strauss developed linguistics-based Saussurean semiotics into structuralist anthropology by drawing on aspects of Russian formalism in his analysis of the story. The result is a schema or model. Unlike Saussure, who was deeply concerned with linguistic models, Lévi-Strauss goes further by proposing a model of social behaviour or social structure. A structure in Lévi-Strauss's view is similar to Saussure's concept of 'deep structure' in language which provides a 'schema' or a cognitive framework for the ordering of meaning. In other words, Lévi-Strauss and Saussure are more interested in studying the structure of phenomena on a synchronic level (*langue*) than phenomena in use (*parole*). Pragmatic semiotics (the study of phenomena in use) is derived from the theory of signs introduced by Peirce. He stresses the importance of semiosis in which signs can grow as human culture grows. Unlike Saussure who freezes the sign in synchronic analysis, Peirce locates signs within process and points explicitly to the importance of the 'interpretant'. This view is very important in understanding the complexity of culture, particularly in the post-modern and post-colonial period where Saussurean and Lévi-Straussean views of cognitive patterns are challenged by the rapidity of social and cultural transformations. For Peirce, the sign is accordingly fluid rather than frozen.

To comprehend Peirce's semiotics we have to know his main doctrine of the sign. According to Peirce, "A sign, or representamen, is something which stands to somebody for something in some respect or capacity…" (Noth 1990: 42) Accordingly, there are three conditions that permit a phenomenon to qualitfy as a sign. First, it should be come to our perception. Second, it should refer to a referent, and third, it should be interpretable or generate interpretation. Furthermore, signs should be anchored in a context and in time. The Saussurean paradigm omits agency or the subject in the process of semiosis, but Peirce opens the way to research on the interpretations made by people. (Rochberg-Halton 1986: 45-70)

Later theoretical investigation reveals that a process of signification not only deals with the conventionalised relation between signifier and signified but also other kinds of relations which provide the framework for other unintentional signs, both linguistic and non-linguistic (Eco 1979: 190-216). In other words, a process of communication cannot always be assumed to have just a 'sender' and 'receiver'. The signification can be actively engaged without the existence of a sender. In this regard, Clifford Geertz (1973) asserts

> ...what Lévi-Strauss has made for himself is an infernal culture machine. It annuls history, reduces sentiment to a shadow of the intellect, and replaces the particular mind of particular savages in particular jungles with the Savage Mind immanent in us all (1973:355).

In his *Religion of Java* (1960/1976) Clifford Geertz answers the shortcomings of Saussurean structuralism by utilising local knowledge. Unlike Lévi-Strauss and Saussure, he focuses on *parole* rather than *langue*. The variants of Javanese religion are a fabulous example of his phenomenological framework. If we follow structuralist semiotics, the main project in Pamijahan would focus on linear and contrastive analyses of signs, finding the regularity underlying the system of signs functioning in the area. It would be like studying a building by making inventories, classifications and generalisations in order to get a view of the structure behind the building. This project would not be interested in the 'cultivation' of signs where the building might later be used by other tenants, or be sold, or even be neglected. Yet, in reality there is much opportunity for the owner of the signs and for the receiver of the signs to negotiate or to make transactions regarding the building, or structure. This does not mean that our knowledge of the formal regulation of the building is unnoteworthy. It is just a choice we make.

There is no room in this volume to detail further the intersections and disjunctions between the views of Saussure and Peirce. I am not concerned with the debate about the nature of signs but rather will refer to their work in general terms for the important insights it gives into the signification process in the society of Pamijahan. The utility of Peircean semiotics in studying culture, to some extent, has been drawn upon by Turner (1967) and Geertz (1976) even though these masters of 'cultural performative' and 'interpretative' analysis do not mention explicitly the connection between their analytical frameworks and Peirce's work (Parmentier 1997: 13-14). Both Turner and Geertz apply an analytical framework that to some extent displays triadic concepts similar to those of Peirce (Colapietro 1996, Mertz 1985). Accordingly both Turner and Geertz can also be located in the domain of pragmatism where the problem of 'subject' or 'agency' is central. Geertz's fascinating 'thick description' is seen as a preliminary semiotic project in anthropology. As argued by Parmentier (Parmentier 1997), Geertz' interpretative study is lacking in the area of epistemology.

> His work does not advance the technical grasp of semiotic anthropology. His work does not advance the technical grasp of the types and classification of sign relations; his ethnographic demonstrations fail to explore the structure of semiotic codes as presupposed systems of interpretants. ...his focus on textually mediated self-understanding neglects the powerful ways that symbols can be manipulated to constrain,

confuse, and control the understanding of those not in a privileged position in a society. The Geertzean program of a 'natural history of signs and symbols, an ethnography of vehicles of meaning (1983:118) is only the prologue to a full-fledged semiotic anthropology (Parmentier 1997, 13-14).

To follow Parmentier's argument, Geertz's interpretive legacy does not provide the student of culture with a strong analytical tool. In my view, Geertz (especially 1993 and 1973) is able to fill a gap in the Saussurean tradition by accessing local knowledge, making it a cultural category that can be compared and tested by other scholars or researchers. However, Geertz's lack of explicit analytical unities (Geertz 1973) makes his interpretative program difficult to imagine for the student of semiotics or anthropology. His famous categorisation of the variants of Javanese religion is a good example of how problematic this issue can be. Recent studies argue that what has been drawn by Geertz in the *Religion of Java,* the *santri, priyayi,* and *abangan* categories, are not strict iconic or indexical signs referring to certain domains in Javanese culture but rather 'fluid' and 'cultivated' signs (Bachtiar 1992). In my perspective, this gap can be filled by pragmatic semiotics where signs flow through the times.

If customs, or *tali paranti* are seen as signs, they can be examined in terms of three semiotic levels. The first is as signs as people understand them. The second is the position of the signs in relation to other signs in the same cultural framework. The third is the way signs are used in everyday life. Turner's 'ritual forest' (Turner 1967), for instance, to some extent reflects the triadic dimension of the Peircean sign: icon, index, and symbol (see also Rochberg-Halton 1986; Parmentier 1997).

D. Narratives

The study of narrative has passed beyond the borders of the discipline of literature (Prickett 2002:2). An economist recognising the importance of narrative states "Economists cannot predict much, and certainly cannot predict profitability. If they were so smart they would be rich" (McCloskey 1990:10). McClosky claims that economists work partly as storytellers whose studies would be better if their explanations could be shown in accepted narrative form. The same argument has been used by Jackson in the field of legal practice. (Jackson 1990: 27) Jackson found that judicial mechanisms are undoubtedly influenced by strategies employed in narrative. The jury is not concerned with the relevant facts only but also with "the manner of telling the evidence". He gives the example of middle class witnesses who tend to be called rather than people of a marginal class because jurors, who also come mainly from the middle class, can easily 'translate' such witnesses' stories. The same narrative mode is found in historical writing. White (1986) asserts that historians describe events according to stock narratives which live in society or in the minds of readers. In other words, narrative can be found in every domain of culture so that, according to Miller "Nothing seems more natural and universal to human beings than the telling of stories". (Miller 1990: 66) It is arguable then that narrative has penetrated different disciplines in spite of the fact that 'narrative' as an epistemological unit has been overtly neglected by disciplines other than cultural studies and the humanities (Kreiswirth 2000: 293-294).

However, the disciplines of rhetoric, literary studies, sociolinguistics and anthropology have produced a vast array of literature studying homo-*fabula*. In this volume I shall not describe the historical study of narrative but rather discuss the utility of narrative frameworks, particularly those influenced by semiotics. These theoretical departures are relevant in clarifying the nature of narrative in traditional societies where characteristically narrators and audiences interact intensively.

Structuralism has led literary studies into the spirit of scientific inquiry, where critics seek to find a model of a particular genre based on various works studied in the light of structures. They try, for instance, to find universal plots. Northrop Frye's book, *The Anatomy of Criticism* (1969) is based on such assumptions. His followers such as Scholes (1974) modify the framework by focusing on how narrative changes over time. They found that changes only occur on the level of social topics, while the stock of characters and actions remains fundamentally stable. They set up a hypothetical, deductive method based on their assumptions about the nature of narrative, which they have applied and tested on particular literary narratives. Collective awareness is a crucial point of departure for the structuralist: societies are recognised as have an underlying mechanism to organise and classify experience. Following Lévi-Strauss, myth, with its paradigmatic deep structures, is the primary source of meaning (Harari 1979: 19-21).

Somewhat later, post structuralism tried to modify the work of its predecessors; post-structuralists are structuralists aware of their previous mistakes. They argue that literary meaning not only depends on the material content of texts but also on the meaning created by the readers (Culler 11975b:192). On such assumptions, narrative theorists have expanded their frameworks to incorporate reader response. Such an approach resembles communication theory which, in some respects, has provided a foundation for theorising the role of the reader. The audience can grasp meaning only in the complete utterance. Messages are delivered through a particular context of references and codes. Communication also rests on contact between the sender and receiver. Reader response approaches develop a perspective of narrative by "producing its own 'reader' and 'listener'. In creating meaning, readers use their own conventions to understand a narrative or a text (Culler, 1975b: 192). In the last few decades, there has been an emergence of Jakobsonian and Peircean frameworks for studying 'narrative in culture' in the Austronesian region as found in the work of Fox and Parmentier.

James Fox, in his study of Rotinese narratives (Fox 1986), provides a good example of how structuralism must be anchored in context. In Roti, structure is often negotiated and used differently according to a context of 'precedence'. A metaphor of itinerary in Rotinese narratives, which has created a 'trajectory and sedimented path' in society, is subject to multivocality in daily practices (Fox 1997:6).

I apply the semiotic-anthropological perspective of Fox and Parmentier to Pamijahan for several reasons. The nature and function of narrative in Pamijahan are very different from narrative as it is conceived by modern Indonesian literary scholars, where fictionality, stylistics, aesthetics, canon and genre have been important foci.

Indonesian and Malay critics of literature are to some extent indebted to Winstedt who, unlike Dutch scholars, at an early stage attempted to theorise the concept of literature (*sastra*) in the Malay world in his History of *Classical Malay Literature* (Winstedt 1969). On the first page, Winstedt states clearly what *sastra* is and how it is related to history.

> Literature strictly came into being with the art of writing, but long before letters were shaped, there existed the material of literature, words spoken in verse to waken emotion by the beauty of sound and words spoken in prose to appeal to reason by the beauty of sense... (Winstedt 1969, 1)

So *sastra* should 'appeal to reason by the beauty of sense'. The simple syllogism that 'what is not beautiful is not *sastra*' applies. Winstedt's definition is useful for the discussion of the verse forms of the *pantun* and *syair*, or Malay romances, because these genres are regulated by the 'canon of beauty'. However, undergraduate students in Indonesia may be somewhat confused when they glance through *A History of Classical Malay Literature*. Within his concept of 'beauty', Winstedt includes a range of various written and oral genres to which 'canon', 'fictionality' (in Rene Wellek's terms, 1976/8), authorship, and other Western literary concepts cannot easily be applied. In what terms can we define the concept of beauty in, say, the Malay romance *Hikayat Sama'un* on one hand, and the 'theological catechisms' written by Nur al-Din al-Raniri in 17th century Aceh on the other?

Furthermore, another difficulty met by the student lies in historically based definitions like *sastra modern* and *sastra lama*, or 'modern literature' vs 'classical literature'. The mere concept of *sastra tradisional*, or 'traditional literature' is fraught with difficulty. For example, there is an implicit suggestion in Winstedt's book that any written material not published in Latin script by some 'publishing house' or other, or not printed on a 'Gutenberg machine' should be classified as 'classical literature'. Winstedt is probably right, if he is taking his definition from the dictionary of Malay compiled by Wilkinson. Wilkinson (1959:1025) states that the term *sastera* is originally from Sanksrit *shastra,* meaning the Hindu sacred books, or in the Malay Archipelago, books of divination and astrological tables.

The word *sastra*, or literary work, in the contemporary Indonesian context is equally ambiguous. Critics divide *sastra* into two main categories based on period, patronage, content, and canon. These are *sastra lama* (old literature) and *sastra modern* (modern literature). *Sastra lama* is associated with literary works written in pre-modern Indonesia. Zuber Usman (1963: 9) defines *kesusastraan lama* as "literary works produced before Abdullah bin Abdulkadir Munsyi". The reason is simply that Abdullah had departed from tradition and his literary expression, in content and style, was close to that of daily life. He states:

> ...pokok jang ditjeritakannya sudah agak berlainan dengan jang ditjeritakan oleh pengarang-pengarang sebelumnja. ... Tentang tjeritranya bukan lagi mentjeritrakan dewa-dewa, raksasa-raksasa atau dongeng jang muluk-muluk dengan puterinya jang tjantik djelita serta dengan istananja jang indah permai... Abdullah mentjeritakan kehidupannya sendiri.... (Usman 1963: 9-11)

> ...the story told is different from those of previous authors (in 'old literature')... The story is no longer about the gods, giants, or fabulous fairy tales with beautiful princesses and magnificent castles... Abdullah tells about his own world...

Thus, the *Hikayat Sri Rama, Tuhfat al-Nafis, Babad Tanah Jawi, Babad Pajajaran, Sejarah Melayu* can all be found under the one heading of *sastra lama*. On the other hand, students reading Teeuw's *Modern Indonesian Literature* (1979) are led to believe that Pramoedya Ananta Toer's *Bumi Manusia* and Achdiat K. Mihardja's *Atheis* are examples of *sastra Indonesia modern*, Indonesian modern literature, because they were written after the creation of the modern Indonesian state. Clearly the boundaries between 'modern' and 'pre-modern' literature represent more ideologically loaded categories than definitions according to internal literary properties. Furthermore, there is a tendency for critics and literary students to pay more attention to the aesthetics and canonicity of the texts. Thus in modern Indonesian literature, as in Western literature, there are *belles lettres* and pulp works (also called *sastra pop* or *sastra picisan*) and in the category of traditional literature there is chronicle, fable, myth and legend. A work of literature may be seen solely as an artistic work without any reference to the real world, or it may be perceived as having reference in the real world. There are many debates in the weekly columns of newspapers addressing these issues, for example whether a particular work is good enough to be classified as *karya sastra* or not.

Such notions about modern Indonesian literature seem to be alien when applied to so-called *sastra lama*. I once acted as an examiner in an honours level examination, or *ujian sarjana*, in literary studies in the Faculty of Letters of the University of Indonesia. I put a simple question to the student candidate: what is literature? One of the main variables in literary studies - a variable important to my discussion here - is 'fiction' or fictionality (in Indonesian *rekaan*). Literature is fiction! Because I had been trained in 'old' Indonesian literature and philology, I brought to the examination three kinds of manuscript: the *Hikayat Sri Rama* (a Malay romance), the *Sejarah Melayu* (a chronicle) and *Hill al-Zill* (a mystical work on the 'Shadow of God' in the world). I asked whether these manuscripts were literature. The answers were interesting enough to be outlined here. The *Hikayat Sri Rama*, said the candidate, is a work of literature (*karya sastra*), the *Sejarah Melayu* is a work of historical literature (*sastra sejarah*), and *Hill al-Zill* is a work of literature (*karya sastra*) but not fiction. My student was rather hesitant to describe the last one because she had previously defined *karya sastra* as fiction. *Hill al-Zill*, according to her reading of the manuscript was not fiction. Thus, she tactically redefined her answer. The student demonstrated her reliance on Wellek' book (Wellek 1955-1992) which had become the most famous text book in the Faculty in the late 1980s. It is devoted to the notion of fictionality in literary works.

What is *sastra* is not so easy to describe, not only for undergraduate students but also for literary critics and scholars. 'Fictional narrative' is made up, invented, a product of the imagination. For Lamarque however, 'fictional' narrative and 'factual' narrative resemble each other in terms of their "formal features - time, structure, voice, perspective; an in semantic features - truth, correspondence with the facts, or reference" (Lamarque, 1990; cf. Culler, 1975a). Ambiguous assumptions about traditional literature, *sastra tradisional,* and classical literature, *sastra lama*, need further explanation. Ambiguities are not only reflected in the definitions of the genres but also in the methodologies and frameworks applied to research on such materials. No doubt philologists have been among the principal agents providing us with information about these genres. Starting with the need for teaching materials for colonial administrators and missionaries, they collected and carefully studied written materials from the archipelago. In time, philological studies have made important contributions to defining what should be recognised as *sastra* and what not.

Sometimes problematic transmission occurs. Scribes may use various 'horizontal' or contemporaneous sources as materials to write their own 'hybrid' versions of a text. In Indonesia, the Dutch translated, transcribed, and transliterated texts from the local bibliotheca. The locals often retranslated or copied the Dutch version back into their tradition. Accordingly, Robson proposes that the main task of philology is 'making a text accessible' (Robson 1988) by trying to identify some putative 'original' lost in the past. However, the originality as often imagined by the 'stemma students' cannot be applied properly (e.g. Brakel 1977: 105:113). Works of traditional literature are created in 'open tradition' where originality and authorship are not crucial issues. In the eyes of the traditional communal society, the text should be useful, not just beautiful in Winstedt's terms.

Robson (1988) observes that the urge to demonstrate the usefulness of classical literature by Indonesian scholars is rather an emotive endeavour due to the notion of 'cultural heritage' (*warisan kebudayaan*). He states,

> In an Indonesian context this is especially emotive because it calls to mind those from whom one receives a 'warisan' (inheritance) - one's elders and ancestors, and it is well known that these are deserving of high respect, so that it becomes no less than a moral duty to care for what they have left behind for us, their living descendants… Indonesian scholars on the other hand like to point to the moral lessons to be found in classical literary works (Robson 1988, 6)

Robson's proposal has brought a new perspective to the study of Indonesian classical literature within a philological approach. However, 'reader expectation' is also problematic, particularly in the light of recent developments in post-colonial theory, where the task is to see post-colonial discourses from the point of view of colonized subjects. There is a legitimate post-colonial question that can be applied in the field of manuscript study in Indonesia: the necessity to re-read a discourse that is related to the colonized people but created in post-colonial times (Becker, 1989).

It is important to provide access to the wider world, but it is even more important to understand why a certain community might have no proper access to their own heritage. In this case, the Indonesian philologist, Sri Wulan Rujiati Mulyadi (1994:79) highlights the disappearance of manuscripts, their very extinction, or *kemusnahan naskah*. Mulyadi clarifies two kind of extinction: unintentional and intentional. Climate, natural disasters, and unskilled conservation practices cause the loss of manuscripts or deterioration in their quality (Mulyadi 1994: 79-86). But there is also a lot of evidence that manuscripts have also been burned during or seized for political reasons and borne off to overseas collections wars (Alfian 1987: 130-136). The Balinese and Achenese experienced a huge loss of manuscripts in their holy wars with the Dutch invaders. In the 19th century, when orientalist scholars and Christian missionaries travelled through the interior of Java, they too started collecting manuscripts. Indeed, these are legitimate questions regarding the manuscript acquisition. Even more than this, colonial policy in culture and education influenced what people should read and write in the archipelago. The dynamic intersection with colonial powers, war, national government policies, and pseudo collectors has created a number of 'lacunae' in the local bibliotheca.

We cannot stop the times. However, there is in all of this a critically important lesson for me as a responsible student of culture and philology, that is, to look at manuscripts which record various local narratives in the context of the communities that produced them (Becker 1995). In other words, the work of a diligent philologist should extend to the people, the scribes, and the communities that sustain these materials. Before I decided on Pamijahan as my field site, I had trekked through various old villages around Tasikmalaya and Garut in the southeastern quarter of West Java. I was confronted with a situation in which the main written narratives of villages had been removed from their local contexts by various agencies, whether deliberately or not. The people of Kampung Naga near Tasikmalaya, for example, told me that their connection to their past had been broken when what they called "the colonial apparatus" borrowed their manuscripts in the 1920s, and then when the army of the Darul Islam Movement burned their village in about 1959. The same situation also occurred in Pamijahan. Only a few manuscripts of good quality are now available for reading in the village. There is also the irony that when Indonesian Government tried to preserve traditional manuscripts by giving funding to the researchers, some researchers abused this by borrowing sacred manuscripts from villagers and 'forgetting' to return them. In other cases, the researchers copied manuscripts, giving the copies to the villagers while retaining the originals.

In Pamijahan and its neighbouring areas, there are a number of written and oral narratives about the past. These narratives are not only used in reading performances, or as manuals, or as cultural reference works but are also perceived as sacred 'signs of' and 'signs in' the past. It is very evident that the meaning of narratives is constructed through diverse decoding modes. Thus for my purposes, I will use the term 'narrative' instead of *sastra* for the narrative materials I encountered in Pamijahan.

E. Research Questions

Providing local narratives to 'the world' within philological projects is an important task that deserves attention. However, in the case of Pamijahan, it is also legitimate to go beyond the role of text provider. We can ask the question how do the villagers or the owners of the texts, or the scribes, relate to the references suggested by particular narratives? What role does a particular narrative have in local history? Who told, and who still tells, the stories? How does the group identity of the narrators affect this history? Which are the most important groups appreciating or listening to the stories? We can also posit other questions in temporal perspective. For example, how did the narratives develop? How have certain stories followed different paths of evolution? What impact do different narratives have on villagers' daily activities? What do certain narratives have to tell us about historical awareness? Which stories are crucial for villagers and which not? In addition, we might list still other legitimate questions on narratives, depending on our interest.

The 'Gutenberg' culture of print, colonialism, and the globalisation of information have penetrated to the level of local culture. Unlike the people of cosmopolitan societies who can easily and conveniently go to fine book stores or libraries or to the internet, the Pamijahanese have to understand their practice, ritual, identity and the past from the only available narrative sources in the village. They have to negotiate with the changing times and the external world, including a capitalistic mass media and often devious and predatory politicians. They have to comprehend all the scattered signs around them. More than that, they have to negotiate diverse signs, religious texts, *tali paranti*, the management of sacred sites, *ziarah* and *tarekat*. Their narratives are one of the media they possess to understand what is happening in and around their village. This volume builds on the various accounts of traditional narratives, popular practices and custom, or *tali paranti*, to address the following specific questions:

1. What narratives are the most important to the people of Pamijahan?[2]
2. What kinds of references are designated by the people's narratives?
3. How and why do the people of Pamijahan, as interpretants, make particular interpretations of these narratives?

My argument in relation to the first question is that the peoples' narratives are vastly more complex than is assumed in studies based on literary or philological approaches. In Pamijahan I observed that manuscripts are perceived not only as written materials but also as artefacts and as evidence in various cultural debates. All the important manuscripts preserved in the village are concerned with the founding of the village, Sufism, and pilgrimage, or they are collections of written amulets. Access to these manuscripts is generally only possible through ritual and initiation. Because this access is limited, there is room for manipulating the significance of the artefacts to bolster social precedence within the village. The manuscripts supply people with a cultural category related to the concept of space and place. To be a cultural representamen is to be approved by the *tali paranti* or 'grounding' of village culture. So my first question relates to the first dimension of Peircean semiotics where the properties of signs are questioned.

My argument concerning the second question – the semantic dimension or references of signs in the village - is that most narratives (or signs) in the village appear in three modes: as icon, index, and symbol. For most villagers a manuscript can exist as an iconic sign when it refers to the words of ancestors. In this guise, it is a 'sign in the past'. Such iconic references are found in the narratives of ancestors, 'the path', space, places, Sufism and pilgrimage (*ziarah*). The arrangement of spatial concepts and social structure carries reference to the ancestors' itinerary or the metaphors of kinship and the imagined space of the *pongpok* (sides). In this respect, iconic signs, whether present in narratives or in material artefacts of the culture, are oriented to the past without, to borrow Parmentier's words, "the actual spatio-temporal existence of the represented object" (Parmentier 1994). It is necessary to add that all narratives concerned with the village founders are also present in 'contiguity mode' or as indexical signs. The narratives in indexical modes function as a discourse or experience in the present of the Pamijahanese. They are narratives pertaining to the past but they tell about the references of the past from the point of view of present narrators. The written and oral material collected and broadcast by the guild of custodians are framed in this mode.

Finally, my research in Pamijahan suggests that the signs *of* the past and the signs *in* the past are not necessarily coherent and frozen. In fact, it reveals fluid signs where the *tali paranti*, ritual action and sacred text are continuously negotiated. The regimentation of meanings is often undertaken by the custodians at the sacred sites, but at the same time different groups in society contest this process by focusing on different source narratives. Precedence becomes a crucial topic in the village. More than that, the practice of pilgrimage in Pamijahan invites outsiders such as pilgrims, government functionaries and religious organizations to become involved in village affairs. There is no doubt that tradition and sacred narratives are thereby opened to pragmatic perception.

F. Volume Structure

This volume is divided into three main parts. The first part, Chapters 2 and 3, provides an overview of signs in the village of Pamijahan. Chapter 2 describes Pamijahan as a cultural domain and a modern political entity within the Republic of Indonesia. Chapter 3 describes in philological style the most important signs appearing in traditional written narratives. The discussion focusses on the manuscripts found in the village of Pamijahan and in neighbouring areas that are perceived by villagers as important references.

The second part of the volume, Chapter 4 to 7, examines the references of the signs, whether these appear in written or oral narrative form, in artefacts or in social performance. Chapter 4 describes the references of narratives based on their internal and external properties. The chapter argues that the formal synchronic and pragmatic regulation of the narrative of the ancestors is expressed schematically and iconically in the social structure of the village. Chapter 5 discusses a further implication of the references of narratives described in Chapter 4. In essence, this chapter argues that iconic signs are related to the itinerary of journeys undertaken by Shaykh Abdul Muhyi, the founding ancestor of the village. These signs become the references of the narratives of space. Chapters 6 and 7 discuss the nature and meaning of Sundanese Sufi narratives in the villagers' context. I argue that these narratives of Sufism not only connect the village to the wider world of the orders (*tarekat*) and of Sufi teachings but also have profound symbolic significance for those who hold the manuscripts in their possession. In sum, the second part of the volume examines the semantic dimension of narratives in the village. I argue that the references of the narratives are heavily contextualized by various modes and actions. The meaning of signs is not fixed and can appear in various modes of semiosis.

The third part of the volume examines the interpretants or the process of negotiation between people and the sacred signs in narratives by focusing on the phenomena of a Sufi order (*tarekat*) in Pamijahan and of pilgrimage (*ziarah*). Both *tarekat* and *ziarah* provide a dense web of signs and agencies. The main argument of these chapters is that the relationships between custom or *tali paranti*, religion and the people are complex. The concept of *ibadah,* the issue of precedence, popular practices, and external influences are all intermingled and shape the villagers' daily activities. Through these narratives, people try to comprehend this scattering of signs.

ENDNOTES

[1] I will use the term *tarekat* instead of Sufism.

[2] In Sundanese literary genres we find a number of terms that are associated with narrative, most notably *riwayat, carita, sajarah, babad, sasakala, dongeng* and *cario*s.

Chapter 2: Signs in the Valley

> This village was formerly a wild forest. No one lived here. Then came 'animist' urang Hindu[1] who performed witchcraft. Finally our holy man (wali) came here and defeated Batara Karang, the Hindu. These places become prosperous. Pilgrims come here without being invited because of the blessing of the holy man radiating from this place. (Custodian of Pamijahan, 1996)

In the Pamijahanese view, various signs significantly 'tow' the past into contemporary Pamijahan culture. Both verbal and non-verbal signs emerge as a configuration of propositions regarding ritual practice, ancestors and identities. They create cultural arguments subscribed to by the villagers. An example is given by the quotation above, made by an ordinary man as he chatted with pilgrims in a cafe stall outside the sacred space in the centre of Pamijahan. In the view of the people of Pamijahan, this space which was initially empty, was then crisscrossed by, borrowing Pannel's term (Pannell 1997:165) "various collective ordered representations".

All Pamijahanese share the same narrative regarding the early period of settlement in their village. The quotation mentions three important key words representing three episodes in the myth of Pamijahan, namely 'the wild forest', 'the animist', and 'the *wali*'. The climax of the narrative is in the third episode in which the *wali* brings Islam and grace to the people. He is a protagonist who is able to clear the land of its wildness and give the villagers identity and a moral foundation. This fragment of narrative refers to the conversion of Pamijahanese by Sufis in the 17th century. The villagers, accordingly, are very proud to be descendants of a Sufi saint. They established a cult springing from the family of the founding Sufi. Later they were able to extend this family cult incorporating into it the popular tradition called *ziarah* (pilgrimage to a holy man's gravesite). These phenomena clearly involve a process of transformation that needs construction and creativity.

According to one of the custodians in Pamijahan village, some time in the 1660s, a *wali* (holy man) from Mataram, at the end of a sacred journey, made a clearing in a wild forest in the southern area of West Java. In the course of doing this the *wali*, Shaykh Abdul Muhyi, fought with a local animist ruler known as Batara Karang who surrendered to the *wali* and was converted to Islam. He then continued his mission to find a sacred cave for meditation as his *guru* had instructed. After trekking through the forest, he found the cave in a hilly area. He called the place Safarwadi.

Today the custodians of Pamijahan say that the term Safarwadi[2] or 'walking in the valley' has a metaphorical meaning, namely that a human being should follow the right path as if traversing a muddy sloping riverbank. If he takes a wrong step, he will slide into deep misery. The metaphor in fact has become an important motif in Pamijahan culture, a motif which will be discussed in later chapters. After the death of Shaykh Abdul Muhyi people began to call the village after its river, Pamijahan. *Pamijahan*, according to them, means a natural fish hatchery *(lauk mijah)*.[3] After the *wali* settled in the valley, his fame was such that his followers swarmed to the valley like hatching fish.

In contemporary terms, *Pamijahan* refers to two different concepts. The first is a cultural concept referring to the area believed physically to be the place of various historically important artefacts *(patilasan)* and narratives of the *wali*. According to one of the custodians Pamijahan in this sense includes the area of the valley of Pamijahan and the surrounding mountains.

The second is a modern political concept. In this sense, Pamijahan refers to a village or *kelurahan*, the smallest unit of government. This area in turn consists of various sub villages *(kampung)*. The villagers themselves use 'Pamijahan' for the first concept and 'Desa Pamijahan' for the second. Pamijahan is led by the chief custodian *(kuncen)* of the tomb of Shaykh Abdul Muhyi, while the Desa Pamijahan is administered by the village head *(kepala desa)*. Following this distinction, in this study I use the term Pamijahan to refer to the first concept and Desa Pamijahan to the second. To complicate matters, there is also a Kampung Pamijahan which refers to one of the neighbourhoods or hamlets, a 'sub-village', within Desa Pamijahan.

Desa Pamijahan is in the southern part of the regency *(kabupaten)* of Tasikmalaya in the Priangan Timur area of West Java. Tasikmalaya is a prosperous regency covering an area of 2,751 square kilometres, and is divided into seven subdistricts *(kacamatan)*.

Tasikmalaya has been shaped by various Islamic movements in the course of its history. It was touched by Islamic rebellion in the 17th century promoted by the followers of Bantenese and Macassarese religious leaders who retreated there from the north coast. In 1945, there was a rebellion there instigated by the *Ajengan* [4] of Sukamanah in which hundreds of unarmed young Muslims were killed by the Japanese. Later, between 1956 and 1962 Tasikmalaya was a base for what is probably the best known of Indonesia's post-independence religious rebellions, that of the *Tentara Islam Indonesia* or *TII* (the Islamic Army of Indonesia) which fought for the realisation of *Darul Islam* or *DI*, a 'place for Islam' or an Islamic state in Indonesia. DI/TII was established by Kartosuwiryo, a Javanese who gained considerable support from the Sundanese elite in the more remote areas of West Java. Kartosuwiryo was able to combine Islamic spirit with a political and military movement. (Jackson 1980:27) In the late 1940s he took advantage of the conflict between the Dutch administration, which controlled the main cities of West Java, and the Indonesian army which ultimately retreated to Central Java. DI/TII controlled the territories abandoned by Indonesian army and promoted Islamic rule in these areas. Consequently, the DI/TII had to face two enemies, the Dutch, and the Indonesian army.

At the time significant ideological polarities emerged among the people of the region. Later, after the Dutch left Indonesia, the Indonesian army succeeded in wresting control of West Java and capturing the rebel leader, Kartosuwiryo. In some areas of Tasikmalaya, Kartosuwiryo is today still regarded as a legend and a hero of the people. Even now, some people are still trying to promote Kartosuwiryo's concept of Islamic rule, particularly in the area where the DI/TII first proclaimed its message.

In 1997 there were deadly riots caused by conflict between the police and students (*santri*) at Islamic boarding schools. The riots caused destruction of police installations, Chinese shops and churches in Tasikmalaya. The people of Pamijahan share a similar language and religious identity with people from other subdistricts of Tasikmalaya. Almost all claim to be descendants of the holy Sufi saint, Shaykh Abdul Muhyi. They have, however, given this claim a uniquely spatial form (see Chapter 4) which makes them slightly different from the rest of the people of Tasikmalaya.

Desa Pamijahan is situated in a hilly area some 70 kilometres to the south of the city of Tasikmalaya, or around 400 kilometres from Jakarta. It is administratively subsumed under the Bantarkalong subdistrict, which consists of fourteen villages scattered across undulating terrain. In the Dutch literature (Haan 1912, 462), the Desa Pamijahan was a part of the Karangnunggal subdistrict, which is why Shaykh Abdul Muhyi was also called the '*Haj* from *Carang*' or 'Hadje Carrang''. Since the 1980s, Karangnunggal has been divided into two subdistricts: Karangnunggal and Bantarkalong. Desa Pamijahan is located in the western part of Bantarkalong, which lies between the latitudes $7^0\,3'$ and $7^0\,35'$ South and the longitudes $1^0\,15'$ and $1^0\,20'$ East. The village stretches across the valley and the hills some 120 to 200 metres above sea level.

The terrain of Desa Pamijahan is dominated by a garden area, a grazing area, mahogany and albasia forests, as well as paddy fields. The mahogany forests are on the hills surrounding the village. In the garden area villagers plant coconut, albasia, bananas, bamboo and betel. The paddy fields are mainly scattered in the foothills. The main river is the Ci Pamijahan that flows through the village. Desa Pamijahan has enough water for daily activities and farming, particularly after the government built a tertiary irrigation system across the foothills. Previously, durian and mangos were the main commodities. Now, due to changes in land use, these expensive and exotic fruits are rarely found in Pamijahan. Compared to other parts of the southern area of Tasikmalaya, Desa Pamijahan gets little rain in the wet season. The daytime temperature is around $25\text{-}27^0$ C, three degrees hotter than in the northern part of Tasikmalaya, which is close to the high mountains of Galunggung and Sawal.

To reach Desa Pamijahan from Tasikmalaya you may use a private car or public transport. Taking a bus, you can reach Desa Pamijahan in about two and half-hours. Approaching Desa Pamijahan from Tasikmalaya, you pass through the subdistrict of Sukaraja (the old city of Sukapura), the subdistrict of Karangnunggal, and finally the subdistrict of Bantarkalong where Pamijahan is situated. The government has recently built a sealed road to connect Pamijahan with the city of Tasikmalaya, but ten years ago the area was still regarded as remote and backward by city people.

As in other districts of Tasikmalaya, statistics on religious affiliation show clearly that Pamijahan is one hundred percent Muslim. The *kabupaten* of Tasikmalaya is known as a major religious centre in West Java, ranking only after Cirebon and Banten in importance. Statistics on religious affiliation bear this out. According to data from the Tasikmalaya branch office of the Department of Religion, in 1996 there were 800 registered traditional Islamic boarding schools (*pesantren*) scattered around its villages.

In general, these *pesantren* are affiliated with Nahdatul Ulama (*NU*), the huge, traditionalist Islamic organisation. The Cipasung *pesantren*, for example, is the biggest of NU's traditional boarding schools in Priangan Timur. Only a few *pesantren* belong to Muhammadiyah[5] and Persis,[6] the modernist organisations, and these are mainly to be found in the city of Tasikmalaya. There are also *pesantren* which focus on Sufism. The Surialaya *pesantren*, for example, about hundred kilometres to the north of Pamijahan, is the best-known Sufi *pesantren* in Tasikmalaya and is also known internationally as a centre of the Sufi order of *Qadiriyyah wa Naqsabandiyyah*. Another is the Pagendingan *pesantren* which follows the Idrisiyyah order.[7]

According to data from the Department of Religious Affairs, thirteen of the *pesantren* in Tasikmalaya are located in the subdistrict of Bantarkalong, and three of these are situated in Desa Pamijahan. However, based on data from Desa Pamijahan itself, there are 385 *pesantren* there, as well as 715 smaller, traditional elementary-level Islamic schools (*madrasah)*, and 85 other traditional and informal religious education centres (*Pendidikan Keagamaan*).[8]

There is some confusion in the Department of Religion with regard to data on Sufi orders. The Department has not compiled a list of the Sufi orders in Tasikmalaya. However, complete data on Sufi orders is available from the local office of the district attorney (*Kejaksaan*). The Suharto government, in power from 1966 until 1998, sought to control all religious movements within a political framework. In this period Sufi orders were regarded not as religious movements to be registered with the Department of Religion, but as *kebatinan* (mysticism) movements. *Kebatinan* groups were defined not as religions or religious movements but as groups merely engaged in spiritualist exercises which consequently had to be registered in the district attorney's office.

In Desa Pamijahan, in 1996, there were 1155 households and 4,624 people scattered through six sub-villages (*kampung*): Pamijahan, Panyalahan, Parungpung, Karanji, Pandawa and Cicandra. Only in Kampung Cicandra and Kampung Karanji are there no sacred sites. Each sub-village is headed by a village chief called a *punduh*. However, the *punduh* only acts as a land and building tax collector or *Pengumpul PBB* (*Pajak Bumi dan Bangunan*). For this reason traditional leaders such as the custodians of sacred sites (*kuncen*) and religious leaders (*ajengan*) are more popular among the villagers. (This will be further discussed in Chapters 4 and 8.)

Kampung Pamijahan emerges as an important point in Desa Pamijahan. It has attracted settlers from the neighbouring villages. This is shown clearly in the population figures. Compared to the neighbouring villages, Kampung Pamijahan has the biggest population. This is a consequence of the role Pamijahan plays as the site of the shrine of Shaykh Abdul Muhyi. The sub-village with the second biggest population is Panyalahan with 216 households and 921 people. Panyalahan also has an important sacred site, but it is less popular than that of Muhyi in Pamijahan. The third in size is Cicandra (704 people), followed by Karanji (504), Pandawa (492) and Citapen (489 people), respectively. All the villagers from the six *kampung* claim that their ancestors had close ties with Shaykh Abdul Muhyi. However, the villagers in Pamijahan claim that they are related by blood with Muhyi and therefore are closer to him than the people in other *kampung*.

The villagers from Desa Pamijahan are recorded in the Village Office (*Kantor Bale Desa*) as farmers, peddlers, labourers, and members of the military. However, in reality it is difficult to rely on such statistics. Although the villagers may have paddy fields, they do not claim to be farmers. They prefer to identify themselves by jobs that are not associated with farming activities. According to them, to call yourself a true farmer (*patani*) you should have larger amounts of land than they have. They also argue that they rarely go to their paddy field as farmers because they always hire labourers (*buruh*) to work their lands for them. This claim is partly due to their activities associated with pilgrimage (*ziarah*). Men in Pamijahan and Panyalahan, for example, are quite often involved in guiding pilgrims around the sacred sites. This provides them with money for daily needs, while their wives help by selling souvenirs and take-home gifts to the pilgrims. During my fieldwork, I hardly ever observed women in the fields cultivating their lands. This contrasts with other villages where women have to care for their own gardens. Instead of cultivating their gardens, the women of Pamijahan prefer to buy fresh produce from people who come from neighbouring areas, particularly in the busy ritual or pilgrimage months such as Rabiulawwal (*Maulid*), the month in which the Prophet Muhammad's birthday is celebrated, or the seventh month, 'the revered month' (*Rajab*), when pilgrims come in their thousands each day.

In this setting, the practice of negotiating, creating, and interpreting the signs of the *wali* proceeds with great intensity. I use the term 'sign' as Peirce and his followers use it. As indicated in the previous chapter, according to this school there are three conditions for something to be regarded as a sign. A sign is perceivable, referential, and interpretable. As will be seen in the narratives of Pamijahan, the signs of blessing, holiness, ancestors, and mysticism are all linked. We will see that villagers try to negotiate with the tradition passed down to them by their ancestors. They do this through pilgrimage practice, mystical associations, and in the rewriting of their history.

ENDNOTES

[1] Hindus (*urang Hindu*) in this sense are not real Hindus. The term Hindu is today used by people to refer to the people or period before Islam.

[2] According to Rinkes *pamijahan* is derived from the word 'tree' since the names of villages in Java are often associated with the name of a tree. He also states that Safarwadi has "nothing to do with Safar, the second month of the Muslim year". (Rinkes 1910)

[3] In Sundanese, the word *mijah* is also associated with moving and growing.

[4] *Ajengan* is a title and a synonym for an Islamic scholar. In Central and East Java, Islamic scholars are called *kiai*.

[5] Muhammadiyah is often said to be a reformist or modernist organization. It combines religious teaching with modern social studies and activities in its schools.

[6] Persatuan Islam or Persis is probably the most puritan Islamic organisation in Indonesia. It promotes Islamic values in the literal spirit of 'back to the scriptures'.

[7] *Idrisiyyah* is a variant of the *Sanusiyyah* order. *Sanusiyyah* is the famous order of North Africa founded by Sayyid Muhammad Ali al-Sanusi al Mujahiri al Hasani al-Idrisi in 1787. In Tasikmalaya, the Idrisiyyah order was founded by Kiai Haji Abdul Fatah in 1932. In North Africa, Idrisiyyah is a very progressive order. It provides the local Bedouin not only with mystical teachings but also with the identity and ideology that, in the past, made it possible for them to confront colonial rule. In Indonesia, the name Idrisiyyah was adopted in preference to Sanusiyyah to disguise the order's international links.

[8] This difference in figures is mainly due to the registration system. The government has not registered some *pesantren* in Pamijahan. Others have been disqualified as *pesantren* because, according to the government, they lack organization and buildings.

Chapter 3: Manuscripts in Pamijahan: *Kakantun Karuhun*

A. Introduction

Kakantun, in Sundanese, is a polite word to specify something that is left by someone who has special position in the speaker's perceptions. It may be used to signify action or culture from the past. *Karuhun* is a kinship term referring to predecessors at least two or three generations back and is often used in ritualised language. The Pamijahanese understand the meaning of *kakantun karuhun* as a reference for *tali paranti*, or custom, as well.

The manuscripts, or *naskah kuno,* in Pamijahan are mostly written in Sundanese and Javanese using *pegon*[1] script. This is clear evidence of a Javanese scholarly influence in the interior of Sunda. (For more on this see Chapters 4, 6 and 7.)

Philological research on Sundanese manuscripts found in the land of Sunda is just in its beginings. Of course, there has been research on old Sundanese epics such as *Lutung Kasarung* and *Mundinglaya* (Pleyte 1910) conducted by Dutch orientalists. Continuing this task, local Sundanese scholars, in particular Ekadjati (1983), Atja (1969 and 1981) and Atja and Ayatrohaedi (1984/1985), have made preliminary inventories of manuscripts. It is due to their contributions that Sundanese scholars today have unprecedented access to their written heritage. In contrast to orientalist accounts of Sundanese and Javanese manuscripts, Professor Ekadjati and his colleagues have recorded diverse genres of Sundanese written material in the hands of local collectors, many of which are still in use within their communities. The living use of manuscripts adds a post-colonial dimension to a tradition whose place was once believed to be the sterile 'safety' of public library collections. For instance, many manuscripts dealing with the isolated Kampung Naga community (a mere 60 km. north-west of Pamijahan) and with Pamijahan itself have been taken away for study, not only by Dutch researchers but also by Indonesians. Their actions may well have been agreed to by the owners of the manuscripts, but today I believe there is room for scholars to discuss the functions and continuing significance of manuscripts in the communities from which they originate. We are well aware of the question: how can we study a manuscript when it is no longer in the possession of its true owners? The desecration of a ritual object by its removal from its environment is a real possibility. We need a new framework in philological studies, an 'ethno-philology' to provide an better understanding of both the artefact and the narrative it transmits as well as the functions of both in the view of the people who own the manuscript.

I now turn my attention to the manuscripts found in Pamijahan. They have not been previously described in any catalogue or scholarly study. As suggested in manuals of philological practice, it is important to make a preliminary note listing the manuscripts relating to Shaykh Abdul Muhyi that are held in various places. For this purpose I will refer to the Library of the Rijksuniversiteit in Leiden, the National Library of Indonesia (Perpustakaan Nasional) in Jakarta, as well as personal collections in West Java, particularly in and around Pamijahan. However, for further analysis I will only use the manuscripts found in Pamijahan.

The Library of the Rijksuniversiteit in Leiden holds at least 33 manuscripts mentioning the name of Abdul Muhyi. These manuscripts are Cod. Or. 7461, Cod. Or. 7265, Cod. Or. 7717, Cod. Or. 77176, Cod. Or. 7527, LOr 7412, Cod. Or. 7432, Cod. Or. 75333, Cod. Or. 7764, Cod. Or. 7721, Cod. Or. 7705, Cod. Or. 7526, Cod. Or. 7743, Cod. Or. 7857, Cod. Or. 7446, Cod. Or. 7414, Cod. Or. 7705, Cod. Or. 7486, Cod. Or. 7454 (Mal. 2225), Cod. Or. 7419, Cod. Or. 7455, Cod. Or. 7540, Cod. Or. 7465, Cod. Or. 2235, Cod. Or. 7708, Cod. Or. 6534, Cod. Or. 7432, Cod. Or. 7753, Cod. Or. 8634, Cod. Or. 7459, Cod. Or. 6461, Cod. Or. 6457b, LOr. 7689. These manuscripts contain both mystical doctrines and chronicles (Ekadjati 2000).

I shall deal with texts from outside the village first, since these were what I first encountered in the field. There are a number of manuscripts owned by private collectors who are mostly Shattariyyah followers or their heirs. Ekadjati (2000) reports that many Shattariyyah manuscripts have already been identified in various parts of West Java, but there are many others still awaiting description, not only in West Java but also in the farther provinces of Central and East Java. It is interesting to note, however, that the National Library of Indonesia in Jakarta holds only one manuscript associated with Shaykh Abdul Muhyi, namely SD 180 (Kossim 1974). This manuscript appears to have been vandalised; its binding is intact, but only one page of the text remains.

At the outset, it is important to make an inventory and a description of manuscripts associated with Pamijahan, both those which are kept in the village and those that are scattered through neighbouring areas. D.A. Rinkes (1909) has supplied us with preliminary information in manuscripts held in Tasikmalaya and Cirebon which reflect Pamijahan genealogies, but he has not given us an adequate description of those found in the village itself, nor does he offer any text edition of Javanised versions of Shattariyyah practice and belief. In response to this lacuna, I will now brief sketch the Shattariyyah teachings found in the Pamijahan manuscripts and in other manuscripts closely associated with Shaykh Abdul Muhyi.

During my fieldwork, I discovered seven works that could be characterised as historical chronicles (*babad*) or that relate to mystical orders and to Shattariyyah in particular. I surveyed five Shattariyyah texts (described below as mss. A, B,

C, D, and F), one Qadiriyyah text (ms. E), and two *babad* texts (mss. G, H). I believe there are other manuscripts in the hands of villagers which demand further research.

Certain individuals have inherited the role of custodians who preserve the chronicles (*babad*) and Sufi writings (*kitab tarekat*). These are Ajengan Satibi (85 years of age at the time of my fieldwork), Ajengan Endang (47), Pak Apap (65), and Pak Beben (35). In theory, these individuals have high status and may play an important role in the community, partly by virtue of their blood relationship with Shaykh Abdul Muhyi. Ajengan Endang, for example, is the brother of a recent custodian of Pamijahan, and Ajengan Satibi is the son of the immediately previous custodian. Both of these men are respected as *ajengan* and they are often invited by people from other villages to give lectures or to deliver sermons. Ajengan Endang is more popular than Ajengan Satibi, even though he is younger, because he is recognised as having *ilmu laduni*,[2] and his lectures quite often attract larger audiences. Pak Beben is formally recognised as a Shattariyyah leader because he holds both an *ijazah*, or religious license from a Shattariyyah master, and a certificate of recognition from the government.[3]

The *kitab tarekat* found in Pamijahan have three main features in common in terms of form and content. The first is an historical feature telling of the legitimation of the master. This is the genealogy or *silsilah*. The second is a practical aspect outlining methods of recitation and contemplation. The third is a more philosophical aspect under which are described the foundations of the metaphysical doctrine of the Shattariyyah referred to as 'The Seven Levels of Being', or the *martabat tujuh*.

Unfortunately, not all of the Pamijahan manuscripts are wholly legible. Some have been damaged or are incomplete, though comparison with manuscripts from neighbouring areas may turn up clues to missing or unclear contents. Let us now turn to a description of the manuscripts found in Pamijahan. To provide a further illustration of these texts, particularly of Shattariyyah manuscripts, I will include a manuscript from Limus Tilu which has been examined by Ekadjati.

In this part I use the form of description suggested by Professor Hooker (Hooker 1991:91) in her study of Malay manuscripts.

A Shattariyyah Manuscript (ms. A)

This manuscript has not been described in any catalogue. It is in the Javanese language. There is no title, but the first sentence states "This is a *kitab* which tells about the genealogy of Shattariyyah" (*Utawi ikilah kitab ingdalem anyatakaken turunan-turunane dadalan Shattariyyah*).

> Dating and place: There is no date but it is believed to have been written by the villagers or a forebear of *Ajengan* Endang.

Scribe: -

Owner: Ajengan Endang Pamijahan, Tasikmalaya

Script: Pegon

Dimensions: 29 cm x 21 cm

Paper: locally made paper or dluwang

Pages: 28

Lines per page: 10—11

Colour: brown

Figure 2. Manuscript A

Comments:

On the cover, which was probably added by the latest owner, there are some words written in Latin script which include "Lent to Memed: sugar, salt, tobacco, paper and ink. 1956", (*Memed hutang gula, uyah, bako, kertas, mangsi. 1956*) indicating the latest year in which the cover might have been added.

The manuscript is evidently a copy but there is no mention of the date when the copy might have been made. The original would have been composed long before the copy was made. *Ajengan* Endang said that the original text was written in the 18th or 19th century by one of his ancestors (*eyang*). According to *Ajengan* Endang it would have been copied three generations before his own time. He further claims that this *kitab* was given to him by his father, Jabidi, whom he believes to have been the last Shattariyyah follower in Pamijahan to possess a traditonal letter of authorisation (*ijazah*).

On pages 7 and 8 of the manuscript, mystical diagrams illustrate the Shattariyyah doctrine of the Seven Levels of Being. The technical 'area of *dikir*' is also schematised on page 24. It shows how the *dikir* should be started and incorporated into the rhythm of breathing.

A Shattariyyah Manuscript (ms. B)

Dating and place: There is no date, but the manuscript is believed to have been copied by villagers or ancestors of Mama Ajengan Satib

Scribe: -

Owner: Mama Ajengan Satibi, Pamijahan, Tasikmalaya

Script: Pegon

Dimension: 21 x 29 cm

Paper: locally made paper or *dluwang*

Pages: 9-71 = 62

Lines per page: 10

Colour: black and brown

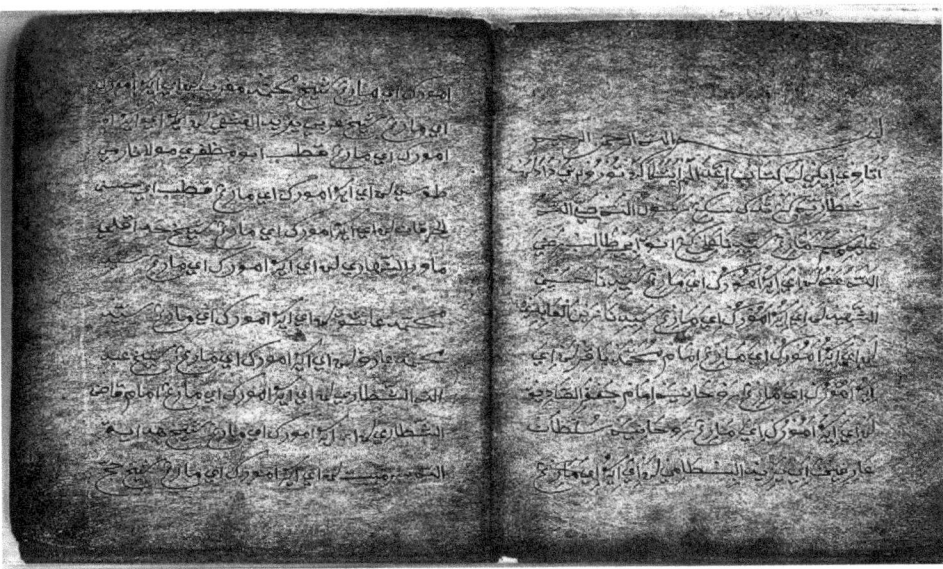

Figure 3. Manuscript B

Comments:

On the first page, the name of the current owner is written: Satibi of Pamijahan. According to Satibi, he inherited the manuscript from his grandfather. Ajengan Endang often borrows it. The first to ninth pages comprise a collection of favourite prayers assembled over generations, quite separate from the Shattariyyah content. This manuscript is therefore a collation of texts.

The Shattariyyah *kitab* itself is in Javanese. It begins with a line of transmission beginning from Muhammad and ending with Shaykh Abdul Muhyi of Safarwadi and his sons. (pp. 9-10). Interestingly, in this *silsilah* section, after the name of Muhyi's son, there is an unfinished sentence which reads "The son Kiahi Mas Nida Muhammad Muhyi in the village of Karang and in Safarwadi and he taught..." (*Kang putra kiahi Mas Nida Muhammad Muhyi ing Karang desane lan ing Safarwadi padukuhane lan ia iku amuruk maring...*) The empty space at the end of this sentence is to be used by other followers who have obtained the *ijazah* and who are allowed to inscribe their names there. This raises the possibility that this manuscript was copied from manuscripts dating from the period of Kiahi Mas Nida Muhammad Muhyi, who is believed to have lived some time in the late 18th or early 19th century as the grandson of Muhyi.[4]

On page 13, in bold letters, there is the phrase "There is no God but Allah" (*la ilaha illa l-lahu*) and the Sufi interpretation of this testimony to instruct the disciples. The doctrine of the Shattariyyah begins on page 14 with:

"In the name of God the Compassionate and Merciful... this is the reality of God at the level of His mysteriousness. We tell of the time of emptiness before the universe had been created."

Bismi l-lah r-rahman r-rahim, punika martabat Allah Ta'ala tatkala ingdalem ghoib sang karihin cinaritaken tatkala awang-awang uwung-uwung bumi langit durung ana.

A full diagram portraying the metaphysical doctrine of the Shattariyyah is given on page 14 and the way Shattariyyah chant (*dikir*) should be performed is set out on pages 50, 52, and 55.

A Shattariyyah Manuscript (ms. C)

This manuscript is also not described in any catalogue.

Dating and place: There is no date but it is believed to have been written by an ancestor of Abdullah Apap in Pamijahan.

Scribe: -

Owner: Abdullah Apap, Pamijahan-Tasikmalaya

Script: Pegon

Dimension: 32 x 20 cm

Paper: book paper

Pages: 40

Lines per page: 1 = 13, 2--40 = 14

Colour: black, almost illegible

Comments:

Raden Abdullah Apap is a retired primary school teacher and a member of the local Sundanese aristocracy. By insisting on the use of his title, *Raden*, he affirms his linkage to the old aristocratic house of Sukapura, Tasikmalaya. He is author of the first book of *Sejarah Perjuangan Shaykh Abdul Muhyi* (The History of Shaykh Abdul Muhyi's Mission) published in Pamijahan. The book concerns the mission, or *perjuangan*, of Muhyi based on this manuscript and on oral sources collected from his family. However, he admitted to me that he is not capable of reading and interpreting the *kitab* properly, although he is aware that its contents derive from the teachings of Abdul Muhyi.

A Shattariyyah Manuscript (ms. D)

Scribe: Muhammad Akna

Dating and place:

Owner: Muhammad Akna

Script: Pegon

Dimension: 33 cm x 21 cm

Paper: book paper

Pages: 40

Lines per page: page 1 = 13 lines, pages 2-40 = 14 lines

Colour: brown

Comments:

This manuscript contains seven fragments of text. The first talks about jurisprudence (*fiqh*) and includes instructions on correct practice of *salat* prayer. The second tells about the essence of the confession of faith (*syahadat*), the third describes Sufi teaching, the fourth presents the Shattariyyah *silsilah*, the fifth section schematises the main points of Shattariyyah doctrine, and the sixth and seventh describe *dikir* ritual and the categories of student, or *murid*.

Unlike manuscripts A, B and C, this manuscript uses both the Sundanese and Javanese language. For example, the manuscript describes the essence of *syahadat* in Javanese. "This is the essence of the *syahadat Asyhadu an la…* that is to say, the radiation of *syahadat* merges into the Oneness." (*Punika jatining syahadat Asyhadu an la tegese gempuring syahadat lenyeping tunggal*.)

Sundanese appears instead of Javanese in the third part of the text which tells about the teaching of *tasawwuf*. "The third *kitab* tells about *ilmu tassawuf*" (*Ari kitab anu katilu mertelakeun ilmu tassauf. Kanyahokeun…*). In other places, it switches between Javanese and Sundanese, particularly in the section recording the *silsilah* of the Shattariyyah. "This is the genealogy of Shattariyyah starting from God's Emissary." (*Punika nganyataken turunan nana perjalanan tarekat Shattariyyah anu kawit ti Kangjeng Rasulullah*). The same pattern is also used in elaborating the *dikir*recitation, which it says is derived from the great-grandson of Shaykh Abdul Muhyi, Kiai Bagus Hijaya. The text here reads: "This is an invocation of Kiahi Bagus Hijaya or Kiai Bagus Haji Irfan, the son of Kiai Bagus Nida Muhiddin. After the invocation…" (*Punika wiridna Kiai Bagus Hijaya atawa Kiahi Bagus Haji Irfan puterana Kiahi Bagus Nida Muhiddin. Sanggeus dikir…*). Such patterns are probably influenced by the manuscript's use in the community. In contemporary Pamijahan, Sundanese texts are often cited in sermons. Indeed the Javanese text may not be intended for use in a communal teaching session at all but rather as a source or reference for the leader (*guru*), or the adherents of the order, the *ikhwan* who want to develop their knowledge.

Kitab Istiqal Tarekat Qadiriyyah-Naqhsabandiyyah (ms. E)

Scribe: Idoh of Kebon Manggu, Cibalanarik, Sukaraja, Tasikmalaya

Dating and place: date unknown. Sukaraja, Tasikmalaya

Owner: Idoh, Kebon Manggu, Cibalanarik, Sukaraja, Tasikmalaya

Script: Pegon

Dimension: 24 cm x 17 cm and 20 cm x 15 cm

Paper: HVS

Pages: 84 pp

Lines per page: 14

Colour: brown

Comments:

According to the villagers, this work is called *Kitab Istiqal Thariqah* Qadiriyyah *Naqshabandiyyah* (The Book of the Way of the *Tarekat* of the Qadiriyyah and the Naqshabandiyyah) and was "copied" from an old manuscript written by Shaykh Abdul Muhyi himself.

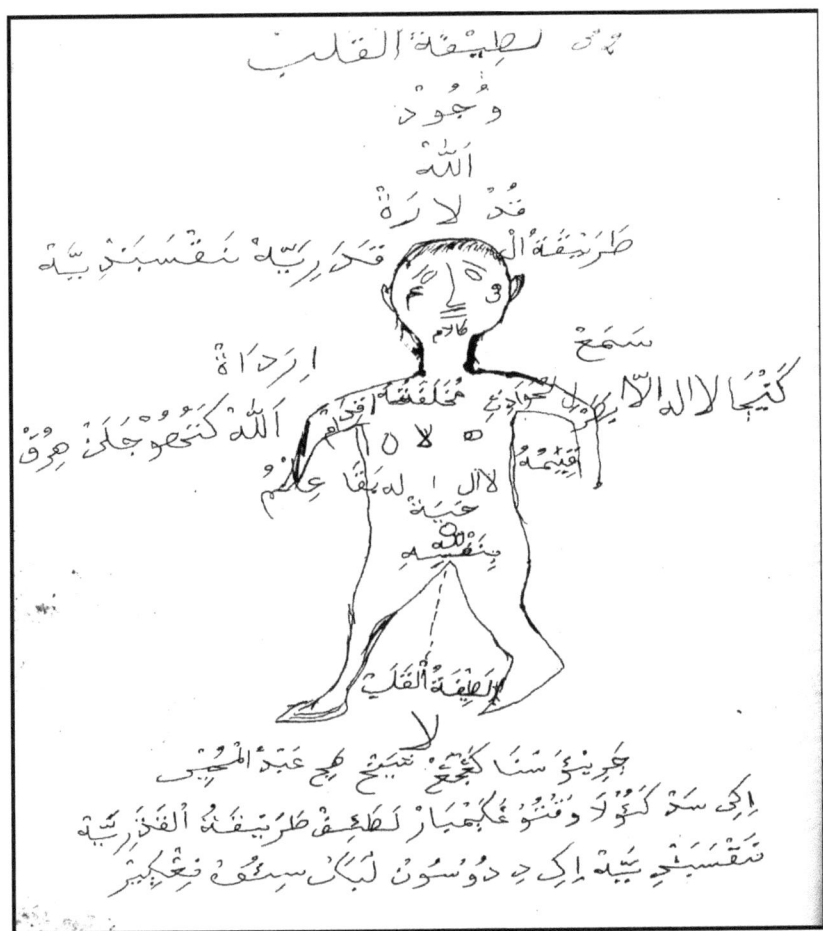

Figure 4. A page from Kitab Istiqal Tarekat Qadiriyyah-Naqshabandiyyah

The opening colophon reads:

> "This is the Kitab Istiqal Tarekat Qadiriyyah Naqshabandiyyah. The copying was begun on Monday in the month of Jumadil Awal, coinciding with the day of Kliwon on the second day of Jumadil Awal, 1390 Hijrah. This coincides with July 6, 1970. It was finished on Saturday, 5pm, the 21st day of Jumadil Awal, 1390 which coincides with July 25, 1970."

Ieu Kitab Istiqal Thariqah Qadiriyyah Naqshabandiyyah ngawitan diturun dina dinten Senen bulang Jumadil Awal meneran dina Kaliwon tanggal 2 Jumadil awwal 1390 Hijrah meneran tanggal genep Juli 1970 MaShaykhi tamatna diturun dina dinten Sabtu jam 5.00 sore ping 21 Jumadil awwal 1390 Hijrah meneran tanggal 25 Juli 1970 Masehi.

Comments:

Initially I heard about this manuscript from a custodian of the sacred site at Panyalahan, but at that time, he could not show it to me. According to him, a colleague had taken it away. The custodian of Panyalahan subsequently lost contact with the manuscript following his colleague's death and he could no longer trace where the it was.

After I had been six months in the village, I received information that a retired army officer, Pak Syafii, now held the manuscript. Pak Syafii was a man of influence in the community, not just because he was a custodian reputedly with supernatural powers, but also because he was a retired Major. Through the efforts of an intermediary, he finally permitted me to view the manuscript and made a copy of it. This small incident is interesting for the light it throws on the preservation of manuscripts in Pamijahan. Traditionally, it is the site custodians *(kuncen)* who must keep, or at least monitor the whereabouts of sacred texts dedicated to their village and their ancestors. However, because of tensions among the main families of the village, each has felt more secure safekeeping his own manuscripts and not reporting them to the custodians.

This *kitab,* as far as I know, is quite different from other Pamijahan manuscripts, or indeed manuscripts from other places. It incorporates various Sufi texts. Its title indicates two well-known schools, the Qadiriyyah and the Naqshabandiyyah, which are indeed traditionally linked.

However, in the introduction, the scribe also talks eclectically of other *tarekat,* namely the Shattariyyah, Asrariyyah, Anfasiyyah and Muhammadiyah. There is no information as to why the scribe chose to limit her title in the way she did, without mentioning the Shattariyyah and other orders. It seems to me that Ms. Idoh, the scribe and owner of the manuscript, may have thought that Shaykh Abdul Muhyi was also a follower the Qadiriyyah---Naqshabandiyyah movement.

In the matter of the *silsilah,* the confusion goes further. First, we would expect Ms. Idoh, who confesses to be the wife of a follower of Sufism, to identify herself according to the protocol of the *tarekat* by positioning herself within the *silsilah*. This she has not done.

Furthermore, the manuscript does not provide us with a *silsilah* which might be compared to other manuscripts of Pamijahan as mentioned above. What is given is a hybrid version. For example, Abdul Muhyi is inserted into the *silsilah* of both the Naqshabandiyyah and the Shattariyyah. On page 75 of the text, this genealogy of Abdul Muhyi is presented, but the scribe has confused the genealogy of Sufism with the genealogy of the Shaykh's family. This can be seen, in the following fragment

...puputra Shaykh Abd al-Qadir al-Jaelani Baghdadi, puputra Shaykh Abd al-Jabar, puputra Shaykh Abd al-Rauf Waliyullah Kuala Aceh, guruna Shaykh Haji Abdul Muhyi Waliyullah Safaril Wadi Pamijahan.

This fragment erroneously states that Shaykh Abd al-Rauf of 17th century Aceh, the master of Shaykh Abdul Muhyi, is the grandson of the famous Sufi of Baghdad, Shaykh Abd al-Qadir Jailaini (b. 1077). Furthermore, the author uses the words 'had a child' *(apuputra)* which is also discordant, since Abd al-Rauf was not the natural son of Abd al-Jabar. Their relationship was one of precedence in the line of teachers.

We know that Abd al-Rauf appears in various *silsilah,* one of which is that of the Qadiriyyah, but there is no evidence that Abdul Muhyi was ever a follower of Qadiriyyah-Naqshabandiyyah. Thus, as long as there are no other manuscripts with a title or contents resembling this *kitab,* we cannot decide whether Muhyi also practised Sufi disciplines other than the Shattariyyah.

Although this *kitab* has obvious weaknesses in terms of its *silsilah,* its explanation of the nature of Shattariyyah doctrine is important. The whole idea of the Seven Levels of Being resembles other Pamijahan manuscripts, but this *kitab* has its own style when explaining the relations between a view of cosmology, the seven *martabats* and the *salat* rituals.

A Shattariyyah Manuscript (ms. F)

Scribe:

Dating and place:

Owner: Enok Sariah Yatmikasari, Limus Tilu, Cikajang, Garut

Script: Pegon

Dimension: 19 x 26,5 cm; 15 x 23,5 cm

Paper: HVS

Pages: 81 pp

Lines per page: 14

Colour: black

Comments:

To a certain extent, this manuscript resembles other Pamijahan manuscripts in terms of its contents. However, it has more detail and examples when it comes to the doctrine of the Seven Levels of Being. The manuscript has been transcribed into Latin characters by Edi S. Ekadjati.[5] According to Edi, Kiayi Haji Muhyidin wrote the manuscript before 1821. If this information is true, it is likely that this *kitab* preserves the original teachings of Abdul Muhyi. The doctrine of the seven *martabats* in this *kitab* is close to that expounded in manuscripts C and D. However, there is no explanation about *silsilah*. According to villagers, Kiayi Haji Muhyidin is a grandson of Shaykh Abdul Muhyi (see Chapter 6)

Babad Pamijahan (Ms. G)

Scribe:

Dating and place:

Owner: Ajengan Endang

Script: Pegon

Dimension: 33 cm x 21 cm

Paper: European paper

Pages: 34

Lines per page: page 1 = 12 lines, pages 2-32 = 14 lines

Colour: dark brown

Comments:

This manuscript is damaged on almost every page of the first half and is difficult to read. There is a clue in the paper of the second part however, which indicates the origin of the material: the trading name of '*M. van Dorp & Co., Batavia*'. This indicates that the paper was made in Europe during the 19th century. The paper is similar to that of Ms Sd. 211 held in the National Library of Indonesia, Jakarta. The text does not reveal the scribe or any other information regarding the origin of a first owner or collector. The current owner says that the manuscript was bequeathed to him by his ancestors. However, I speculate that the paper comes from the time of Snouck Hurgronje in the late decades of the 19th century. Snouck had contacted some of Muhyi's descendants in Manonjaya and Mangunreja, Tasikmalaya, in his search for Islamic materials. A manuscript now held in Leiden University Library (Cod. Or. 7708) tells this story. In his search for manuscripts and ordering of copies he provided European paper to a number of scribes. This paper could have been the van Dorp paper on which this manuscript is written.

The manuscript was later translated into Sundanese by the previous *kuncen*, Zainal Mustopa (Ms. H) below.

Babad Pamijahan (Ms. H)

Scribe: Zainal Mustopa

Dating and place: 1977

Owner: Ajengan Endang

Script: Latin and Pegon

Dimension: 33 cm x 21 cm

Paper: book paper

Pages: 52

Lines per page: 28-30

Colour: white

Comments:

The scribe clearly states that this is a copy of the *Babad Pamijahan*. The text claims that the

> Babad Pamijahan was translated from Perimbon Kuno, an older reference work, by Zainal Mustopa Bin Muhammad Jabidi".
>
> Babad Pamijahan disalin saking perimbon kuno dening Zainal Mustopa Bin Muhammad Jabidi (Babad Pamijahan, 1)

Manuscript H contains a chronicle, a contemporary genealogy of the scribe, and some Arabic formulaic chants. The manuscript seems to have been used as a manual by the chief custodian. The chronicle is used in this volume for further analysis (see Chapter 4). The historical sequence is complete and the text is more legible than Ms G. Furthermore, similar to the case of Ms. G, it is important that the person of the scribe and owner of this manuscript was a prominent figure in Pamijahan. Equally important was the social purpose to which it was put as a reference for the villagers' identity.

Conclusion

The manuscripts both confirm the importance of Shaykh Abdul Muhyi in his own time and are witnesses to his continuing significance in the imagination of the Pamijahanese. I believe there are other manuscripts preserved in the village and surrounding areas, as well as those lying unidentified in major manuscript collections. For my present purposes, however, I have limited my discussion to the living use of manuscripts in Pamijahan.

ENDNOTES

[1] *Pegon* is the term for Arabic script used to write the Sundanese and Javanese languages.

[2] *Ilmu laduni* is spiritual knowledge which allows some one to go beyond a material boundary. Pamijahanese mention that Haji Endang is able to preach sermons in two places at the same time. This is possible, they say, because his mastery of *ilmu laduni* allows him to appear at the same time in different places.

[3] The *ijazah* is a letter of authorization given by a Sufi master. Whoever possesses such an *ijazah* is eligible to lead *dikir*, or the recitation of selected verses from the Qur'an, and to establish a new branch of the order. The issue of Pak Beben's status as a Shattariyyah leader is taken up in detail in Chapter 6

[4] Information provided by Beben Muhammad Dabas, 1997

[5] Edi Ekadjati et. al. (1984), unpublished research report.

Chapter 4: The *Babad Pamijahan*: Sunda, Java and the Identity of the Pamijahanese

Shaykh Abdul Muhyi of Karang came from the East. He was a descendant of Susunan Giri Kadaton (Babad Pamijahan)

A. Introduction

The *babad*, or historical chronicle, is widely known as a genre of traditional Javanese literature. The genre came to Sunda in the 18th century through the Javanese administrators who occupied certain territories of Sunda. In Javanese, it is a narrative of past events telling, for example, about the founding of a new settlement or insurrection against an older power. The Javanese chronicle is a literary work written in a poetic metrical form which is intended to be sung. From the perspective of narrative, the *babad* to some extent is similar to the *hikayat* or *sejarah* in traditional Malay terms such as *Sejarah Melayu*. Like these texts, the *babad* was traditionally addressed through performance to real and present audiences. Structurally, the *babad* consists of genealogical and narrative elements. Writing about the very similar Balinese genre, Worsley (1972:4-5) observes that the author of a *babad* inserts various narratives into particular segments at critical points in the dynastic linkages. This mixture of genealogical and narrative components is especially dense in major *babad*.

Another characteristic of the *babad* is that it is written within an 'open tradition' of composition, by more than one author, from the same or from different periods. Accordingly, there is an evolution in the structure of *babad* (Djajadiningrat 1965). This open tradition, in which the author is free to mix various texts from different variants, reflects an important function of the *babad* in its society.

The genre legitimates the contemporariness of the scribe and the authors. This phenomenon, according to Ras, can be found in the Banjarese chronicle, the *Hikayat Banjar*. Based on his linguistic analysis of this text, Ras (1968) finds that the chronicle was written by at least three authors. The scribes or copyists attempt to bring the past into their contemporary conditions. For instance, from an external historical perspective, the fall of Majapahit (probably around 1527) was a very important event in its scale and its impact, yet the authors and the copyists in Banjar view this event as being of relatively small significance. Their main objective is to declare their own contemporary dynastic linkages. Furthermore, as a product of an open tradition, the *babad* also appears in various versions. A good example of this is the emergence of long and short versions of a particular chronicle corpus (1991:18). The combination of genealogical and historical narrative in *babad* attracts the attention not only of philologists and literary scholars but also historians and anthropologists. Ras states that the study of the *babad* must be based on the internal character of the texts. He identifies *babad* as

> "a specific form of expression by means of language, either oral or written, always artistic in character, recognised as such by the community involved and differentiated from the daily use of language for purely communicative artless purposes" (Ras 1992:182).

From a different point of view, the *babad* stands between an expressive and persuasive discourse, reflecting the ideological point of view of the author or the patron. The question of whether the *babad* also supplies historical evidence does not concern those who approach the text as a literary genre. For the literary scholar, the task at hand is to describe the poetics of the text. There are also researchers who locate *babad* as both history and literature *(sastra sejarah)*. However, the genre of *sastra* will theoretically conflict with *sejarah* particularly in the modern sense in which history is usually understood. Winstedt (1969: 223) argues, with reference to classical Malay literature, that *sastra* tends to refer to a belle lettristic tradition. In fact, however, what is called *sastra* in the Nusantara region is any narrative material recorded in written and oral tradition. These may range from theological catechisms to plantation manuals to romances and proverbs.

For the purposes of this study, I will try to use the concept of 'narrative', in Indonesian, *tuturan*. I do not pretend to characterise narrative or *tuturan* in the *babad* as belle-lettristic *sastra,* but rather simply as 'telling'. *Tuturan* in Sundanese is also called *pitutur* or *kasauran*. It seems to me that *pitutur* or *tuturan* is close to the *tutuik* Fox has described on the island of Roti (Fox 1979, 16)

> Tetek, in the compound term tutui teteek, is a reduplicated form of tete. In strict etymological terms this form tete is probably derived, by the loss of medial consonant, from tebe. Tete (in ordinary language) and tebe (in some versions of ritual language) denote what is true, real or actual'.... For a tale to be acceptable as tutuik teteek, it must be fixed in time and place and must establish its authenticity according to Rotinese criteria of evidence. (Fox 1979: 16-17)

In this chapter, I will treat the *Babad Pamijahan* as a narrative and, to borrow Fox's phrase, a "culturally acceptable chronology and location" (Fox 1976: 10). In Austronesian as suggested by Fox, there is an indication that 'historical narratives' project the image of a people in time. (ibid. 10)

For students of Javanese and Sundanese literature, the *Babad Pamijahan (BP)* is extremely concise. It is nevertheless evident that it retains the general character of *babad* as found in other places such as Central and East Java. The *Babad*

Pamijahan becomes a very important reference for the villagers who want to trace the linkages of their ancestry. Through a close examination of it we find that the chronicle not only lists various names but also recollects the myth of the two kingdoms of Sunda and Java. Foremost among the mythic stories relating to the relationship between Java and Sunda is that of the Perang Bubat, an incident that traumatised relations between the two regions. According to the story the intended bride of the King of Majapahit and her father, the king of Sunda were executed at the gate of the palace of Majapahit (Atja 1984/1985; Zoetmulder 1985: 528-532). However, Sunda also received religious enrichment when some Javanese *ulama* penetrated to the heartland of Sunda and introduced Islam there. The *Babad Pamijahan,* in fact, illustrates the myths of these two kingdoms from a Sundanese perspective. Custodians call this text the *Sejarah Babad Kuna* (in a Javanese version) and the *Babad Pamijahan* (in a Sundanese version), the Sundanese version having been copied from the Javanese. The villagers believe that it was members of the *wali's* family, living close to him, who wrote the *Sejarah Babad Kuna*.

B. The *Babad* in Sunda

The Sundanese adopted the genre of the *babad* from their neighbours, the Javanese, during domination of the region by the Sultanate of Mataram in the 17th century. Sundanese contact with the genre created a slightly different variant. For Sundanese, the term *babad* does not always refer to historical narratives as it does in Java. *Babad* can also refer to non-historical narratives, such as for example the *Babad Kawung,* a manual on how to make palm sugar. Furthermore, the farming cultures in remote areas of Sunda have preferred very short versions of the *babad*. Unlike the case in the city, good quality paper is very difficult to find and is a luxury, so these communities tend to rewrite the long version of written materials into shorter versions. This situation may also be influenced by the persistence of a strong oral tradition in which people only need to know (or record) the skeleton of a story.

The structure of the *babad* in Sunda, particularly those conveying historical narrative, retains the major characteristics of the Javanese, Sundanese and Balinese *babad*. Like the major *babad* from these traditions, such as the *Babad Tanah Jawi,* the *Babad Dipanagara,* the *Babad Pajajaran* and the *Babad Buleleng,* the *Babad Pamijahan* also contains the two elements of genealogy and narrative. To treat it as an historical document in modern terms would be rash. Similarly, it is also difficult to analyse it in terms of its poetics, particularly if we are in search of sophisticated story sequences or episodes. However, this does not mean that such written material is not invaluable for our purposes.

Although the *Babad Pamijahan* has a poor literary structure and lacks historical data in the modern historical sense, the village council nevertheless treats the manuscript as a legitimate source for explaining the identity of villagers as descendants of Abdul Muhyi. However, the way villagers generate this concept of identity from the manuscript is complicated and needs to be clarified.

For the people of Pamijahan their *babad* is as important as other items of sacred material culture. Although many of them do not understand the language of the text, they can still generate meaning from different directions. We find here that the *babad* is not only a book of history but also an artefact of the *wali*. As is the case with other artefacts in Pamijahan, it too is believed to have spiritual power which comes directly from Shaykh Abdul Muhyi and his contemporaries. So villagers conserve the manuscript as well as the words of its text.

To understand the meaning of the *Babad Pamijahan* in its context we have to treat this narrative both as a self-telling text and as a text which functions in social and cultural discourse.

C. The *Babad Pamijahan* (BP)

There are sufficient extant copies of the BP to provide material for a philological study of the transmission of the text and its various recensions. The custodian of Pamijahan holds two manuscripts. Leiden University Library in the Netherlands holds three manuscripts. I believe that there are other manuscripts preserved by various collectors both in Indonesia and overseas. For instance, at the end of my fieldwork I learned that there are also manuscripts in Garut, Sumedang, Ciamis, Bandung and Sukabumi recounting the history of Shaykh Abdul Muhyi. In this volume, however, I will focus only on the Pamijahan manuscripts, while referring to a number of other manuscripts as further 'witnesses' of the Pamijahan collection.

The custodians of Pamijahan have two manuscripts. The first manuscript (listed as ms G in Chapter 3) is in Javanese and the second (ms H) is in Sundanese. It seems that ms. H is derived from G which is written in Pegon, or Arabic-derived script. The two manuscripts show similar structure and contents. However, manuscript ms H is more complete than ms G, since the first two pages of ms G are missing and it is damaged in some parts.

The Pamijahan materials and Ms. SD120, a manuscript concerning Shaykh Abdul Muhyi which is held in the National Library, Jakarta, are close to those of the Brandes' manuscript in Jakarta (Br. 283) and the manuscripts collected by Snouck Hurgronje's (LOr. 7858, LOr 7708) held in Leiden. The *Babad Pamijahan* is also similar to the text preserved in the Rinkes' collection (LOr. 8588) which was copied from Snouck Hurgronje's LOr. 7858. There is an indication that Snouck Hurgronje obtained his manuscript directly from its owner, or perhaps via another collector in Tasikmalaya, whilst touring the religious sites of Java. A religious officer, the Penghulu of Mangunreja, copied LOr. 7858, for example, in about 1890. In LOr 7708, the owner clearly states, "the Penghulu of Tasikmalaya freely submits his manuscript to his master", evidently Snouck

Hurgronje. According to my informants in Pamijahan, the Penghulu of Mangunreja (70 km to the north-west of the village) as well as the Penghulu of Tasikmalaya, were descendants of Shaykh Abdul Muhyi.

One custodian of Panyalahan told me that his ancestors bequeathed to him a *Kitab Papakem Kuning,* a manuscript probably concerning Shaykh Abdul Muhyi. According to him, the *Kitab Papakem Kuning* was taken by the Dutch to be held in the Netherlands. The villagers have never seen this manuscript. However, as close relatives of Shaykh Abdul Muhyi, they have inherited various oral narratives from their forebears in a traditional fashion. I tried to reconcile this information with all the catalogues of the Leiden University Library and of the National Library in Jakarta. There is, however, no manuscript corresponding to such a title.

However, I did find that the manuscript given by the *Penghulu* of Tasikmalaya in 1914 to 'Kangjeng Tuan Snouck Hurgronje' (Cod.Or. 7708) entitled *Kitab Patorekan Shaykh Abdul Muhyi* apears to be close to the *Papakem Kuning* on several counts. The title *Papakem Kuning* means 'the yellow guide'. In the traditional religious teaching of Javanese *pesantren* schools, we also find a similar term, *kitab kuning,* to refer to books written and disseminated by traditional means. Often the paper used is old or of low quality and hence yellow in colour. It is probable that the *Kitab Patoreka*n Shaykh Abdul Muhyi is in the same cast as the *Kitab Papakem Kuning* reported to me by the custodian in Panyalahan. This speculation can be related to my informant's story. Between 1950 and 1980, he worked in the office of the Penghulu of Tasikmalaya. He had access to certain information relating to his predecessors in the office. Office records show that the *Kitab Patorekan* (Cod.Or. 7708) is, in fact, the one submitted to Snouck Hurgronje by one of his predecessors. We read on the first page of this text:

> The book of the history of Shaykh Abdul Muhyi, submitted to my master Kangjeng Tuan Snouck Hurgronje. The head Penghulu of Tasikmalaya, Haji Muhammad Idriss copied this book on 18th August 1915.
>
> Kitab Patorekan Shaykh Abdul Muhyi kang haturan Kangjeng Tuan Snouck Hurgronje turunan Haji Muhammad Idriss Hofd Penghulu Tasikmalaya 18.8.1915.

For the present discussion however, I will focus on manuscript H of the *Babad Pamijahan* preserved by a previous custodian, Zainal Mustafa bin Muhammad Jabidi, who passed away couple years before I came to the village. Ajengan Endang, the younger brother of Zainal Mustafa, now has safekeeping of the manuscript because it is the more complete of the two versions held by Pamijahan custodians. I will present here a full translation of the *Babad Pamijahan,* making annotations to facilitate the discussion.

D. Translation of The *Babad Pamijahan* (Ms H)

This recension of the *Babad* Pamijahan was translated from *Perimbon Kuno* by Zainal Mustafa Bin Muhmmad Jabidi, 5 Juli 1977/18 Rajab 1397. The *Perimbon* or *Paririmbon* is known as a collection of the oldest manuscripts. It contains various texts important for the villagers. Here I will present a paraphrase of the *Babad Pamijahan*. The segmentations are based on a category of event which will be used for subsequent analysis.

[A]

The benefit of this tale was derived from our ancestors. They were people who received grace and blessings from God.

In the name of God, the compassionate, and the merciful.

Our brothers came to me, asking me to write a clear *Hikayat* or *Babad Pamijahan*. I performed *tawassul* to Tuan Paduka Shaykh Haji Abdul Muhyi [din] Panembahan in Pamijahan-Karangnunggal. I was asked to write this *Hikayat* in accordance with the ancestral stories taken from the *Sejarah Babad Kuna*.

[B]

This is a genealogy of the Panembahan's ancestors. Shaykh Abdul Muhyi of Karang came from the east. He was a descendant of Susunan Giri Kadaton. Susunan Giri Kadaton had a son. His name was Pangeran Giri Laya. The prince of Giri Laya had two children: one son and one daughter. These were the children from his marriage with a daughter of Kiai Haji Demang Malaya. Raden Giri Laya' son was Raden Wiracandra. Raden Giri Laya's daughter was Raden Malaya. Raden Malaya then married Kiai Gedeng Mataram. They had a son named Kiai Tumenggung Singaranu in Mataram. After Raden Malaya had this son, her father, the prince of Giri Laya, went to Mataram to celebrate the birth of his grandson. He set off for Semarang. However, on the ocean between the island of Karimun and the island of Mandalika his boat sank. Therefore, he was called the 'Prince Who Died on the Ocean' or *Pangeran Seda Lautan*.

[C]

The son of Giri Laya was Raden Wiracandra. He married the princess Haris Baya of Madura. After half a year, his wife died. He was desolate. In order to reduce his depression he sailed to Lampung.

[D]

When he came to Lampung, he taught the science of invulnerability to the royal family, including Patih Haji Panji Lalana Mas Wisesa. From Lampung, Raden Wiracandra travelled to Pathani to teach the same knowledge. From Pathani, he travelled to Pariaman. From there, he moved to Minangkabau and then back to Palembang. He stayed for a long time in Palembang. Kiai Gedeng Mataram received the news that Raden Wiracandra was staying in Palembang. Then Kiai Gedeng Mataram requested an elephant of Pangeran Sumedang.

[E]

Pangeran Sumedang commanded one of his men to go and meet Raden Wiracandra in Palembang. Pangeran Sumedang delegated Pangeran Singamanggala to invite Raden Wiracandra back to Mataram. Raden Singamanggala went to Palembang with an elephant. After a time Raden Wiracandra went with him back to Sumedang. In Sumedang, Raden Wiracandra met his relative from Madura. Pangeran Sumedang had been ordered by Kiai Gedeng Mataram to defeat the Madurese. Kiai Gedeng Mataram gave him booty slaves from the battle. They then settled in Sumedang.

[F]

After this, it is told that Susunan Ranggalawe Malangkabo clashed with people from Nagara Gung. Therefore, Susunan Ranggalawe faced the enemy in Timbanganten and asked Wiracandra to help him attack Nagara Gung. Thereupon Wiracandra attacked the Nagara Gung and defeated them. Raden Wiracandra was then rewarded with a daughter of Susunan Ranggalawe from Lebak Wangi. Wiracandra married her and settled in Timbanganten.

[G]

After a long time, the news came to Kiai Ngabehi Jagasatru in Nagara that Raden Wiracandra was living in Timbanganten. Kiai Ngabehi Jagasatru ordered him go into battle against the people of Lampung. Raden Wiracandra went to Lampung in order to fight them. After he came into the field, the fighting between the Lampungese and Cidamarese ceased, because both factions were the pupils of Raden Wiracandra. Instead of fighting, Raden Wiracandra ordered Haji Panji Lalana Mas Wisesa of Lampung to release his captives. Some of them had been taken as wives by the Lampung aristocrat. Other captives were returned to Raden Wiracandra. Only seven families were left in Lampung. Most of the captives went back to Kiai Ngabehi Jagasatru and settled in Citamiang. Except for one beautiful woman, Raden Tangan Kandi - she was most attractive.

[H]

Better than that, Kiai Ngabehi Jagasatru gave two women to Raden Wiracandra. The second woman was the daughter of Ngabehi Jagasatru himself. After that, Kiai Ngabehi Jagasatru of Mataram initiated Raden Wiracandra as Santana Agung Kiai Pamekel Tempuh. Kiai Pamekel Tempuh then settled in Mataram.

[I]

After long time, it is told that Kiai Rangga Gede in Karang invited Kiai Santana Agung Pamekel Tempuh to come to Karang. However, at that time he declined to go to Karang but he said, "Well, then, some other time I will come to Karang."

After that, the son of Kiai Santana Agung from his wife from Lebakwangi, who was the son of Sunan Ranggalawe Malangkabo, who was called Wirasantana, married Ayu Pathani, the son of Kiai Rangga Gede.

[J]

There was a son from the marriage of Kiai Santana Agung and Raden Tangan Kandi. His name was Entol Sambirana. Ayu Pathani married Kiai Rangga Gede. The brother of Ayu Pathani was called Entol Wirasantana. Ayu Pathani had one son and one daughter. The daughter married Wirayuda and had two daughters called Nyi Tasik and Nyi Wulan. Nyi Tasik married Ki Wirung, the son of Pangganan and he had two daughters and one son: Nyi Sutadinata, Ki Duriat, and Ki Mas Tuwan. Nyi Wulan had two daughters: Nyi Wanakerti and Nyi Kertasantika.

The child of Kiai Agung Pamekel Tempuh from Raden Tangan Kandi, called Entol Sambirana, married the daughter of Kiai Ngabehi Jagasatru.

[K]

Entol Sambirana had three daughters and one son; these were Nyi Tangan Imbasari who married Raden Singabangsa, Nyi Raden Tanganjiyah, who married Lebe Warta, and Nyi Tangan Koncer who married Ki Nurman from Batuwangi.

Nyi Tangan Imbasari had one son and one daughter: Ki Mas Wangsakusumah and Nyi Mas Panjang Jiwa.

Nyi Tanganjiyah had five sons and one daughter: these were Abdul Arif, Abdul Rosid, Panembahan Haji Abdul Muhyi, Nyai Chatib Muwahid, Tuan Haji Abdul Kohir and Abdul Halek.

Tangan Koncer had two daughters; these were Bibi Yaqin and Bibi Jakanta. Kiai Lebe Warta, the son of Entol Panengah had a brother called Ki Wanta, the father of Kersajati. Entol Panengah was the son of Serepen Nebol. Serepen Nebol was the son of Mudik Cikawung Ading. Mudik Cikawung Ading was the son of Kuda Lanjar. Kuda Lanjar was the son of Ratu Buhun. Ratu Buhun was the son of Galuh.

Ki Nurman from Batuwangi was the brother of Aki Boko, Aki Tindak, and Aki Munawar. Paman Jakanta's son was Aki Wangun. Aki Wangun's son was Aki Pangganan. The mother of Paman Jakanta was from Karang. She was the daughter of Ki Wana Baraja, the brother of Nini Madari, Nini Wiradinata, and Aki Ambu, the father of Aki Misin. The mother of Kiai Lebe Warta was from Gusti. She was a friend of Aki Codong, Aki Subang, Aki Bolang, Aki Salam, and the mother of Kiai Haji Abdul Qahar Pandawa, Aki Pagon the son of Entol Panengah and the brother of Kiai Lebe Warta from a different mother. The father of Aki Salam was Entol Panengah and his mother was Kiai Haji Abdul Kohar Pandawa.

The End.

E. The Structure of the *Babad*

The chronicle consists of signifiers referring to various things and concepts. In this referential perspective, the chronicle shows special arrangements of signifiers. To reveal the configuration of signs in the chronicle, I will first use some concepts of signification proposed by Saussure and then tried to interpret them further by using Peircean semiotics. An examination of the *Babad Pamijahan* shows that it is structured according to two sign configurations that may be called the vertical and horizontal axes. A horizontal axis is used by structuralists to analyse language and mythical narratives (Levi-Strauss 1968-1977: 145, 206-230) at the synchronic level. Saussure focuses on the abstract system of language based on the relation between the elements of *langue* called paradigmatic.

In the present study, I will use the concept of syntagmatic and paradigmatic only for describing the structure of the narrative as signs. After that, I shall try to place the whole narrative of the *Babad Pamijahan* within the discourse of the people of Pamijahan.

F. The Narrative of East and West

The *Babad Pamijahan* (BP) was written in the simplest of narrative forms. There is no flash back, insertion or maintaining of parallel plots. The plot is arranged entirely in a linear direction. In some sections we cannot find a time sequence, but instead move into a list of names. However, in its brevity and simplicity, BP conveys meaningful signs to its audience. Our task is to unmask the structure of the narrative by asking how meaning arises from its structures. Given that the narrative was written in the traditional genre of the *babad*, the organisation of events suggests itself as a good point of departure for our discussion.

It is evident that the narrative structure of this chronicle reveals a mythic abstraction of space, suggested by the travelling motifs related to Abdul Muhyi's ancestors who moved from the east (the Javanese space) to the west (the Sundanese space). From an anthropological perspective, such a narrative has implications in that it gives expression to the mythical space which provides the ground for the ancestors' mythical travelling, or topogeny (Fox, 1997: 91). This is the way people trace their ancestry through the metaphor of the journey in narratives. (ibid.) Fox states that "By 'topogeny' I refer to an ordered succession of place names. I see the recitation of a topogeny as analogous to the recitation of a genealogy." (ibid.) Therefore, at the same time, narratives can also illustrate genealogical lines. Fox observes that genealogy focuses on personal names while topogeny focuses on place names. (ibid) Elsewhere, Fox (1995: 225) has elaborated the metaphor of space and name by proposing the concept of 'apical' and 'lateral' expansion. These concepts refer to the structure of cognitive schemas which function as mnemonic devices. I believe that to some extent the Babad Pamijahan also employs these two metaphors, providing people with a cultural framework relating to their origins. This in turn is used for structuring cultural and social organisations crucial in managing the sacred sites and pilgrimage. Let us see how the Babad Pamijahan meets these assumptions. In doing so, I will first examine the linear structure, the 'horizontal axis', of the Babad Pamijahan.

G. The Horizontal Axis

Although BP is structured in a short and simple way, in fact it covers a wide geographical range, mentioning various places scattered from Wetan, or the East (in Java) to Banten, Lampung, Palembang and even Pathani on the Malay Peninsula. Altogether the chronicle mentions 23 places, in succession: Batuwangi, Cidamar, Cikawung Ading, Citamiang, the East (Wetan), Galuh, Karang, Lampung, Lebak Wangi, Madura, Malangkabo, Mataram, Minangkabau, Nagara, Palembang, Pandawa, Patani, Pulo Karimun, Semarang, Sumedang, the Nagara Gung, the Ocean, Timbanganten. These places are attached to the movement of the protagonists in the story. I will show that they are part of the signifying order provided by BP. The numbers of places are important in describing the range of the places designated by the text.

The custodian, who introduces the aim and the purpose of the chronicle, opens the narrative. In episode [A], the custodian appears to be the actual narrator for the reader or audience, or more precisely, to be the 'presenter' responsible for the story. His narration reveals two important factors in local reading conventions. First, the narrator reveals that BP should be received as a historical narrative (*sajarah*). *Sajarah* is a term found widely in Indonesian languages. It is derived from the Arabic *sajarat* (tree). Second, he states that the narrative is not only a 'history', but is also sacred material. In his introduction, the 'presenter' recounts that he needed to conduct a ritual purification before he translated the story from the Javanese language into Sundanese. These two factors 'regiment', to borrow Parmentier's term (1996), audiences or readers. It 'influences' the signification process concerning the narratives.

After that, there are episodes describing a number of characters, who later become known as the chief forebears in Shaykh Abdul Muhyi's genealogy [B]. Then come narrations of movements of characters such as Raden Malaya and Kiai Gedeng Mataram. The story mentions Sunan Giri Laya, who celebrated the birth of a new baby by his daughter, Raden Malaya, and journeyed to Raden Malaya's palace. However, on the way back to his palace, Sunan Giri died, his boat sank in the ocean. Sunan Giri was then called Pangeran Seda Lautan 'The Prince who Died on the Ocean'.

There follows an episode recounting Raden Wiracandra, who, it soon becomes apparent, is a key character. He travelled to the West, settled in various places, married and fought as well as taught. He was the son of Raden Malaya and the grandson of Sunan Giri Kadaton. Raden Wiracandra married the princess of

Harisbaya of Madura. However, after only six months, his wife died. He became depressed and set out towards the West. This episode, from a formalist perspective, is significant in transforming the plot. It is a point of departure for the whole story and contains a motif which generates the flow of the story. The dead princess of Harisbaya of Madura prompts 'the hero' to travel to the West. He sailed to Lampung. In Lampung, he taught the knowledge of invulnerability to royal families such as that of Patih Haji Panji Lalana Mas Wisesa. From Lampung he moved to Pathani, which today is in southern Thailand, and later settled in Pariaman in Minangkabau. After that, he returned to Palembang. According to the narrator, he lived in this region for a long time.

After that, BP delineates good relations between three important rulers: the king of Mataram, the king of Sumedang, and the king of Palembang. Meanwhile, there is also information regarding the tension between the two kings in 'the East', that is, between Mataram in central Java and Madura.[1] Unable to overcome this, the King of Mataram then recalls Raden Wiracandra to Mataram. In doing so, the King of Mataram asks his colleague from Sumedang to send an emissary to Palembang with an invitation for Raden Wiracandra. Raden Wiracandra then sets out for Java. He is ordered by the Sumedangese to go with the King of Sumedang to make war on Madura. They succeed in vanquishing the Madurese. The King of Mataram rewards Raden Wiracandra. Some followers return with Wiracandra to the West, i.e. to Sumedang. I mentioned the early episode of 'the dead princess' which triggers the main character to move westwards. From this episode, we can identify other motifs. The King of Mataram, who recalls Raden Wiracandra to Mataram indicates the importance of Raden Wiracandra as a protagonist.

The king of Mataram gives him a daughter as a wife in reward for his services. We find that the protagonist's problem, which appeared in the first episode, is solved: Raden Wiracandra at last has his new wife. This motif is then transformed in subsequent episodes where the protagonist is also rewarded by various local kings in the West in recognition of his bravery.

The episodes recite, for instance, that Wiracandra is invited by Ranggalawe to defeat his enemy from Nagara Gung. Wiracandra defeats Nagara Gung and is rewarded with the daughter of Ranggalawe from Lebak Wangi. This episode also tells us that Wiracandra then marries the daughter of Ranggalawe and settles in Timbanganten. Then, he also is invited by another ruler to fight his enemy from Lampung.

Important events, which are grouped in the episodes in a linear direction, can be schematised as follows:

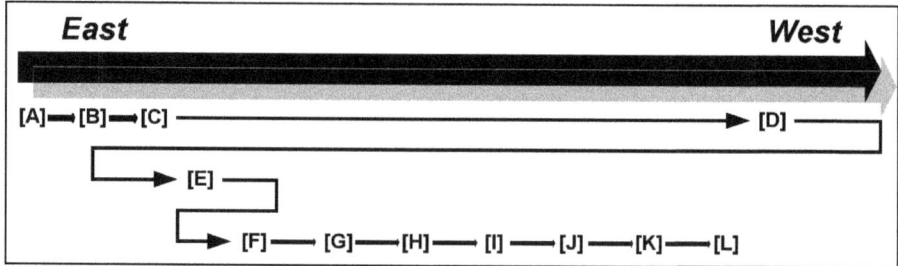

Figure 5. The zig-zag linear direction of the *Babad Pamijahan* narrative

It is clear that the movement of Raden Wiracandra is contained along the horizontal axis. The protagonist travels from the East [A] to the West [D], back to the east [E] and returns finally to the West [G→K].[2]

To borrow Levi-Strauss' term (1967:17), we have a 'geographic schema'. For Levi-Strauss, the linear story or myth represents the cognitive pattern of the people. This 'unconscious category' (ibid.) appears to be a cultural composition. He says that

> ...these sequences are organised, on planes at different levels (of abstraction), in accordance with schemata, which exist simultaneously, superimposed one upon another; just as a melody composed for several voices is held within bounds by constraints in two dimensions, first by its own melodic line which is horizontal, and second by the contrapuntal schemata (settings) which are vertical.

Thus, the horizontal line in the narrative creates a dimension of mythical space, the geographic schema. What should be kept in mind here is that the metaphor of travelling clearly becomes an important theme grouping the episodes. It marks the structure of events associated with a particular character.

H. The Vertical Axis

We have seen that in BP the plot is arranged linearly following the contrast between the East and West. There is another logic that supports the plot, which is called the 'vertical axis'. It constitutes the genealogy of Shaykh Abdul Muhyi from two ancestral lines. Here the contrast is between socially 'high' and 'low'. Sunan Giri, the Javanese saint-king of Gresik in East Java and Ratu Galuh of Sunda represent the highest points. While very much shorter than other *babad* in the Javanese tradition, BP contains almost 80 different names in its genealogy. These are integrated into a genealogical structure which is divided into two parts: the first section illustrates the relationship between Shaykh Abdul Muhyi and Sunan Giri; the second between Shaykh Abdul Muhyi and the King of Sunda.

The genealogy given in BP shows the importance of Javanese linkages. From the number of names identified, Javanese names make up a larger proportion than Sundanese. The author gives more detail to the Javanese than to the Sundanese ancestors. BP traces the Javanese line through Shaykh Abdul Muhyi's mother, Raden Tanganjiyah. She was a daughter of Entol Sambirana, who was the son of Raden Wiracandra. Raden Wiracandra himself was the son of Giri Laya and the grandson of the saint, Sunan Giri Kadaton.

Furthermore, from his father's line, that of Lebe Warta, the Shaykh is linked to the kingdom of Galuh through Entol Panengah, Serepan Nebol, Mudik Cikawung Ading, Kuda Lanjar, Ratu Galuh, and Ratu Buhun.

There is an indication that these vertical 'schemas', to use again Levi-Strauss' term, tie the story firmly together. We will see that 'vertical' lines have an abstraction similar to the 'horizontal' lines. Both contrast two similar things. Let us see how the vertical lines are structured and joined to the horizontal lines.

The vertical line is a selection of names. The author puts these names, his characters, into the slots of events. For example, the series of episodes A to H are filled by figures from the Javanese world while the next cluster of episodes, I and J, is supplied with figures both from the East as well as from the West. Finally the last episode, K to L, is filled by Sundanese figures only. When these arrangements are schematised, the repertoire becomes apparent.

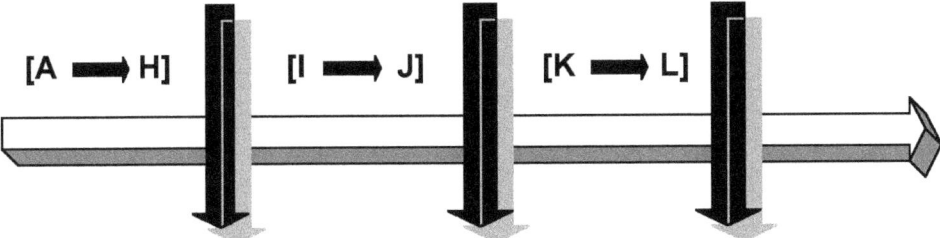

Figure 6. The paradigmatic schema in the *Babad Pamijahan*

The first vertical line shows the events filled by the Javanese ancestors. The second vertical line presents the events filled by a combination of people from the East and the West, in the third line there are only those from the West. For the names identified (refer to the text), the Javanese names constitute a larger proportion than the Sundanese. The author also supplies more detail for the Javanese than for the Sundanese ancestors. It would appear that the author is more concerned with creating a narrative than a genealogy from the point of view of the Sundanese kingdom. He appears not to be familiar with Sundanese history relating to Raja Galuh, the King of Sunda. Thus, the text gives the genealogy of the king of Sunda only at the end of the narrative.

The two genealogies can be represented schematically as follows.

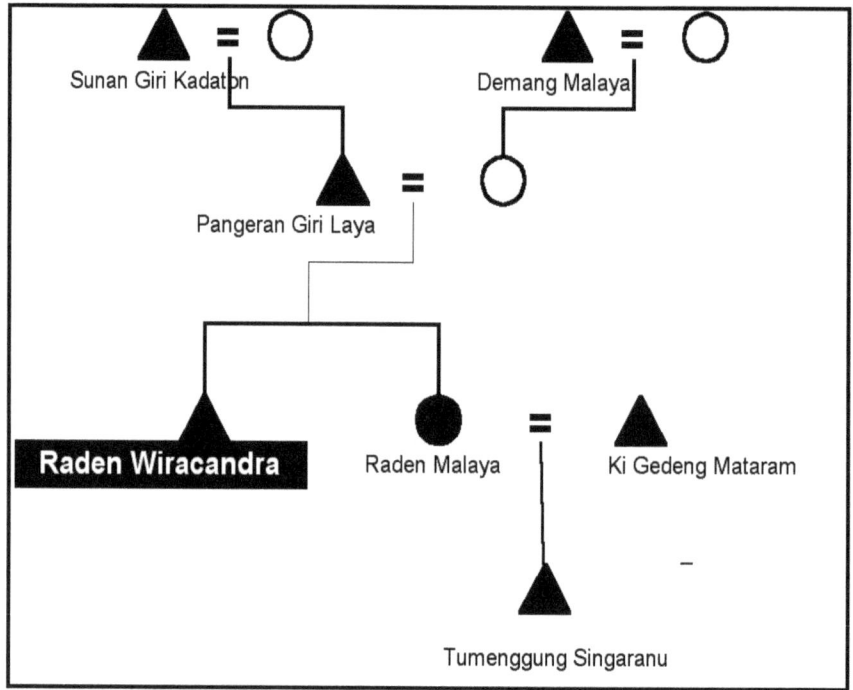

Figure 7. The genealogy of Abdul Muhyi through his mother's line from Raden Wiracandra, his mother's father

I. *Saur Sepuh* or 'What the Ancestors Say...'

The informant in Pamijahan who discussed the *Babad Pamijahan* with me was not the owner of the *babad,* nor he was able to read the manuscript, but he had had an opportunity to see the manuscript and had received an explanation of its contents from the owner, a site custodian. It was easy for him and other villagers like him to believe that Shaykh Abdul Muhyi was a real holy man because he is mentioned in the *Babad Pamijahan*. However, the term "real" here goes beyond the referential. It is experienced. The elder, like other villagers, shares the ground[3] regarding their ancestors' signs, without any obligation to check references given in the narrative. The manuscript and the elder's narrative itself are an 'index'[4] of their shared knowledge.

In my interviews with the villagers, I tried to put open questions, such as 'how do you know X?' or 'what is the meaning of X'? Responding to this question, the phrase "my ancestors told me," *saur sepuh*, recurs frequently at the beginning of their answers. This key phrase is used particularly in historical narratives, or when villagers have to explain certain aspects of material culture preserved by the custodians. In Sundanese, *sepuh* carries broad meanings. It can refer to ancestors, elders, or parents. The villagers may use *sepuh* when speaking of their ancestors, the older generation, or living elders as well as parents who have already died. The word modifies the whole of the content of the narratives delivered. The elders and the custodians, for example, share the same belief that Shaykh Abdul Muhyi was a real holy man according to *saur sepuh*. The author of BP in [A], mentions that *sepuh* means "one who has received the grace and blessing of God".

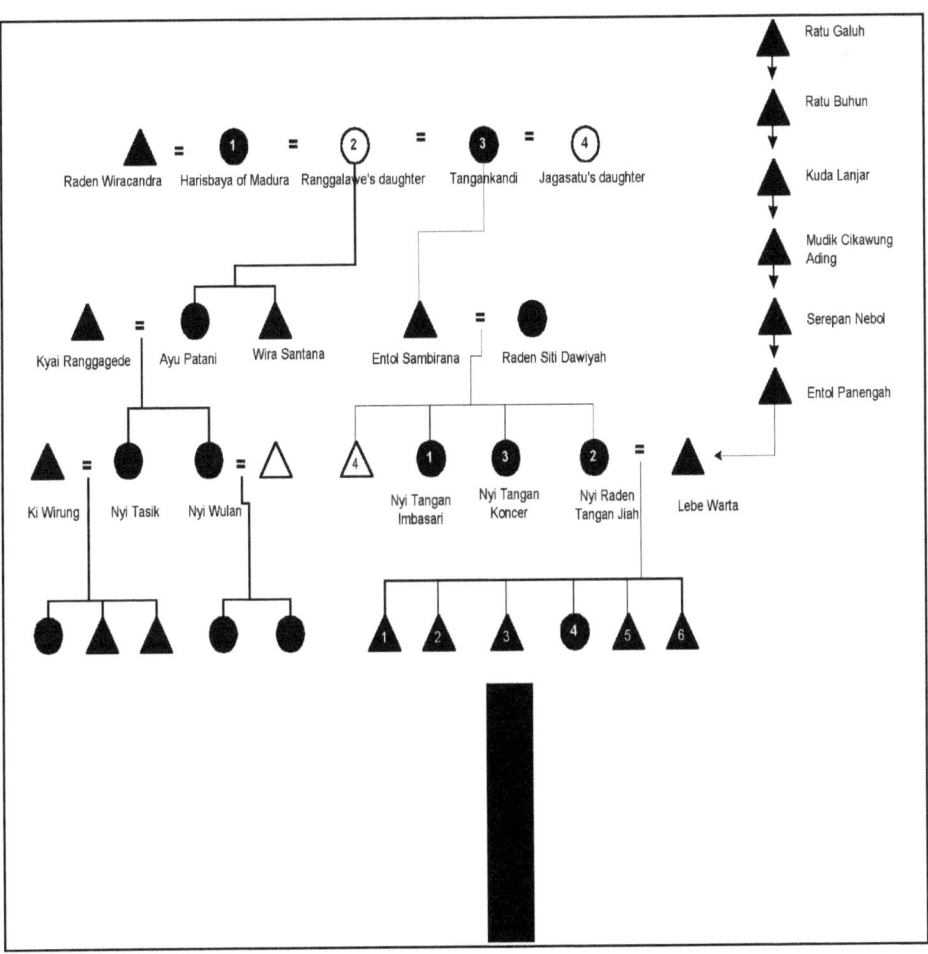

Figure 8. Shaykh Abdul Muhyi's genealogy through his father's line.

These 'words of the ancestors' form a powerful element in all narrative performance. They encapsulate the whole ideology of the narrative. By using such devices, custodians can spread and manipulate belief in the holiness of Shaykh Abdul Muhyi. During my fieldwork, I found that the villagers always use *saur sepuh* to introduce narratives explaining features of the material culture around the sacred village. In the same vein, it is easy for the villagers to assume that if Susunan Giri Kadaton[5] is real, then Shaykh Abdul Muhyi must also be real. Of course, it is difficult for historians to confirm whether Shaykh Abdul

Muhyi actually was a descendant of Giri Kadaton, or whether Shaykh Abdul Muhyi was part of the Wali Sanga tradition, the popular 'Nine Saints of Java'. Krauss (Krauss 1995) suggests that Shaykh Abdul Muhyi stands half in myth and half in history. However, villagers construct the 'historicality' of their Shaykh by a process of abduction. Abduction[6] is defined by Peirce (Mertz and Parmentier 1985) as a way of reasoning where one does not use a 'general rule' explicitly, as may be seen in the relation between the following two propositions.

> Shaykh Abdul Muhyi's name is connected to the genealogy of the Wali, therefore Shaykh Abdul Muhyi is a wali.

The *Babad Pamijahan* provides the villagers with the first proposition. The second is the villagers' own hypothesis. Such abduction is not only generated from the text of BP but also from a complex narrative performance. By a complex narrative performance I mean the actualisation of narratives (signs of history) in daily activities.

On the first day of my fieldwork, I tried to make a 'tour' of the pilgrimage area. A custodian ordered one of his staff to accompany me. In the villagers' terminology, the staff member is called *nu nganteur* or a guide. His main job was to take me to the sacred cave and to other sacred sites outside Pamijahan. *Nu nganteur* cannot perform the ritual pilgrimage within Muhyi's shrine itself. That job is a monopoly of the senior custodian. Accordingly, most of those *nu nganteur* are not closely related to the fourth main family which controls the pilgrimage area. The guide told me to buy the book of the history of Shaykh Abdul Muhyi which he called 'The History Book' (*Buku Sajarah*). When I asked him who wrote the book and why I had to buy it, he said that it was written by one of the custodian's relatives. He said, "You can get the whole story (*sajarah*) of Shaykh Abdul Muhyi from it." He said that he could not recite the story of Abdul Muhyi in detail himself because he was not an expert. I asked him again, who was an expert in history. He said that Ajengan Endang, the most prominent custodian was the expert. He added that contents of the *Buku Sajarah* that I bought were also taken from what the the custodian had said. The custodian was an expert in history because he had a sacred manuscript called *Babad Pamijahan*. "Why do you think that *Babad Pamijahan* contains the real history of Shaykh Abdul Muhyi?" I asked him. He was surprised by my question at first, but then he replied with a relatively long explanation.

> *"For me, Shaykh Abdul Muhyi was real because all the elders as well as the custodian in my village believe so. According to the words of our ancestors (saur sepuh), all the sacred materials (nu karamat) in this village are connected to his life. Many people come here and concur that Kangjeng Shaykh was a wali who received divine favour (barakah). According to saur sepuh, the sacred book called the Babad Pamijahan was also written by a close*

relative of Shaykh Abdul Muhyi's who was his contemporary in time (dina zamana)."

My 'guide' strongly believed that the *Babad Pamijahan* is one of the main sources for reciting his ancestor's history. Interestingly, he has never seen the manuscript but he believes that it contains 'narratives of the ancestors'. Thus, the meaning of the *Babad Pamijahan* came to my informant, not through the process of reading but through its performance. In the narratives delivered by my guide, indeed, there was an 'epidemiology'[7] of the reported speech *'saur sepuh'*. The reported speech has an internal power to generate interpretation.

In this regard, *saur sepuh* is the 'additional software' needed for comprehending the meaning. The narrative of the ancestors recorded in the *Babad Pamijahan* must be activated by another medium, such as ritualised language or action. For instance, the custodian who translated the *Babad Pamijahan* into Sundanese felt that the process of translation itself was a sacred project. Before he made the translation, he performed intermediary ritual or *tawassul,* a rite which is also often conducted during pilgrimage and in mystical practices. The main theme of the *tawassul* is to recite Shaykh Abdul Muhyi's name and those of his ancestors, as well as of the Sufi master, and to ask God to bestow His blessing upon these figures. By performing this ritual, people expect two things. The first is that all the grace and blessings given by God to their ancestors will be transmuted into their own lives. Second, the ritual is also used as a way of asking the ancestors for permission to recite their histories. Every act related to the ancestor's name or identity has a sacred dimension. The custodian who copied this manuscript from the older one also followed this rule. The scribe of manuscript H adds this formulaic introduction into his manuscript.

> [A]
>
> Mangka sarehna pirang-pirang para ihwan, oge badil asdiqoi seueur anu mundut dipangdamelkeun Hikayat (dongeng) Babad Pamijahan anu jelas, janten manah abdi lajeng tumandang kana tawassul ka Tuan Paduka Shaykh Haji Abdul Muhyiddin Panembahan di Pamijahan—Karangnunggal.
>
> When many of my friends asked me to make a clear copy of the story of Pamijahan, I decided to make ritual mediation (tawassul) to Tuan Paduka Shaykh Haji Abdul Muhyiddin in Pamijahan, Karangnunggal.

From this perspective, *saur sepuh* has the power to enhance beliefs regarding Shaykh Abdul Muhyi. So far, I have shown that the construction of meaning is initially triggered by ritualised idioms such as *saur sepuh*. *Saur sepuh* itself is not part of the poetics of the *Babad Pamijahan* but rather an extrinsic element embedded into the text by the performer. However, we will see that *saur sepuh* is not arbitrarily attached to the text. There is a correlation between the attachment of *saur sepuh* and the genre to which it is attached. Only particular narratives have the authority to be activated and validated by *saur sepuh*. Any single word, sentence, typography of manuscript, collector, as well as any place where the manuscript is collected, are signs: perceivable, referential, and interpretable.

For the villagers, the validation of whether a particular phenomenon such as a narrative or a manuscript can function as a meaningful sign rests on their ideology. By ideology, I mean any set of interrelated assumptions which appear as a 'ground' for identifying and using signs. Ideology itself is a product of previous semiotic processes. (Eco 1979: 139-42) It is accumulated through the process of interpretation. In this regard, the idea of closeness to the holy man is crucial. The manuscripts are only held by the close family of the saint who may dwell in the vicinity of the holy tomb.

The *Babad Pamijahan* is meaningful not only because it is part of the *saur sepuh* discourse but because it contains other significant references for the villagers. As stated by Peirce, signs have three elements, the perceptable, the referential, and the interpretable (Mertz 1985; Parmentier 1994). In other words, a manuscript or the text of a manuscript could be a sign because it comes to the villagers' perception as something important, pointing to something, and suggesting interpretation.

J. The References

The total configuration of the signs bound up in the *babad* is part of Pamijahan tradition. In this regard, Teeuw (1984, 38-56) proposes that a particular genre of literature entails a horizon of expectation (see also Culler 1974). If we push this assumption a little further, then we will find that a genre is the system of meaning attached to particular works. The framework or 'horizon of expectations' determines the meaning of the *babad*. Thus, the *Babad Pamijahan* is a configuration of signs for the villagers because the genre, or 'ground' in Peircean terms regiments it.[8]

However, the gap between genre and the signification process and its result is still to be disclosed. We have to describe not only signs as a 'type' but also describe the mode of relation between a sign and its reference, and the relation between the reference and its interpretants. In other words; the schematic approach adopted from structuralism above, as suggested by Saussure and Levi-Strauss, only reveals a linear and an internal regulation, a 'grammar' of the text. We still have to describe the relation between the grammar and its references. In this case, the Peircean perspective is important. Peirce mentions three modes of relation between representation and object and these are icon, index, and symbol. (Parmentier 1994)

References or objects do not always refer to material culture but also to mental concepts. In these terms, there are two kinds of objects. The first is the object within the sign. (Parmentier 1994) The second is the 'object outside of the sign'. Thus, the object can be both 'fictive' and 'real' at the same time depending on how the sign 'indicates' or "leaves the interpreter to find out by collater experience". (Parmentier 1994; Rochberg-Halton 1986) The most important task for us now is to discern the relation between the signs in the *Babad Pamijahan* and their references, as well as their intepretants. It is a question of relations. What is the relation between the signs in the *Babad Pamijahan* and their objects as well as to their interpretant?

K. Space and Place: Limestone (*Karang*)

One of the important words related to the concept of space is *karang*. To comprehend its position in this cultural narrative is to discern, first, the category of relation between the word *karang* which denotes limestone, and its references as well as its interpretants. *Karang* is a word referring to kind of stone. *Karang* itself, borrowing Peirce's terms, is both replica (token) and legisign (type). In other words, *karang* is in actual existence as the word but at the same time it is part of Sundanese vocabulary or type (signsign) which 'shall be significant' according to the convention (legisign). Similar to the word for stone (*batu*), *karang* refers to the concept of 'solid' or 'hard'.

This can be tested against villagers' experience. People in the regency of Tasikmalaya know that the Karang area is a centre of old teaching recognised as a centre of spiritual power such as black magic (*teluh*) as well as white magic.[9] They also have *ilmu karang* or knowledge of invulnerability. There is a saying familiar to people in this area referring to *karang* as a notion and a place embodying magic power.

> Bedas weduk urang Karang, taina teu teurak ku parang.
>
> Strong and invulnerable are the folk of Karang, even their faeces can not be penetrated by swords.

Furthermore, in the Dutch archives, Karang was known as a remote place where rebels were hidden and given assistance by the "Haji Carrang" (Shaykh Abdul Muhyi). Thus, the word *karang* is actually an informational sign or proposition referring to its object by symbol (convention). *Karang* symbolically refers to the concept of invulnerability that ultimately is interpreted as part of identity.

Most manuscripts relating to Shaykh Abdul Muhyi similarly make reference to *karang* as a place. Some of them also describe what they call "the knowledge of *karang*" or *ilmu karang*. My informants and several manuscripts also refer to *karang* as a place of the ancestors known in Sundanese as *kabuyutan*.[10] Recently local philologists have found a number of Old Sundanese manuscripts preserved from the pre-Islamic period. These included the *Amanat ti Galunggung, Shanghyang Siksa Kanda ing Karesyan* and *Waruga Guru*. They were found in Garut and Tasikmalaya, places recognised as *kabuyutan*, or ancestral homes of Sundanese culture (Kossim 1974; Atja 1981: 1-9; Atja 1968). *Urang Karang* or "people from Karang" in the Tasikmalaya district are seen then as belonging to a society with a distinct character. Mysticism and sorcery or *teluh* are often attributed to them. They are part of the 'old world' of Sunda.

Oral traditions from this place mention that before Shaykh Abdul Muhyi came to 'Carrang' (Pamijahan is part of the district of Karang), it was occupied by *urang Hindu*. What they mean by 'Hindu' is not Hindu in particular but Hindu designating pre-Islamic culture in general. According to local lore, once a Batara Karang (Lord of Karang) controlled all of the area now called Karang Nunggal. Batara Karang was a master of black magic. Shaykh Abdul Muhyi was sent to this place in order to defeat Batara Karang and convert him to Islam. Another story recounts how Batara Karang intercepted Shaykh Abdul Muhyi in his mystical journey, intending to kill him. However, Batara Karang was unable to draw his sword. It was stuck fast in its scabbard and its hilt become longer and longer. Batara Karang then summoned all of his powers to point his sword at the Shaykh's face. According to the locals, Batara Karang failed to kill Muhyi because the volume and dimensions of his sword kept increasing so that he could not even hold it. Batara Karang then agreed to convert to Islam and come under the Shaykh's tutelage.

The term *karang* is then permeated with sacred and historical concepts. The concept of *kabuyutan* as a place of the ancestors is, in fact, attached to the Karang area today. The custodian of Pamijahan believes that Pamijahan in particular, and the Karang area in general, have been important sources of religious clerics or *ajengan*. According to the custodian, all famous religious preachers in the eastern part of West Java have linkages with ancestors.

Thus, *karang*, as word, is also a 'conventional sign', and in Pamijahan this word has become an actualisation, or the 'parole' of the ancestors in Saussuerean terms. In other words, the signs of history, narratives, and discourse appear to be cultural narratives regulated by conventionalised signs.

L. The Interpretant: The East and The West

Other spatial concepts can be found in the text. Historically, the Sundanese have been categorised by Dutch colonial and Indonesian governments as *orang Jawa Barat* or 'people of West Java'. Some Sundanese have realised that this label simplifies far too much the complexity of the term 'Sunda' as a label marking cultural identity (see also Ekadjati 1995:12-13). For them 'Sunda' is more mythical than the geographical term 'West Java'. It is important first to outline how the term 'Sunda' has developed and is understood. After that, we will return to the references of space made in the *Babad Pamijahan*.

Dutch administrators, in their first contact with the Sundanese, tended to classify them as people residing in the heartland of West Java. Sometimes, they simply called them 'people from the mountains' because they perceived the Sundanese at that time as the people inhabiting the central part of the region, which is hilly and mountainous. (Stibbe 1929)

From the perspective of the Sundanese themselves, this view is naive and humiliating. There are serious implications when politicians and researchers try to use the term without being aware of the dimension of internal perspectives. As Wessing has correctly observed: "West Java has, for most of recorded history, been considered a cultural backwater" (Wessing 1978: 22). From Sundanese myth and legends, the word Sunda can be traced back to the period of 1030—1333 AD, when the kings of Sunda, such as Jayabhupati, held control of the ports on the north coast. (Wessing 1978) (Wessing 1974; Fruit-Mess 1920) Stibbe speculates further that Sunda existed between the two larger kingdoms of Singasari in East Java and Sriwijaya around Palembang. (Stibbe 1929) Sunda, he says, has existed as a single cultural and political entity in contradistinction to the Javanese or the people of Palembang. It is also not appropriate to call the Sundanese *urang gunung* (mountain people) since the Sundanese king also controlled ports such as Sunda Kalapa or Jayakarta (later Jakarta).

Sundanese historian Edi Ekadjati (1995:12-13) has given an important historical outline of West Java and the Sundanese. According to Ekadjati, the term *Jawa Barat* (West Java) was popularised in 1925 when the colonial government proposed the division of the area into a province. Under the Dutch policy, the boundaries of the province of West Java were close to the map imagined by Mataram and the VOC in 1706. The Province of West Java included Banten, Batavia (Jakarta), Priangan, and Cirebon (Staatsblad no. 235 and 278, 1925; Ekadjati).[11] For some Sundanese, the term 'West Java' suggests a subordinate position to Java. Indeed, the Sundanese were reluctant to use the terms 'West Java' preferring instead 'Sunda or 'Pasoendan' as may be seen in a petition proposed by the *Pagoejoeban Pasoendan* (The Sunda League) in 1924-1925. Furthermore, the Sundanese also proposed a *Negara Pasundan* (State of Pasundan) when Indonesia operated as a federation in 1948-1949 (Ekadjati 1995:13). Similarly, the Youth Congress of Sunda also suggested Sunda as the name of the province instead of Jawa Barat. As we know, none of these petitions were accepted. The word Sunda or *tatar Sunda* (the realm of Sunda) then, remains a term for cultural usage rather than political affairs.

Sundanese antipathy to their Javanese neighbours can be traced back to the Bubat tragedy of 1357 when the king of Sunda along with his daughter and followers were slaughtered on the orders of minister Gajah Mada of Majapahit at the very gate of the capital of Majapahit. Gajah Mada's agenda was to prevent the Sundanese princess from marrying his ruler. (Atja 1984/1985) For the Sundanese, this tragedy etched the differences between Java and Sunda deeply in their minds.

However, the kingdom of Sunda was not to endure for long. It was defeated by Banten in 1579 and most Sundanese embraced Islam. Relations between Java in the East and Sunda in the West developed new dimensions. If Sundanese myth and legend tell of the glories of Sunda and stress their differences from Java, both oral and written works dating from the 17th century indicate a new type of imagery of their ancestors. Sundanese ancestral myths became connected with Javanese kings or with the Nine Saints of Java, the *Wali Sanga*. Of course, there was a need to provide cultural foundations regarding these phenomena. Traditional narratives tend to reconcile the two identities of Sunda and Java in a peaceful manner. We find numerous stories describing marriages between the families of the Sundanese kings with Muslim rulers of Javanese or Arabic extraction, or accounts of the conversion of the King of Sunda to Islam. In the Priangan, this motif is found, for example, in the story of Kiansantang. Kiansantang was the son of a Sundanese king. He converted to Islam and tried to persuade his father to convert with him. According to the local narratives of Garut, the king himself was not swayed to adopt Islam, but he allowed his son to follow the new religion. This is a popular motif in West Java by which the Sundanese try to ease the relations between their previous identity (in this case, religion) and the influence of Islam which, to a large extent, was brought by the Javanese to the highlands of Sunda. The last king of Sunda then retreated to the forest on the south coast and built his own kingdom there with his faithful followers. Sundanese legend says that he is not dead and appears from time to time in the form of a tiger (*maung*). The tiger has become an important icon for the Sundanese and the associated narrative a face-saving device.

In this regard, the author of the *Babad Pamijahan* depicts Shaykh Abdul Muhyi as a 'man from the East', that is, a Javanese. It is also common for Sundanese to refer to their Javanese counterparts as people from the East, *urang wetan* rather than Javanese, *urang Jawa*. *Urang Jawa* is a ritualised term used by the Sundanese of the Priangan to help them indentify and understand the conspicuous elements of Sunda and Java in their culture. This very same atmosphere is found in the *Babad Pamijahan*.

M. Sumedang and Mataram

Other representations of East and West can also be found in the contrast between Sumedang and Mataram. Sumedang is a centre of Sundanese culture, Mataram is the Javanese kingdom to the east. The *Babad Pamijahan* makes clear references to Mataram and Sumedang. Sumedang and Sukapura-Tasikmalaya have common historical legitimacy. Under Mataram's hegemony, their territories were granted to their leader in reward for brave service rendered in capturing a local figure, Dipati Ukur, who led a rebellion against Mataram's authority. (Ekadjati 1982)

There is a marked similarity between local history and the *babad* accounts of the position of Sumedang as a political intermediary between Mataram and the realm of Sunda. In the *Babad Pamijahan,* Sumedang features as a meeting place between the Sundanese (Raden Rangga) and the Javanese (Raden Wiracandra). Raden Wiracandra was the grandson of Sunan Giri, one of the Nine Saints, who travelled to Sunda after the death of his wife. In Sumedang, he married a Sundanese noblewoman. It is from this linkage that the *Babad Pamijahan* derives Shaykh Abdul Muhyi's genealogy.

After the expanding Dutch administration reduced Mataram's influence in Sunda relations between Sukapura and Sumedang became unstable. The colonial power used these two regencies to help them gain control of coffee and other agricultural commodities developed in the area. For instance, when Sukapura rejected the Dutch agricultural policy of forced cultivation known as *tanam paksa,* the Regent of Sukapura was replaced by an official from Sumedang. The Sumedangese then tried to impose their will in Sukapura's territory by replacing certain officials. However, the Sumedangese in Sukapura were not successful in persuading the local people to plant coffee and other plantation crops as were required. The Dutch realised that the Sukapuranese did not have the support of the people of Sumedang. Ultimately the regency of Sukapura was allowed to return to its own lineage. With all of this in mind, it seems to me that *Babad Pamijahan* articulates the position of Sumedang rather than that of Sukapura.

If the historical background has bearing on the authorship of the *Babad Pamijahan,* it is easy to assume that the chronicle is part of the aristocratic tradition, whether of the Bupati of Sukapura or of Sumedang. Our question is how the Pamijahanese or the Karangnese recognise this past.

During my conversations with the elders, the custodians and other villagers, I grasped a different theme relating to their affiliation with aristocratic centres. The Pamijahanese tend to see their village and region as a centre in itself, rather than as part of Sukapura or Sumedang. Again, the priority of the ritualised space of Pamijahan is affirmed. As a consequence, they believe that all the important figures of Sukapura-Tasikmalaya and Sumedang are descendants of, or at least, have mystical relations with, Pamijahan. This assumption was revealed to me by the custodian when the Bupati of Tasikmalaya made a pilgrimage to the shrine of the Shaykh. Unlike other people in other areas, the Pamijahanese did not perform any special ceremonies to honour the Bupati. The custodians and villagers accepted him and his entourage in a modest manner, as they do for other pilgrims.

The next morning I asked the custodian in his office about this phenomenon. "Why did you not perform a special ceremony for the Bupati?" He answered, "All the Bupatis of Tasikmalaya regard it as compulsory to make a visit to Kangjeng Shaykh because they know that their predecessors, the old regents of Tasikmalaya, always came here to remember the important relationship between Sukapura-Tasikmalaya and Pamijahan. Sukapura-Tasikmalaya has a strong bond *(pakuat-pakait)* with Pamijahan." He went on, "One of Sukapura's *bupati* was buried in the area of Shaykh Abdul Muhyi's shrine. He was a follower of Kangjeng Shaykh." The villagers share this story.

Indeed, these areas have been filled by historical energy from various sources. Karang and Pamijahan have perpetuated the concept of *kabuyutan,* an ancestral heartland which radiates spiritual power. Sukapura, Sumedang, and Mataram in contrast are recognised only as political centres. Relations between the two realms have been dynamic, particularly when they deal with foreigners like the Dutch (de Haan 1910-12: 462,674-676). At times political centres such as Sukapura have wanted to occupy all of Karang and Pamijahan. However, they have never succeeded in regulating all the spaces. Even today the Pamijahanese maintain their *perdikan* status with independence from government taxes. (Ricklefs 1998)

When the government wanted to promote tourism in the area by building a bus station in Pamijahan, they had to face the custodians and elders, who questioned the proposal. The elders wanted to show their symbolic authority to the government by insisting that they be consulted about any changes planned for the area. The government had to recognise them because all the lands were in the hands of Pamijahanese. The Pamijahanese, through a local foundation called the 'Holy Place Foundation' (*Yayasan Kakaramatan*), then leased the land to the government to used for the constgruction of the bus station.

N. Conclusion

Our discussion so far indicates that the relation of various signs in the *Babad Pamijahan* expresses certain assumptions about the relation between East and West, as well as about genealogy. In other perspectives, these relations can be meaningful for the society if there is mediation, or an interpretant to bring the synchronic level into a temporal dimension. Between the past and the present, there is a reasoning process. People make every effort to connect the past and the present through certain narrative discourses.

Narratives of the origins of Pamijahan are among the most authoritative in Pamijahan. Accordingly, the custodian has held versions of them for several decades. The guild of custodians (*pakuncenan*) not only serves pilgrims but also delivers these 'true' narratives to them. The *Babad Pamijahan* connects the Pamijahanese with the aristocratic tradition from both Sundanese and Javanese forebears. It not only provides the genealogical sources which connect the Wali with two important rulers in Java, the King of Pajajaran and Sunan Giri Laya, a powerful missionary in early conversion of Eastern Java to Islam (Fox 1991,32-3), but also furnishes the villagers with various schematic categories. (Levi-Strauss 1968-1977; Parmentier 1994) Among these is the shaping of perceptions of space and place, and it is to this I turn in the following chapter.

ENDNOTES

[1] In Sundanese, Javanese are often called *urang wetan*, or 'people from the east'.

[2] Apparently this schema is also close to the sacred journey undertaken by *urang wetan* (people from the east) to Pamijahan. In certain seasons of the year more Javanese make the pilgrimage to Pamijahan than any other ethnic group, including Sundanese. Some of them even come to Pamijahan by foot. In modern times, the motif of the man from the East can also be found in the Darul Islam rebellion in Tasikmalaya. Kartosuwiryo was a Javanese who led Sundanese peasants and religious clerics in opposition to the Dutch in the 1940s, and a decade later in opposition to the army of the Republic. Among his followers, Kartosuwiryo was believed to have spiritual powers similar to those of a *wali*, see Jackson (1980)

[3] In the Peircean paradigm 'ground' is defined as 'frame work', which determines the existence of the sign in relation to its object.

[4] 'Index' is a sign, which refers to its object on the basis of actual connection.

[5] In the Javanese tradition as mentioned in the *Babad ing Sangkala*, the name of Giri refers to the Sultan Agung's opponent in East Java in 1636, see Ricklefs (1998)

[6] One of the methods of inference in Peircean semiotics is called 'abduction'. Abduction is defined as a hypothetical inference where people try to identify that 'something must be the case'. (Mertz 1885)

[7] The 'script' used by these performers was derived from, borrowing Sperber's phrase (Sperber 1990) 'the belief box story'. Any belief is produced and stored in this box. However, as Sperber states, such a record 'machine' cannot play the whole story; there is at least some additional software required called 'inferential devices'. These help us to make coherence out of our experience. According to Sperber: "What we need to add for this to the belief box is some inferential devices which can recognize unrepresented beliefs on the basis of the actually represented ones. Human beliefs are grounded not in the perception of things the beliefs are about, but in communication about these things. Second, humans have a meta-representational or interpretive ability. That is, they can construct not only descriptions but also interpretations." (Sperber 1990). Thus the *Babad Pamijahan* is somewhat like a jukebox by which custodians and villagers can replay the contents in their daily activities.

[8] Regimentation is the sign configuration the design of which is based on a particular ideology. For instance, the way a war memorial diorama is designed reflects the ideology of the regime. The audience is forced to follow the narrative of war as imagined by the regime, see Parmentier (1994).

[9] Black magic is conceived of as a survival of pre-Islamic practice. White magic is believed to be a supernatural power exercised by *wali* and *ulama*.

[10] Archeologists believe that the concept of *kabuyutan* is similar to the Indian concept of *mandala*. *Kabuyutan* was sacred ancestral territory in the Hindu period. People tried to translate and maintain this spatial concept in the subsequence Muslim period.

[11] In October 2000 the four *kabupaten* of Banten broke away from West Java and formed their own province.

Chapter 5: *Karuhun*, Space, Place and Narratives

"Ka luhur moal pucukan, ka handap moal akaran" (Ajengan Endang, custodian of Pamijahan, 1997).

"New green leaves will never grow at the top of the tree, nor will new roots ever grow at the bottom."

A. Introduction

As mentioned in Chapters 2 and 3, the major meaning of the ancestor narratives is to signify a transformation given to the land: the space of the wild forest transformed into '*hindu* land', and later into '*muslim* land'. Written narratives in the form of the *babad* have preserved the villagers' imagination of the past. There is a clear indication that the *babad* functions to freeze the genealogy of the ancestors, the *karuhun* genealogy. However, we see a different focus in narratives of the oral tradition. The *Babad* does not recite clearly how the protagonist, Shaykh Abdul Muhyi, found a cave, converted Batara Karang, and made shelters in the southern part of the Sunda region. Contrasting with the *Babad Pamijahan*, oral narratives retell the *Wali*'s itinerary in this area in a very lively way. If the Babad chronicle tries to draw the importance of Pamijahan in a framework of the Javanese and Sundanese realms, oral narratives tend to focus on the existence of Shaykh Abdul Muhyi in his own time. Oral narratives have implications for the way that villagers imagine their ancestry and territory.

The notion of origin in Austronesian societies has been an important issue for anthropology (Fox 1996 and 1997; Bellwood 1996), history and semiotics. (Parmentier 1986) Fox, for instance proposes two useful concepts related to the tracing of origins. The first is the succession of personal names, and the second is "topogeny". Topogeny is a metaphorical form where people use a structure of metaphor in order to designate the line of origins in terms of 'a succession of place names'. (Fox, 1997:8)

In addition, a similar framework, also suggested by Parmentier, is important in the case of Pamijahan. Parmentier focuses on the meaning of 'path' in traditional society. The path is a 'sediment trace of activity' and a 'trajectory' device. (Tilley 1994; Parmentier 1987) In his semiotic perspective, Parmentier argues that the path relates to three dimensions of semantics. First, the path is recognised as a sign that has an effect on social consciousness. It is able to provide a 'sign in history' as seen in narratives that trace the ancestors' itinerary. Second, the path provides people with a framework or metaphor of hierarchy (cf. Fox 1996:132) where precedence in social rank is linked to the path. Third, the path has a structure which 'influences' a walker. To modify the path is to have a certain power to modify cultural strategy, or local affairs. Arguing along the same lines, Tilley (1994: 31) proposes the concept of 'a serial trajectory' in which 'the best way to go' is written in the path. The path can then be used as hierarchical *mnemonic* device related to the founders of the village. A criss-crossing of the path and texts creates a space which is also open to interpretation. (cf. Eco 1999) Thus, precedence and contestation are important issues. (Fox 1996:146)

While the *Babad Pamijahan* focuses more on the description of the ancestors of Muhyi, the oral traditions, which are used by the custodians as a pivotal source for their history of the Shaykh, tend to focus on the contemporaries of the Wali and his descendants. For instance, oral tradition retells the story of his journey to Aceh and Mecca to acquire the teachings of Islam, his mystical journey to the southern part of Priangan in search of a cave for meditation, or his conversion of the villagers to Islam. The custodians classify these narratives as the speech of ancestors, or *kasauran karuhun,* sometimes is called *pitutur karuhun*. This chapter then aims to explain the relationship between spatial concepts and genealogy as well as the mystical journey of the founder of the village.

B. *Karuhun*

In Sunda, particularly in Pamijahan, 'our ancestors', or *karuhun urang*, can refer to the founding ancestors, a single ancestor, the village ancestors, or to family ancestors.

Karuhun is a central concept in the village culture, referring to the founder, Shaykh Abdul Muhyi, as well as to his companions and to Muhyi's ancestors. The line of descent after Shaykh Abdul Muhyi, which is called *kolot* or *kolot urang* is also crucial. It influences the social interaction in the village. On the other hand, the line of *karuhun* is stable, in so far as it is generally accepted and agreed upon. It connects the villagers directly to the network of the Nine Saints of Java or *wali sanga*, as well as to the King of Sunda. In Sunda, these lines seem compulsory since they help Sundanese to 'domesticate' their conversion to Islam. (Djajadiningrat 1913 and 1965) The narratives reflect the dynamics of 16th century Java when Islam penetrated from Cirebon on the north coast to Galuh and from Banten to Pajajaran. (cf. Lombard 1996) In other words, the story is able to provide a better framework for the villagers to respond to the mixed myth of their ancestors.

In their narratives concerning village ancestors, or *karuhun*, villagers rarely refer to the king of Sunda, but they often make references to the Saints of Java. This is due to the fact that the Islamization of this area was undertaken by people from Cirebon as well as a number of Mataram missionaries. Sometimes, in different settings, villagers will refer both to Sundanese and Javanese ancestors as long as they are Muslims. The Muslim ancestors receive more attention than

Karuhun, Space, Place and Narratives

the pre-Islamic ones. Stories of the past are able to reconcile the contradiction between the winner, the Muslims, and the defeated, pre-Islamic Hindu Sunda.

In the *Babad Pamijahan*, the genealogy of Shaykh Abdul Muhyi starts with Sunan Giri and and continues through Shaykh Abdul Muhyi's descendants from his four wives. Accordingly, in ritual speech, Pamijahanese enumerate ancestral spirits starting from Shaykh Abdul Muhyi. The Shaykh is the founding ancestor of Pamijahan, and in ritual, they call him *Eyang*.[1] An *eyang* belongs the category of founding ancestors, or *karuhun*. The term is used for apical ancestors of Pamijahanese who set up a new village. In rituals they say "Let's recite prayers for *karuhun urang*, all of our ancestors". The second level generation after the *eyang* is called *sepuh urang*. A *sepuh urang* is the origin point of a subgroup within a village, still relatively close to the contemporary life of *eyang*. In the village, the line of succession of names is called the *kokocoran* or the 'source of the river'. It is perceived as a river flowing vertically down from the *karuhun*. According to the custodian Ajengan Endang, "By defining these lines, it is clear that the sacred tomb and other sacred territories, from the death of the Wali until now, have been maintained by four *kokocoran*."

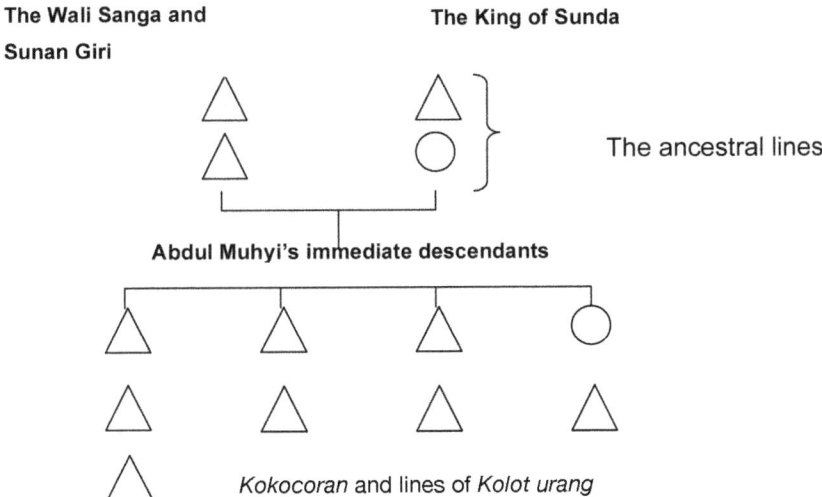

Figure 9. The four main lines of descent

The village's *karuhun* is now a place of pilgrimage and the villagers are mostly dependent economically upon its associated pilgrimage (*ziarah*). In such circumstances, *kokocoran* is pivotal in the contemporary village, as sub-groupings can influence the 'management' of rituals and the balance of power in village politics. The 'flow of the river', the *kokocoran*, or the generation after the Wali's line is unstable and susceptible to contestations of precedence (see Chapters 8 and 9). In this chapter, I will primarily focus on a narrative of space and place.

As will be seen below, a mystical itinerary of the founder and the genealogy are two important 'grounds' for seeing the landscape of Pamijahan.

Before I discuss these two elements of landscape, I will first describe how the contemporary Pamijahanese see landscape. In doing so I will show the villagers' own point of view of their space and places through the map drawn by a local artist under the custodian's supervision.

C. The Sacred Landscape of Pamijahan and its Environs

When I came to the village of Pamijahan for the purpose of fieldwork in June 1997, I met the chief custodian in his house. I asked the general question: how many sacred sites are there in this village? This was the first structured question to which I expected that the custodian would respond at length. But instead of providing an extended answer, he went outside and picked up a book (Khaerussalam 1996) from a vendor on the verandah. He said:

> You will find out everything from this history (book). There is also a map inside that tells you which sites are regarded as sacred. (The custodian, 1996)

> Encep tiasa uninga sagala rupina dina ieu Sajarah. Malih mah di dieu oge aya peta anu ngagambarkeun mana wae anu disebat karamat.

To the custodian, the book and its map of the spatial organisation of the village would tell readers all they needed to know. What you see in the map is what you find in 'reality'. The map also shows the 'path' the pilgrims should take.

The map refers to its referents by similarities and pointing. Thus, a *peta*, a map, functions both as an iconic and indexical sign. If we follow arguments given by the custodian, the map is like a photograph or picture drawn in a realistic mode. From another perspective, the map can be seen as a 'sedimented tradition'. (Tilley 1994) The map is not really an iconic picture that has a contiguous relation with its reference. It is a sign that refers to its reference through a mediation of convention or tradition. This sign may be called a 'symbolic sign' in which people have to learn about it in order to understand it.

The custodian's narratives establish the relationship between the map and its reference. From the point of view of the custodian, outsiders have to know the *sajarah,* or history, and the main source for broadcasting this history is the custodian himself.

Karuhun, Space, Place and Narratives

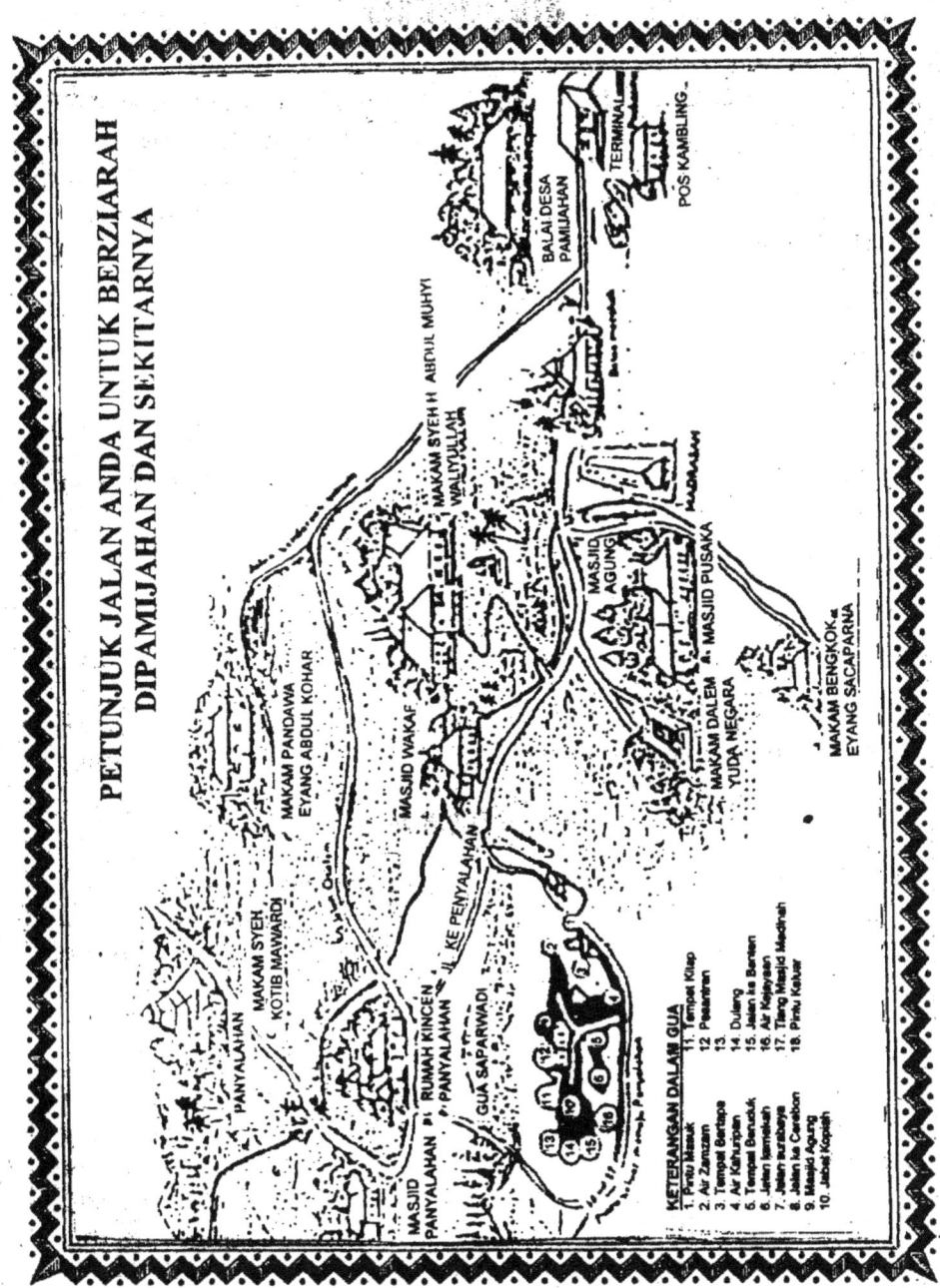

Figure 10. The map of the sacred places of Pamijahan (Khaerussalam 1992: 35)

A wall-map size variant of this map is appended at the rear of this volume.

As a representation, the map cannot be detached from collective views. It reflects a landscape of human rather than physical geography. According to Tilley (1994: 31), "To understand a landscape truly it must be felt, but to convey some of this feeling to others it has to be talked about, recounted or written and depicted."

The custodians supply villagers with a narrative, telling and showing the significance of interrelated places. This can be seen as a collective and ordered representation or symbol. The map is a legisign, that is, through iconic and an indexical modes it creates various interpretants.[2]

So the map of Pamijahan may differ from a geographical map produced by a government or research institution called a 'rational map'. Unlike a 'rational' map, the landscape in the Pamijahan map is not arranged following directional correlates as in an iconic map. Rather it presents them as a medium, contextualised, with temporal stages and contestations, that is as a symbolic map. Distance and hierarchy of place from a particular perspective are retained symbolically. Most notably, the centre is the saint's shrine and other places are peripheral. The custodian's map, like other nonverbal signs such as paintings, photographs etc. appeals to us in various ways. Unlike language which can be read linearly from the left to right or vice versa, the map offers spatial direction where we can start to 'read' from the left, right, top, bottom, or using a diagonal perspective. All elements of images in the map come to our perception simultaneously. In other words, we need a strategy to 'read' the map properly, and the 'method' for doing this is in fact verbalised and narrated by the custodian. Semiotically, if we use a reading strategy, then, we will find that the centre of the map is occupied by a shrine and the sacred village. If we read the map as a linear text then we will find 'a path' functioning as an index which is called a *petunjuk* by the custodian, that is, an indexical sign allowing the pilgrims to explore all the sacred sites shown in the map. Such and indexical sign is derived from tradition. A linear construction imposed on the map is a crucial point in our understanding of village culture. (This is further explored in Chapters 8 and 9.)

In fact, from the point of view of the custodian, the map is a pointing device that refers in particular to the paths in Pamijahan and surrounding areas Although the map's label reads *Petunjuk Jalan Anda untuk Berziarah di Pamijahan dan Sekitarnya*" ("A Pointer to the Path You Should Follow When Undertaking Pilgrimage in Pamijahan and Adjacent Places"), we do not understand the significance of the interconnectedness of the places in the map until we hear the narration given by the custodian. And for the custodian, to give guidance by making the map and providing a commentary on it is obligatory and is an expression of his piety.[3]

The custodian (*kuncen*) told me that the appropriate way to be aware of the meaning of the sacred backdrop in the village was by first disclosing the importance of the trail and places displayed on the map. As he told be this he often put his finger on to the map, explaining the route and the places found on it.

The map points to several sacred places, where, according to the custodian, visitors perform their pilgrimage in Desa Pamijahan. These are: the tomb of Shaykh Abdul Muhyi or *Makom* Kangjeng Shaykh; the grave of Bengkok or *Makom Bengkok*; the grave of Panyalahan or *Makom Panyalahan*; the grave of Yudanagara or *Makom Yudanagara*; and the grave of Pandawa or *Makom Pandawa*. Other sacred sites are the Sacred Mosque or *Masjid Karamat*; the sacred cave or *Guha Karamat* (also *Guha Safarwadi*); and finally the sacred village or *Kakaramatan Pamijahan*.

What is important for our discussion is the fact that two important narratives connect these places. The first five are sacred tombs that are genealogically linked to Shaykh Abdul Muhyi. The others are artefacts that are historically associated with the *Wali's* journey. These associations are evident only if the custodian wishes to narrate the two relevant stories. The map itself doesn't uncover such interconnections. Only narratives can connect them.

Relating the narratives of genealogy to spaces, I will discuss three important phenomena in the sites. First, I will sketch the imagined space and hereditary lines, or *kokocoran,* as reflected in the guild of custodians in the village assembly, or the *pakuncenan*. Second, I will describe the relation between genealogy and particular places such as tombs, the sacred village and other villages in the valley. Third, I will discuss the relation between the itinerary of the Wali's mystical journey, the path, and the places in the valley.

D. Four Symbolic Spaces

When I first encountered Pamijahan and began to grapple with its many issues, I was most struck by the way the villagers manage the thousands of visitors who come to the sacred sites each day. Talking about organizational issues in Pamijahan is to talk about certain aspects of the past and about genealogy. From the chief custodian's explanation of the guild of custodians (*pakuncenan*) it becomes clear how genealogy is used metaphorically for spatial arrangements.

The custodians have published a small book called '*Sejarah Perjuangan Shaykh Haji Abdul Muhyi Waliyullah Pamijahan,* or 'The History of the Struggle of Shaykh Abdul Muhyi of Pamijahan'. (Khaerussalam 1992) The book is regarded as an official written history in contemporary Pamijahan. It consists of four chapters representing historical sequences, starting from the birth of the Shaykh, his mission, his activities in West Java, and the subsequent management of the sacred sites. The most pivotal points regarding the spatial signs, which connect genealogy to the concept of space in the village, are found in Chapters III and IV. In Chapter III the custodian reports that, "The council of the village initially agreed to distribute the right of management of the sites and the territory around the village to three groups (*pongpok*), derived from Abdul Muhyi's three children from his first wife named Ayu Bakta". (Khaerussalam 1992:39) Later a fourth group was added.

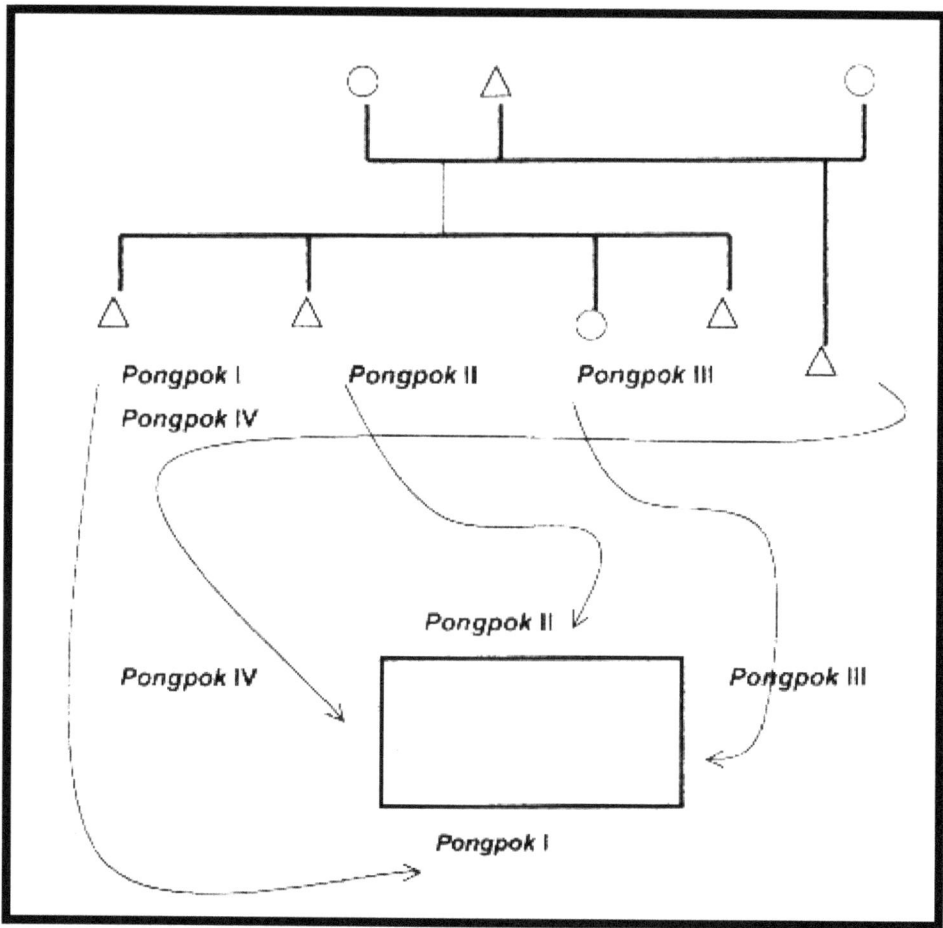

Figure 11. Genealogy and the *pongpok*.

The 'source river', *kokocoran*, as seen from the diagram above, constitutes an imagined place and ritual space. Later, as will be discussed below, these four sources, *kokocoran*, were attached metaphorically to the four sides of the tomb of the Wali.

Genealogies are found in the abstraction of space, or *pongpok*. *Pongpok* literally means 'a side'. It is easy for the villagers to imagine their social relations based on a system of inherited relations. This pattern of relations has been concretized in the form of the four sides, or *pongpok* of the rectangular tomb. *Pongpok* not only refers to the walls or sides of the rectangular shrine or tomb but also is a metaphor for social structure and cultural space where various rituals can be conducted. What is unique to Pamijahan is that lines of descent, or *pongpok,* as a sub group are metaphorically associated with the rectangular shape of the tomb.

Shaykh Abdul Muhyi had four wives. The sacred territory is dominated by a family descended from the first wife who gave birth to four children. But, Muhyi's fourth child, Paqih Ibrahim, moved outside the village and a son from the second wife assumed his right to the sacred space. From there, four sub-groups were derived in which precedence in controlling the *pongpok* of the shrine was accorded to the group from the first wife. From the information given by the custodians, the divisions of space were created later after pilgrims from outside the village began to visit the graveyard. The following is the narrative delivered by A.A. Khaerusalam with regard to the founding of the four *pongpok*.

> After having discussions (musyawarah) the village council decided that the Tomb (makam) and its surrounding area be maintained. Firstly, these tasks were offered to the three families or sides (pongpok) which were derived from the three sons of Kangjeng Shaykh Haji Abdul Muhyi from his first wife, Ayu Bakta. The sons were (1) Sembah Dalem Bojong, (2) Shaykh Abdulloh and (3) Media Kusuma… Furthermore they also agreed to give the status of caretaker to another family, that of Muhyi's wife, Sembah Ayu Salamah… So the division of care of Muhyi's tomb was distributed among these four main families (Khaerussalam: 38-39).

The decision of the village council had a significant impact on the social life of the village. It not only determined relations among members of each family, but also symbolically distributed the *wali*'s blessing among the *pongpok*. It also created a body or 'guild' of custodians (*pakuncenan*) which consists of four of Muhyi's descendants.

The *kapongpokan*, the symbolic spatial organisation based on the four *pongpok* is not a formal right to lands based on government policy. Rather it is a symbolic claim on lands which shows a traditional territory based the loyalty, *karumaosan*, of the people who live in this area. The traditional territory under *kapongpokan* can be divided into four imaginaary sections.

In the past, all these areas were called 'charity lands' *perdikan* or *tanah pasidkah*. (Quinn 2002) These 'charity lands' used to be free from land tax, but today the government has imposed a tax on this area. The term *tanah pasidkah* is now no longer used but rather *kapamijahanan*. In the local language, *kapamijahan* is a further nominalisation of Pamijahan, and in the villagers' view is no less important than *tanah pasidkah*.

This is reflected in the loyalty of the people who live in the four areas to the east, north, west, and south of the shrine. They have the responsibility to maintain the shrine by donating their money, skills and labour. People in these areas have a leader called 'the *pongpok* leader' who will lead them in performing rituals. Outsiders cannot control the *pongpok* system. No-one is able to modify this system because, according to the ancestors' testimony, "Green leaves will not grow at the top of the tree, nor will roots grow at the bottom". (Ajengan Endang 1997)

The division of the space in Pamijahan shows a hierarchy in sign systems. According to the notion of *pongpok*, the shrine is located in the central village surrounded by sub-villages associated with the *pongpok*. The first *pongpok* occupies the South side, the second, third, and fourth *pongpok* occupy the East, North, and the West sides respectively.

Each *pongpok* has a leader (*ketua pongpok*). The notion of *pongpok* functions particularly in rituals, especially pilgrimages, Islamic celebrations and annual rituals associated with the shrine. In these rituals, each *pongpok* plays a very important role. For the ritual renovation of Muhyi's shrine, for example, every *pongpok* brings their own materials to the shrine to maintain the part of the shrine associated with their *pongpok*.

Furthermore, in pilgrimage rituals, the concept of *pongpok* influences social interaction. Custodianship, or *pakuncenan*, is a real translation of genealogy into ritual space in the village, since the custodians of the shrine come from the *pongpok* system. The position of chief custodian is life-long and an elected post. The custodian in charge of staff and the day-to-day running of the pilgrimages, is rotated weekly among the four *pongpok*.

E. *Kokocoran* and the Notion of Proximity

As we have seen, the imaginary landscape of Pamijahan, the abstraction of the space, has a significant influence in social and symbolic interaction. Accordingly, as a text landscape should be conceived, to borrow Umberto Eco's words, as an open text, *opera aperta*. (Eco 1962: 240) There is a point where people can negotiate the structure of the text. Precedence in time is affirmed and even contested by various 'reading conventions'. To manage these 'negotiations', another narrative has come into existence. According to the villagers, the village must also be conceived of as a circle in which the centre where the shrine is located is the most sacred space. As evidence, another custodian has drawn a different type of map (below).

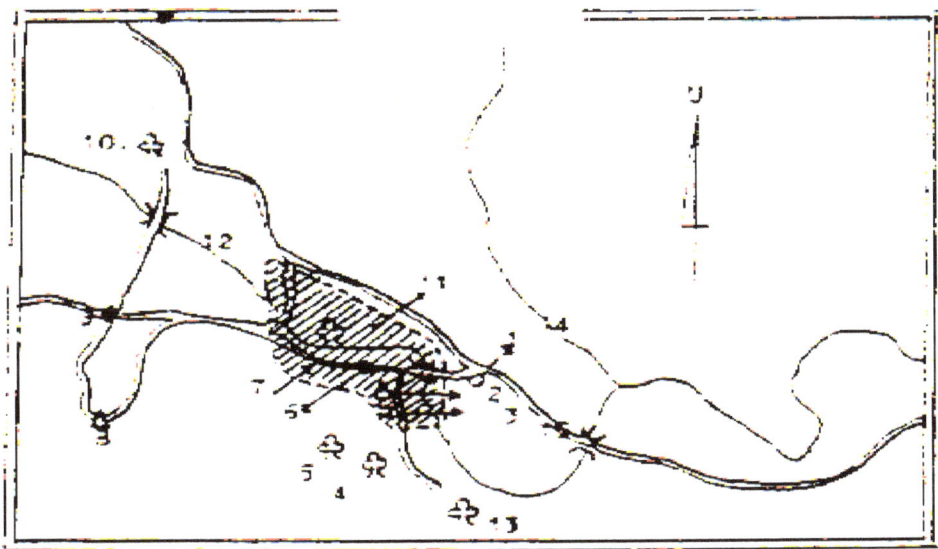

Figure 12. The other map drawn by custodians

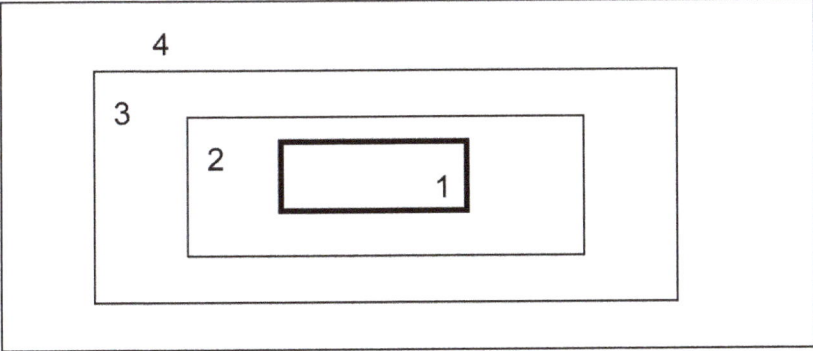

1. The shrine and the graveyard: the most sacred space

2. The sacred village, a non-smoking area inhabited by the immediate descendants of Muhyi. The sacred mosque is also located here.

3. The third sacred domain where the tomb of the Wali's father-in-law, his brothers-in-law and the Safarwadi cave are located.

4. The fourth sacred domain where the grave of Muhyi's companions and the Pandawa *makom* are located.

Figure 13. The nested, or concentric, sacred domains of Pamijahan

A space, which was previously empty or just a 'wild forest', has become an arena where various representations are 'erected'. As seen in the second map (figure 12), the centre is believed by villagers to be the most sacred place in the village where the blessing of the Wali instantly materialises. The map was also drawn by a member of the staff of custodians. Unlike the previous map, the custodian here focuses in more detail on broader topography. This map also clearly supplies a marker for a boundary of the sacred village, or Pamijahan. In the custodian's view, *kapamijahanan* is a cultural concept referring to a rectangular framed space on the map.

This spatial arrangement is associated with two factors. First, according to the villagers, the sacred area was established before Shaykh Abdul Muhyi was buried there. Oral tradition tells that once the Wali 'went' to Mecca to perform the Friday prayer together with another *wali*.[4] Shaykh Abdul Muhyi travelled under the sea, while his colleague travelled on the surface. According to villagers, Shaykh Abdul Muhyi arrived in Mecca later than his friend, because he stopped to smoke a cigarette during the journey. He was unable to see the way to Mecca through the smoke and only after he put out his cigarette could he continue. After he returned to Pamijahan, he ordered his family, as well as followers, to refrain from smoking in his area.

The 'non-smoking area' in the centre of Pamijahan has a root in this narrative. The close relatives of the Wali, including the custodians, mostly occupy this area where the Wali was buried.

To maintain the inner space, the Pamijahanese have built a clear boundary between the outer and inner domains. The most obvious signs which distinguishes the sacred village from the profane one, is an arched entrance gate, or *kaca-kaca*. On each pillar of the gate prohibitions are written, reminding villagers and visitors that they are entering the sacred village. According to the guidelines written on the pillars, known as *tali paranti*, villagers and visitors are forbidden to smoke, to wear hats, to use umbrellas, and to drive vehicles into the inner area. Furthermore, upon passing through the gates, one should wear appropriate clothes based on Islamic tradition. Villagers and visitors believe that breaching this custom is disgraceful and puts them at risk of not receiving the Shaykh's blessing.

The *kaca-kaca*, unlike other artefacts in the village, was devised by the contemporary relatives of the holy man. According to Mama Satibi, a senior custodian, some of the Wali's relatives living outside the village, prominent Islamic scholars, raised funds to build the gate. Abdul Muhyi himself did not erect it. However, the relatives built it in response to the Wali's testimony that all villagers and visitors who come to his place, Kampung Pamijahan, must obey his rules. The area covered by this tradition is marked by its original boundary:

a small river in the North and the East, a small sacred mosque (*masjid*) in the West and a hill in the South.

In contemporary Pamijahan, these boundaries are the subject of reshaping and debate. Members of one *pongpok* have claimed that the present boundary embraces an area larger than the original one but another group believes that the present margin is the original one. This controversy has consequences, particularly for villagers who choose to live both inside and outside the sacred area. According to the first group, the gate should be erected outside the boundary, but, for the latter group, it should be exactly on the border. At he moment, the latter group still lives within the sacred area but many do not comply with rules prescribed for the sacred area. They smoke in this area without fear of their ancestor's prohibition.

F. The Places

a. The Tomb of the Shaykh (*Makom Kangjeng Shaykh*)

Following a path, after five minutes' walk from the custodian's office, one crosses a narrow bridge over the Ci Pamijahan river. Passing through a small gate, the path leads to a small hill, on top of which the shrine is located. At the foot of the hill, taps and showers *(pancuran)* are used for ablutions *(wudu)*. Half way along the pathway, there are also bathing facilities and toilets for visitors who wish to stay for a longer time. From the foot of the hill visitors can walk up the pathway to where the shrine is located.

Approaching the shrine, there is another, smaller *kaca-kaca* decorated with calligraphy, giving the name of the *wali* buried there. This calligraphy has been modified and is now different from what was reported by Rinkes (1909). In changing the inscription, the custodians have ignored criticism from the so-called modernists, namely members of Persis and Muhammadiyah, who have made the accusation that Pamijahan is a *'pamujaan'* or a place for worshipping something other than God. The custodians have removed the previous calligraphy and replaced it with an Indonesian phrase reminding visitors to perform pilgrimage based on Islamic teaching.

The shrine itself is built in a quadrangle, about 18 metres square. The building has three main rooms, separated by walls, each room being connected by a door which is open at all times except for the door connected to the main gravesite, the *makom* itself. The grave of the Wali occupies a small room.

The first room is called the place for pilgrims (*tempat nu ziarah*) and is used by visitors to recite the *Quran*. Pilgrims may also use it to recite particular formulaic chants (*amalan*) given by the custodian, or they may do their own reading there. Pilgrims usually rest there too. Before entering the second room, there is another room called the first place for pilgrimage (*tempat penziarahan pertama*). Here are buried three of Shaykh Abdul Muhyi's wives, his son and his famous aristocratic follower from Sukapura, Subamanggala. Ironically, although Sembah Abdullah, Shaykh Abdul Muhyi's son and his successor as leader of the Shattariyyah order, is buried here, only a few visitors pay their respects at his tomb. Subamanggala, the nobleman from Sukapura, buried in the east corner of the shrine, also receives little interest from visitors. His family have even put an aristocratic symbol, an umbrella (*payung*) on the top of the grave to catch visitors' attention, but it does not appear to add to its sacredness.

The second room, called the *tawassul* room, is often used for the main ritual, which is performed by visitors under the guidance of a *kuncen*. Visitors and the custodian sit around the *makom*. There is a shelf for making offerings or for putting perfume, incense, and other materials to be blessed. Visitors are forbidden to rest or sleep in this second room because visitors are always coming in and out. The third room is the interior of the *makom* area. In this area, there is a grave which is topped by a canopy made from white cotton cloth (*kulambu*). The grave (*paesan*) of Shaykh Abdul Muhyi is marked by a tombstone (*tetengger*). Timber logs extend along each side of the grave. Unlike many other sacred places in Java, Shaykh Abdul Muhyi's tomb does not have a permanent superstructure, or *paesan/cungkup* made from concrete or stones. These features to some extent represent an orthodox view regarding the structure of Moslem tombs, which can also be found at the Prophet Muhammad's tomb. According to the villagers, it is not compulsory to build a permanent *paesan* because it will burden the dead.[5]

Figure 14. The interior of the Wali's tomb. Few people are allowed to enter this space.

The grave of Shaykh Abdul Muhyi is five metres by five metres in area. It is surrounded by a canopy of white cloth which is attached to a frame made from wooden boards. An 8.7 metre length concrete wall encircles the *paesan*, also covered by the white cloth, *kulambu*. Between the grave (*paesan*) and this wall, there is also a space about a metre in width where Shaykh Abdul Muhyi's close family can perform their rituals personally.

b. Kampung Panyalahan

The second biggest hamlet in Pamijahan is Panyalahan. Here there is a second important tomb called the *Makom Shaykh Khatib Muwahid*.

Shaykh Khatib Muwahid married Shaykh Abdul Muhyi's sister Sembah Kudrat. The old custodian in Panyalahan recounts that Shaykh Khatib is also called Shaykh Sembah Abd al-Kedu or Shaykh Abdul from Kedu. He was of Javanese origin and was a follower of Shaykh Abdul Muhyi's teaching. Local narratives also recount that Shaykh Khatib Muwahid was Shaykh Abdul Muhyi's closest companion, who used to teach the master's pupils. Panyalahan custodians say that Khatib Muwahid means 'the best teacher' (in Arabic, *khatib*, 'teacher'; *muwahid* 'one', or, 'the first'). Therefore, his tomb is famous among students of Islam (*santri*) who want to study the Holy Qur'an and books of interpretation and commentary (*kitab*).

Approaching the tomb from the cave to the north, one passes first through the hamlet of Panyalahan then walks to the western part of Panyalahan through paddy fields. Shaykh Khatib Muwahid is buried in the foothills, surrounded by stands of mahogany trees. Approaching the tomb, one passes through another gate (*kaca-kaca*) on the pillars of which are written the name of the holy man. Before entering the shrine, one should make ablutions from a water fountain at the right, close to the gate. The shrine has two main spaces. The first is a place for offerings (*tempat nu ziarah*) and the second in the centre is the *makom* (the grave) which is enclosed by a concrete frame. Unlike the Makom Shaykh Abdul Muhyi, visitors can clearly see the holy man's tomb through spaces in the frame.

According to the custodian of Panyalahan, only ten percent of pilgrims coming to Shaykh Abdul Muhyi's shrine continue their pilgrimage on to Panyalahan. From the point of view of the Pamijahanese, it is not compulsory to perform pilgrimage at this site. Villagers from Kampung Pamijahan (the centre) say that Shaykh Khatib Muwahid settled in the wrong place, and that is why they call it the wrong place or Panyalahan.[6] Another legend has it that Shaykh Khatib Muwahid did not obey Shaykh Abdul Muhyi's instructions perfectly. Indeed, there is significant evidence of the villagers' different interpretations of this.

The Panyalahanese tend to avoid the name Panyalahan due to its negative connotations. According to them, the name is associated with two narratives. The first is a local narrative regarding the origin of the village and the second is a local history regarding a Dutch map-making excursion which was confounded by the topography of the area.

According to the Panyalahanese, there was once a peasant couple who lived in this place. They were the only farmers in the area. They had some domesticated animals, one of which was a tiger. After several years, they found more happiness in their lives after they had a baby. They worked harder than before so that they achieved bumper harvests in every season. If they went to the paddy field, the tiger cared for their baby. One day, they found the tiger waiting at the gate with blood on his teeth. The farmer was very angry. He said, "You cursed animal! I cared for you but you seized my baby in your jaws." The farmer then pulled out his machete (*bedog*) and said, "This is your punishment, and blood must be repaid by blood." He struck the tiger which died instantly.

When they entered their hut, they found the baby still alive with a dead poisonous snake around its neck. They realised that the tiger had saved their son from the snake. After that, the place was called Panyalahan or 'the place of the wrong guess'.

The second narrative relates to the theme of the coming of the Dutch. According to the custodian of Panyalahan, the Dutch came to their village for the purpose of making a map. With some followers, they made several coordinates on the map associated with the rivers which cross the village. After they had finished drawing the lines on their new map, they tried to match it to the real situation. However, they found that they could never find the same pattern that had been drawn on their map. Indeed, they were unable to identify two similar rivers which crossed the village. They had put only one river in their map. Therefore, that, according to the villagers, is why the Dutch called it the 'place of unknown coordinates' or *panyalahan*.

The villagers have yet another legend. According to them, their village was often used by Shaykh Abdul Muhyi and his companion to solve problems (*masalah*) regarding how to convert the pagans around them. According the custodian, the original name for their *kampung* was *Pamasalahan* ('the place for problem solving'). So, instead of using the name Panyalahan they prefer to use Pamasalahan, the name which appears in their later narratives. These days there is a Pamasalahan Mosque, a Pamasalahan Primary School and a Pamasalahan hamlet. Ironically, the name of Panyalahan is already recorded in government archives and they cannot remove it. Later in the chapter we shall return to the effort of the people of Panyalahan/Pamasalahan to create their own tradition, something difficult to do since Pamijahan possesses the dominant sacred symbols.

The Wali is the centre and his friends and relatives (*qaraba*) are the second and third rings of the landscape. Panyalahan lies within the second ring in village culture because the village founder was the brother-in-law of the Wali. Thus, the Panyalahanese do not have access to the custodianship of the saint's shrine.

c. Makom Yudanagara

Yudanagara was a brother-in-law of Abdul Muhyi. Yudanagara's tomb is situated within Kampung Pamijahan but outside the non-smoking area. Some visitors continue their pilgrimage to this tomb to perform a fast in which their intake of food is restricted to rice or non-coloured foods and beverages, mainly cassava and water. This ascetic practice is called *tirakat* or *mutih*. Some pilgrims believe that Yudanagara is the right hand of Muhyi in spiritual power. This is reflected in his name. *Yuda* means 'war' and *nagara* means 'the state'. Yudanagara then is a figure who has both spiritual power in war and is a guardian of the state.

Even though the place is relatively close to the shrine and the non-smoking area, the custodians in the non-smoking area do not manage the site.

d. Makom Pandawa

The fourth sacred site is the grave of Shaykh Abdulqohar in Kampung Pandawa. This site is situated in the northern part of Desa Pamijahan. The Pandawa tomb is another example of how a marginal sacred site has tried with affiliate to Shaykh Abdul Muhyi's tomb. Rinkes reported that Shaykh Abdulqohar was the brother of Muhyi, but the Pamijahanese themselves never claim this. Neither does the custodian of the Pandawa tomb, who describes Shaykh Abdulqohar simply as Shaykh Abdul Muhyi's companion. According to the Pandawa custodian, Shaykh Abd Abdulqohar was Abdul Muhyi's closest companion not Shaykh Khatib Muwahid or Yudanagara. He was the right hand of Muhyi.

From the above it seems to me that the number of related sacred tombs is limited to the number of figures classified as the founders of the villages even though two of them, Yudanagara and Pandawa, do not have a blood relationship with Shaykh Abdul Muhyi.

G. Mystical Paths

In the valley of Pamijahan one of the most important ways of making a serial trajectory is to follow the mystical itinerary undertaken by Shaykh Abdul Muhyi. Villagers make coordinates in their landscape referring to the 'mystical journey' of their ancestors. As we saw above, places in the village of Pamijahan are attached to the past through the metaphor of a mystical journey performed by their ancestors. Each point indicates the place where Shaykh Abdul Muhyi made a shelter, or stopped in his the mystical journey.

The narrative is crucial in this case because the experience of tracing the path has to be broadcast to others. Broadcasting narratives needs a special person such as the *kuncen*. Accordingly, tracing and depicting the path is not only important for making the space and place in a material sense, it is also important in the transformation of the metaphor of genealogy into ritual and social structure. In Pamijahan, everyday activities engage with these narratives.

Every single Pamijahanese can recite that Shaykh Abdul Muhyi came from Mataram and that from his father he had Sundanese and from his mother he had Javanese blood (see also Chapter 4). Through his Javanese blood, Shaykh Abdul Muhyi derived a holy genealogy linking him to the nine Saints of Java[7] and to the Prophet himself. What is significant here is that Shaykh Abdul Muhyi, in his journeys, recognised Pamijahan as a mystical destination because in this place he found the sacred cave suggested to him by the grand master of Sufism, Shaykh Abd al -Qadir Jailani (see Chapter 9). The cave was the final destination in a mystical journey undertaken by Shaykh Abdul Muhyi.

There is a second narrative of a mystical journey relating to the everyday activities of Shaykh Abdul Muhyi after he founded Pamijahan. According to the villagers, after he found the sacred cave he settled in Bengkok. The discovery of the cave created a spatial link between three important places namely the cave, the village of Pamijahan, and the village of Bengkok.[8] These places are connected by the history of the search for the cave and make up the entity called Pamijahan. According to the custodians, the Wali went to the cave for meditation regularly for various periods and returned to Bengkok. In Bengkok, he met a local woman who later became his first wife. Accordingly, in the Pamijahan landscape, Bengkok is important because it was once the Wali's shelter and his father-in-law's home. During periods of meditation, Shaykh Abdul Muhyi often rested in the valley between the cave and Bengkok. In this valley, he built a mosque known as the Sacred Mosque, (Masjid Karamat). These artefacts are recognised as material evidence of his *wali*-hood. The Pamijahanese believe that the holy man bequeathed a sacred heritage to the villagers. This heritage consists of artefacts ranging from material items such as the Sacred Mosque the Sacred Tomb *(Makom Karamat),* the sacred village (the nonsmoking area), a sacred rosary, a sacred robe (*jubah*), sacred manuscripts, and spiritual artefacts such as the *torikoh* Shattariyyah. The following are the principle of these artefacts.

a. Bengkok

Kampung Bengkok is located about ten minutes' walk through the paddy fields from Masjid Karamat in Kampung Pamijahan. This village is classified as being in the second ring. It is called Kampung Bengkok because it is located in the valley close to a bend (*bengkok*) in the river. Here, Shaykh Abdul Muhyi's father in law, Sembah Dalem Sacaparana, is buried. The place is popular among woman pilgrims who are looking for a husband. Unlike Pamijahan and Panyalahan, Bengkok is a rather backward area, which does not yet have electricity. Only specialists[9] or those who want to perform additional rituals will come to this site.

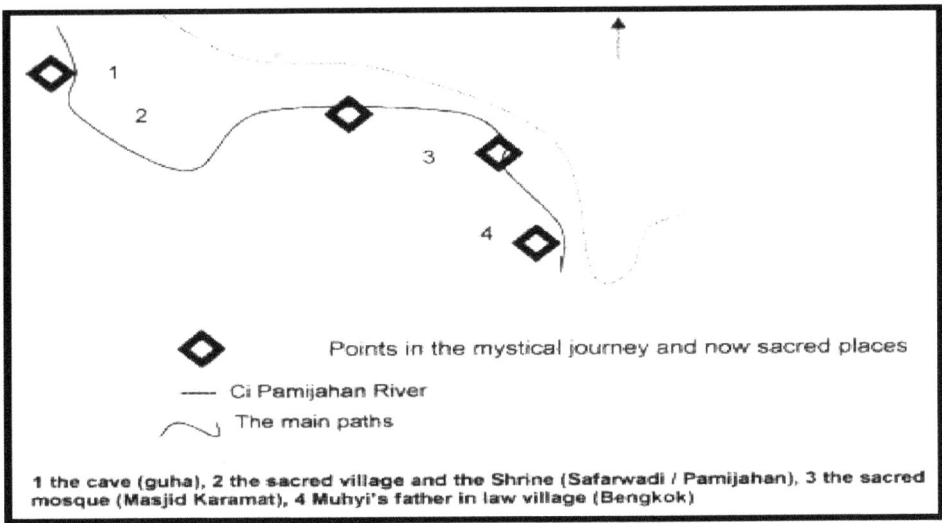

Figure 15. Points in Abdul Muhyi's sacred journey, now sacred places.

In village narratives, Bengkok is recognised as the second station in Muhyi's mystical journey after he found the sacred cave. He lived here for a long time and married a local woman. Unlike Panyalahan, Bengkok has been attached to the mystical journey of the Wali. Thus, even though Bengkok is located in the second ring, situated outside the non-smoking area, its position slightly differs to that of Panyalahan. The arrow sign placed close to the custodian's office mentions clearly that pilgrims are welcome in Bengkok. However, we can not find the same signs for Panyalahan. The place is important because it is touched not only by family linkages but also by the mystical journey. Whatever has been used by the Wali is important.

b. Guha Safarwadi

When he studied Sufism in Mecca, Abdul Muhyi's master Abdul Rauf[10] of Singkel ordered him to meditate in the Safarwadi cave, the place where the famous Sufi Shaykh Abd al-Qadir Jailani obtained an acknowledgment (*ijazah*) from his master Shaykh Sanusi. Now, the cave is recognised as the place of meditation (*tempat tawajjuh*) of Shaykh Abdul Muhyi.

The Safarwadi cave is also reputed to have been the meeting place where Kangjeng Shaykh met other saints of Java. The cave, which is 284 metres long and 24.5 wide has several chambers. Each chamber has a tunnel running off it, which is regarded as a 'door'. These doors 'connect' the cave to the centre of pilgrimage in Mecca and to the tombs of other great *walis* in Surabaya and Cirebon and Banten. Besides the doors, the cave also has a place for meditation (*tempat tapa*), a spring of holy water (*tempat cai zam-zam*), a spring of the water of life (*tempat cai kahuripan*), a mosque which consists of two spaces, one for women and one for men, a vault pocked with round indentations in the roof *(jabal kupiah)*, a space known as the 'boarding school' *(pasantren)*, a space known as the 'kitchen' *(dapur)* and ledges of rock called 'altars' *(paimaran)*.

The cave is open 24 hours a day for villagers except on Fridays. On Fridays from 11 am - 2 pm the cave is closed because according to villagers, at this time, Kangjeng Shaykh often 'performs' communal weekly Friday prayer *(jumaah)* there. For the believers, the Wali is still alive in a different world but he often comes to the village to see his descendants. During his lifetime, he often went to Mecca for the Friday communal prayers` through the cave.[11] Today villagers still believe that the Wali comes to the cave every Friday to perform Friday prayer in Mecca. Thus, during the period of Friday prayer, villagers close the gate of the cave.

In the cave, visitors first take holy-water *(cai zam-zam)* and put it in his plastic containers *(jariken.)* After that, they climb to the mosque or Masjid. This place is believed to be another holy mosque where Kangjeng Shaykh Haji Abdul Muhyi used to perform prayers *shalat* when he was undertaking meditation. Visitors often chant a calling prayer *(azan)* in the dome *(quba)*. For older visitors, it is difficult to stay in the Masjid for long during the peak seasons because the oxygen is reduced by the hundreds of pilgrims and the guides to the cave *(nu jajap ka guha)* who bring push lamps. However, in the low season, the place is silent and some visitors prefer to perform meditation *(tapa)*. Most ordinary pilgrims *(nu ziarah biasa)* stay here for ten minutes, reciting their own supplication *(doa)*.

There are rivers that flow in the lowest bed of the cave. Pamijahanese believe that anyone who takes a bath in the water of life *(cai kahuripan)* will be free from disease and anyone who takes a bath in ' the water of gloriness *(cai kajayaan)* will succeed in business.

c. Masjid Karamat (*The Sacred Mosque*)

All mosques are sacred, but not all the mosques in Pamijahan have the title Masjid Karamat or 'the blessed mosque'. *Karamat* is derived from the Arabic word meaning a miracle given to a *wali* as a close friend of God. This mosque has the title *karamat* because it was built and used by a *wali*.

In 1909, when Rinkes came to Pamijahan he still found that the dome, or *quba*, of the mosque was the one made by Kangjeng Shaykh. Today, no original materials from the Muhyi period remain or are visible to visitors. However, the custodian recounts that the original materials of the sacred mosque were buried in the same place when they renovated the mosque. At this time, the mosque has more permanent and modern construction material than before. The mosque is designed following the architecture found in Arabic countries with the big dome on the top. The style differs to the old mosque, which uses the pyramid structure on the top as 'the dome'.

Event though the mosque has experienced massive renovation, the sacred material are still in there. One elder Pamijahanese recited his experience to me when he renovated the mosque in the seventies:

> When I was restoring mosque in the 70's, if I am not mistaken, I found the old stone still there, very clean. Then, when we were trying to move one of these stones close to the altar, there was a distinct stone radiating a light. Then friends and I buried this stone again. Accordingly, everything still on the site, particularly the solid materials; even, the dimensions of mosque and its main pillars are close to the original. This is an evidence that this mosque is the one originally built by our ancestors (karuhun).

Although visitors and younger villagers are unable to verify such narratives, the fact that this narrative is attached to the existence of the sacred mosque has a powerful association for them.

H. Conclusion: The Growing Signs

In Pamijahan, and popularly among Muslims in general, a *wali* is recognised as having blessing and grace. He is a Friend of God and an intermediary between the common people and God. The radiation of his power spreads into the place where he lived and was buried. As shown in India, Morocco, and elsewhere, the tomb of a saint is a principal coordinate in mapping the landscape of a village. As a central point in space, the tomb or the shrine must be protected and maintained, particularly by the *wali*'s descendants (*turunan*). What is significant in the notion of place is that villagers assume that the place can be classified according to degrees of sacredness ranging from the most sacred place to the less sacred and the profane.

In contemporary Pamijahan, people move from one place to another so that the place where people stay does not always reflect their membership of a side (*pongpok*). However, the notion of *pongpok* is still important in every ritual being linked to Shaykh Abdul Muhyi.

The Pamijahan places described here are spaces where various 'historical energies', borrowing Pemberton's phrases (Pemberton 1994: 270) criss-cross the village. The history of Shaykh Abdul Muhyi is materialised in the form of the sacred signs namely the tomb; the mosque, the cave, the village, as well as the symbolical territory called Kapamijahanan and *pongpok*.

In such setting, the shrine, the sacred narratives, the sacred mosque, the sacred village appear to be dominant symbols. In this, place villagers orchestrate these various signs in order to support their cultural ideology. For instance, the relation between genealogy and places is metaphorically conceived as the relation between the sides of the tomb of Shaykh. These metaphors are indicated by the formation of custodianship where the leader of custodians always comes from the first *pongpok*.

Semiotically, the transformation can be drawn as follows:

Pongpok (S1) → *the concept of sides (O1)* → *the sides of Shaykh Abdul Muhyi (I1, S2)* → *the concept of genealogy (O2)* → *four main lines (I2, S3)* → *the four abstract spaces (O3)* → *the four managers of the sacred sites (I3)* etc.

Figure 16. The semiotics of Pamijahan

The first sign is the word '*pongpok*' (S1). This term means 'the side'. In Peircean terms it becomes an object of the first sign (O1). Later, it acquires an interpretation as 'the sides of the wali' (I1) and also appears to be a new sign (S2) that is the concept of 'genealogy'. This second sign has a new reference (O2), that is the concept of genealogy which is later interpreted as the four main lines (I2). This interpretant becomes another sign (S3), which has a different object (O3) that is the four abstract spaces. This connotation is then interpreted as the four managers of the sacred site (I3). This chain of semiosis theoretically could be endless as long as there is homo-semioticus who can comprehend external phenomena based on their perception. However, as Umberto Eco says, the culture could resist such a process.

The map of Pamijahan is a collective interpretation where the meaning will be generated for one who is able to access such collective interpretant: but, accessing intepretants are the mater of negotiation, which is called by Eco (1999) a "chewing-gum" process The blessing, *barakah*, of their *wali* is subject to dynamic interpretation. Such different interpretations, for instance, can be seen clearly from the different perceptions of two villages, Kampung Pamijahan, and Kampung Panyalahan, regarding the spatial concept and the sacredness of their village. Although both villages share the same ancestors, Pamijahanese recognise himself or herself as closer to the saint than Panyalahanese. Furthermore, there is also a different interpretation regarding ancestors' value that should be converted into their daily life.

As we have seen, the increase in the number of people undertaking pilgrimage visits to Pamijahan is due to the holiness of the founder of the village, Shaykh Abdul Muhyi. In village culture, the centre of *barakah* is situated at the centre of village where the shrine is located. Thus, the centre, which is marked as a non-smoking area, is also the focal point for interpretation. This is due to that fact that the villagers apply two different systems of meaning when they read the map of the village as a text. As we saw above, the genealogical system is used by the people who live in the centre. This system has created what might be called 'the ideology of proximity (*qaraba*) or closeness'. The notion of closeness has been applied to space. Thus, one who are close to the wali's line may have access to the sacred sites, particularly the centre. Conversely, those who are not so close do not have the same access. The second system is derived from narrative, from sacred reported speech. It is evident in the village that there are groups that use both ideologies, and there are groups that tend to emphasise just the second one. The applications of these systems of meaning have significant implication for villagers in their social and symbolic interaction. To elaborate this issue, I will illustrate with the case of Pamijahan and Panyalahan.

Lets us start with the narratives concerning spatial order as understood by the people of Panyalahan. The quotation given below is taken from a testament copied by Nyi Raden Nuri, a Panyalahnese, from the testament of another Panyalahanese, Mama Halipah.

> Now, let us recite the history of the pasidkah land that passed from Shaykh Haji Abdul Muhyi to his brother (Eyang Kudrat). The boundaries of this land are: from the west the tip of the tree on the mount of Tangkil then to the Satus to the south, then to the west in Bongas, up the hill of Bubuway, then to Pandawa Tengah, to the mount of Gadung, to the river of Cisela, to the Angsana tree planted in the north graveyard of Dalem Yudanagara, then east to the graveyard of Bengkok, to Madur in the southeast of Parungpung, to the river of Cihandiwung Jero, to the Cikeuyeup, to Cigaru, to Cikangkareng, to Nagreu, to Burujul, to the Bed Stone, to the river of Cijalu where Eyang Nurdin planted four incense trees brought from Demak, to the Cibentang, to Cilingga, then to the top of the hill along the mountain of Tangkil. (The Testament of Mama Halipah Djainal Aripin)

This excerpt defines the boundary of the sacred sites given by the Shaykh, the *tanah pasidkah*. Both Pamijahanese and Panyalahanese, to some extent, agree about this boundary. However, both Pamijahanese and Panyalahanese take opposing positions when it comes to the terms of custodianship and settlement in the sacred sites such as Kampung Pamijahan.

The polysemic interpretation of space is shown, for instance, by the appearance of 'letters of testimony'. The Panyalahanese have produced letters of testimony (*surat wasiat*), using them in a campaign rejecting the privilege of people who live within the sacred site (*kampung Pamijahan*). In their campaign they state

> Those who live in Panyalahan, Cioga, Ledar, Cibentang, and even Tujul, must be careful. Those who settle in the sacred heritage site (tanah wasiat) who originate from whatever families, must shows their loyalty to Pamasalahan [Panyalahan].

It is clear that for Panyalahanese, settlement in the centre of Pamijahan, which is the most sacred space in the village, is forbidden because it is the *wali*'s space and should be kept unpolluted and pure. should be cleaned and purity. The Panayalahanese also recite that they too have a right to the sacred land and the people who live in the centre of Pamijahan should even pay tribute to Panyalahan. On the other hand, the Pamijahanese absolutely reject these statements. For them, it is unthinkable to send tribute to Panyalahan. According to them, it is the Panyalahanese who should in fact respect the privileges of the Pamijahanese, who, from time immemorial have lived in the sacred territory bequeathed to them. In more recent time times, the ever increasing revenued coming in to Kampung Pamijahan from pilgrimage, has attentuated this long-standing controversy.

Previously I have discussed a cognate icon and index, as well as symbol used to identify the position of people in space and other mnemonic devices to trace the point of origin in the cultural space of the village. Various devices have been identified namely: the metaphor of a flowing river, the sides, and closeness or proximity. However, I have to present another important cognate icon, which is hardly used in villagers' daily activities, but it is used occasionally in crucial narrative performances. By crucial narrative, I mean a process of telling a sign in history to warn any villagers, and non-villagers, to perceive the space and places in the appropriate way as required by the Wali.

To prevent people from taking an undefined or unsanctioned 'path', according to the chief custodian of Pamijahan (1997) the Wali has said that "New green leaves will never grow at the top of the tree, nor will new roots ever grow at the bottom." This tradition strongly interdicts any superfluous semiotic process. There are two important key words in the testimony: 'green leaves" or *pucuk* and 'root' or *akaran*. In other words, the community, which is likened to a tree, will never have new roots into the past, nor ever fresh grwoth and branches into the future. Nevertheless, as an open text, space and place are always subject to precedence and negotiation, and for this reason the 'leaves' and the 'roots' need to be maintained - the signs need to be 'cultivated'. This process will be explored in Chapters 8 - 10.

The Pamijahanese have another source of genealogy that is quite different from the linkages set out in the *Babad Pamijahan*. If the *Babad Pamijahan* links the people of Pamijahan with the two biggest kingdoms in Java, and lays foundation for spatial and social organisation in the village, there are other narratives that connect villagers to a wider Islamic world through Sufism. This will be taken up in the next chapter.

ENDNOTES

[1] *Eyang* in Pamijahan is close to the concept described by Sakai (1997: 49) in Gumai society of south Sumatra. Sakai argues that the Gumai *puyang* is an ancestor associated with a particular origin place.

[2] The interpretant, according to Peirce, is part of the third trichotomy which he calls "A sign addressed to somebody that creates in the mind of that person an equivalent sign, or perhaps a more developed sign. That sign which it creates I call the interpretant of the first sign." (See also Winfried North, 1995:43)

[3] In this case Marcel Danesi and Paul Perron (1999:188) state that "A map is, overall, an indexical sign, since it indicates where the territory is located on the terra firma. Its layout is iconic, because it shows the features in a territory in topographical relation to each other. It involves symbolicity because it is interpretable on the basis of conventional notational system..."

[4] This is a widely told story with several variants. For example, a similar story is told in connection with Shaykh Bela-Belu and his friend Maulana Magribi whose tombs overlook the coast at Parangtritis south of Yogyakarta.

[5] See also Rinkes (1910). Only large pebbles cover the graves of the saint's disciples. According to local conception, this leaves them free to rise on the Day of Resurrection, almost an impossibility had the graves been closed with cement. On both sides there are simple gravestones called *tutunggul* (or *tetengger* in high Sundanese). Sometimes the term *paesan* is used.

[6] The root *salah* means 'wrong' or 'mistaken'. Panyalahan is a derivative of *salah* meaning 'where a mistake happened' or 'where mistakes happen'.

[7] The nine Saints of Java (*Wali Sanga*) are the well-known, semi-legendary first missionaries of Islam in Java. The nine Saints are Sunan Ampel, Sunan Bonang, Sunan Giri, Sunan Drajat, Sunan Gunung Jati, Sunan Kalijaga, Sunan Kudus, Maulana Malik Ibrahim and Sunan Muria.

[8] In Sundanese *bengkok* means 'bent' or 'curved'. In Bengkok, the river Ci Pamijahan makes a sharp curve.

[9] Among the pilgrims there are those who are recognised as pilgrimage 'specialists' (*ahli*). They have experience in pilgrimage rituals and other additional rituals. Specialist are also recognised by their spiritual powers.

[10] In the history of Sufism in Indonesia, Abd Rauf al-Singkel is known as the master of Shattariyah. He stands between the two opposed groups groups led by Hamzah Fansuri and Nur al-Din al-Raniriri. The former promoted a rather heterodox mysticism derived from that of al-Hallaj and the later was influenced by very orthodox teaching.

[11] Sultan Agung has the title of *prabu pandita* (king-priest) because he was also able to perform the shalat prayers each Friday in Mecca (see W.L. Olthof, trans. *Babad Tanah Djawi, Javanese rijkskroniek*, Dordrecth: Foris for KITLV, 1987 p. 122).

Chapter 6: Linking to the Wider Worlds of Sufism

A. Introduction

Sufism, or *tasawwuf* prescribes not only ascetic rituals but also provides a model of social practice. As a social practice, it is in intensive contact with other branches of Sufism and with local traditions which impact upon its articulation. This can be seen in the development of various Sufi orders, or *tarekat*, in which divergent paths of development become salient features. Some Sufi orders, for example, have had to modify their teaching and organisation in order to be able to attract new followers and to gain political support from local authorities (Muhaimin 1995: 231; Zulkifli 1994: 232) while others have lost followers because they failed to reformulate their positions in a changing society.

One of the most important phenomena shaping the development of Sufi orders is the *silsilah* or the intellectual genealogy of Sufi masters. *Silsilah* are of special significance in providing the orders with cultural legitimacy and doctrinal authenticity. *Tarekat* have an international character. Through their *silsilah* they trace their origins and development across national and cultural boundaries as well as across time.

The role of the *silsilah* parallels that of the *isnad*, the chain of transmitters that authenticates a *hadith*, or tradition relating to the Prophet Muhammad. As in the Sufi orders, the authenticity of a *hadith* is established from its chain of transmitters going back to the Prophet Muhammad. Both the *silsilah* in Sufi orders and the *isnad* in *hadith* literature are regarded as foundations for the development of Islamic knowledge (Voll 1980: 246-73.). A *silsilah* characteristically involves a number of leading *ulama*, or Muslim scholars, in the transmission of a facet of Islam, specifically mystical knowledge. The line of transmission traces back to the *ulama* credited with founding the order. A *silsilah* therefore gives form to an intellectual community and plays a crucial role in the establishment and continuing cohesion of further intellectual networks, not only within Indonesia but also those linking Indonesian *ulama* with those of the Middle-East (Azra 1995).

Therefore, the *silsilah* plays a major role in determining the existence of a Sufi order. To some extent, it can also be seen as presenting an argument and an ideology, enabling the order to be socially accepted and religiously justified. The Shattariyyah tradition in Pamijahan is a good example of the dynamics of a particular Sufi tradition in Java, especially with regard to the role in it of a *silsilah*-based narrative centred on a Sufi master.

To date there has been no adequate description of the Shattariyyah tradition in West Java, particularly in Pamijahan, which has been a famous Shattariyyah centre from early times. The present study will contribute to our knowledge of the Indonesian Shattariyyah tradition in general, and this chapter will focus on the *silsilah* of the Shattariyyah in Pamijahan, exploring its implications for the village culture where, as has been outlined above, all kinds of narratives are subject to negotiation.

The veneration of *wali* is widespread in the Muslim world. I argue in this chapter that in Pamijahan the *silsilah* of the *wali* functions to perpetuate the teaching of the master and connects the valley of Safarwadi to the wider world of Sufism. It is important to emphasise that in the case of Pamijahan, the *silsilah* is used not only for tapping into the master's blessing, *barakah*, but also for framing and shaping social practice in the village.

B. The Roots of Shattariyyah

On theological and sociological grounds, Sufism is a problematic concept in Islam. The pilgrimage to Mecca introduced the international character of the Islamic world into the Malay Archipelago.[1] In its early period in Indonesia, the Shattariyyah teaching reflected this international character. At its earliest stage, particularly in Sumatra, the influence of Meccan masters dominated the interpretation of all Islamic teachings, including those of Sufism. The best documented instance of this is the influence of al-Qushashi and Ibrahim al-Kurani on their Indonesian pupils in the 17th century within the interpretation of the doctrine of the the Seven Levels of Being (see below). All Indonesian Shattariyyah *silsilah* relating to Abd al-Rauf of Singkel, Acehcarry the names of these two men.

However, in other areas of the archipelago such as in Java, Sufism underwent various changes of direction that cannot be so completely or immediately attributed to international influences. The transmission of Sufism seems to have been made more complicated because the Javanese were more interested in practice than in theology or interpretation. For example, some followers of Shattariyyah in East Java believe that the order provides a means to acquire and exercise magic power. In some places in West Java, particularly in the area south of Bandung, there are communities claiming links to Abdul Muhyi which practise certain martial arts and cultivate alternative healing practices.

It is important here to recall the Dutch scholar Rinkes' findings about the Shattariyyah order and its links with Abd al-Rauf of Singkel in 17th century Aceh. Part of Rinkes' doctoral dissertation (Rinkes 1909, 160) examined the foundations of the Shattariyyah's metaphysical doctrine called the 'Seven Levels of Being' or *martabat tujuh*. Rinkes found that the Javanese Shattariyyah consisted of common general characteristics of the order, as well as elements incorporated from various other parts of the world. He made the following points about its Javanese variant: first, disregarding possible inaccuracies on the part of Javanese writers, the Javanese language, like most other languages, does not lend itself to an exact rendering of notions from other languages (in this case, from the Arabic), especially if the author intended to re-express them in his own words. Second, the writing in Java, without being a direct imitation of some earlier version, does not express the scribes' thought, but only indicates which ideas they have absorbed. Third, because of the religious sentiments of the Javanese, which, according to Rinkes, might be said to be generally lacking in lively exchange of thought, one should not expect to find sharply outlined dogmas and can expect even less of their mystical speculations.

I agree with Rinkes, particularly in view of the facts of contemporary Pamijahan. Mystical speculation, lively debates on the Shattariyyah, and even the creation of new mystical texts are rare. Such phenomena have been influenced by a social dynamic in the village. The Pamijahanese could not maintain their mystical tradition properly because a number of their prominent Sufi leaders moved away to settle in other places, or have passed away. So the transmissions are halted. Furthermore, various external influences, such as the introduction of different *tarekat* and the increase in pilgrimage activities have modified their views on their ancestor's teachings. Nowadays it is hard to imagine Pamijahan from a perspective of 17th Sumatran Sufism, where the star of Sufism sparkled, and debates on mystical speculation were at their liveliest. However, the Shattariyyah followers in Pamijahan survive in a modest way, still important in village affairs. In this regard, the local manuscripts appear as short manuals of Sufism.

Although Rinkes's study has contributed much to our understanding of the development of the Shattariyyah in Java, Rinkes did not pay great attention to local practices, particularly those of Pamijahan, where around 1660-1715 the order was first introduced into West Java (Krauss 1995: 112). This is reflected in the manuscripts which Rinkes used. Although he visited Pamijahan in 1909, it was the Cirebon manuscripts which he consulted, rather than manuscripts then available in Pamijahan itself, even though he probably had seen manuscripts of Pamijahan origin in the collection made by his teacher, the great Islamologist C. Snouck Hurgronje. Some important manuscripts from Cirebon present a different *silsilah* from that of the manuscripts of Pamijahan. The Shattariyyah order in Cirebon, particularly as practised within the court, is socially exclusive. It is a palace order. Rinkes (Rinkes 1910) also does not inform us whether any manuscripts were extant, or if any mystical circles were active in Pamijahan at the time of his visit – leaving a gap in our knowledge of the history of the order there.

It is therefore all the more important to describe the *silsilah* of the Shattariyyah in contemporary Pamijahan, particularly in the light of the fact that the villagers have transformed Pamijahan into one of the most famous pilgrimage sites in Java today.

Recent studies confirm that the *silsilah* is part of the intellectual network linking various scholars from different places in Indonesia. In his important historical study Azra (1992) identifies various interrelated figures influenced by the idea of neo-Sufism. According to Azra, neo-Sufism is an effort to reconcile mysticism, or *tasawwuf*, and law, or *sharî'ah*. The *silsilah* of the Shattariyyah, particularly in Indonesia, is part of this process. Azra's work uses extensive primary sources written by the figures in the networks he studies. Nowadays, in several places in Java, including to some extent in Pamijahan, the order has been overwhelmed by other orders and has lost followers. Muhaimin (1995: 333) argues that the decline of the Shattariyyah in Cirebon is partly due to its complicated teaching. Other *tarekat* such as the Tîjâniyyah, for example, have gained much popularity from propagating simpler doctrines. Pamijahan stands out as an exception. Even though the Shattariyyah is facing problems in other places in Java, the villagers of Pamijahan who claim a close genealogical connection with the master are steadfast in their attempts to perpetuate the tradition. Today a Shattariyyah congregation is held every week in a certain villager's house in Pamijahan (described in Chapter 8).

C. The Shattariyyah Order in the World of Islam

The Shattariyyah tradition is largely shaped by a Transoxanian tradition of Central Asia, but over time it has also come under Indian and Arab influences (Trimingham 1998: 96-104). The tradition has also been 'domesticated' in Indonesia in order to meet local needs. In the Shattariyyah's *silsilah* we can sense these dynamics.

The *silsilah* is linked to Abu Yazid al-Ishqiyyah of Transoxania, who was influenced by Imam Jafar al-Sidiq (d. 146/763) and Abu Yazid al-Bistami (d. 260/874). Abu Yazid al-Ishqiyyah's order was known as the Ishqiyyah in Iran and the Bistamiyyah in Ottoman Turkey. The Ishqiyyah was popular in 15th century Central Asia. After the Qadiriyyah-Naqshabandiyyah order began to receive more attention in the same area, the Ishqiyyah's popularity decreased (Trimingham, 1998: 41). One of Abu Yazid's successors, Shah Abd Allah al-Shattar (d. 1428–9) who appears in the genealogy of Pamijahan manuscripts as the ninth master before Shaykh Abdul Muhyi, brought the order to more prosperous soil for his teachings, namely India. There, Shah Abd Allah became associated with the Shattariyyah, which had then become another name for 'Ishqiyyah (Rizvi 1983).

After 'Abd Allâh al-Shattar, the Shattariyyah was led by Shaykh Hidâyat Allâh Sarmat (the eighth predecessor), and Shaykh Hâjji Udârî (the seventh predecessor). The most important of 'Abd Allâh al-Shattar's successors was the famous Muhammad Gawth of Gwalior (d. 1562–3). According to Rizvi (1983), he extended the popularity of the Shattariyyah among the local population by retranslating Yogi's manuscript, the *Amritkunda* and incorporating its practices into Shattariyyah *dikir* formulae. He was known as a Sufi who respected the followers of Hinduism. Furthermore, he was a writer of numerous mystical works. During his period the doctrine of the Shattariyyah was codified and strengthened, as may be seen in his work *Jawâhir al-Khamsah* (The Five Precious Things). Another factor which stimulated the Shattariyyah tradition was that its leaders were able to co-operate with the royal courts of North India. This can be seen in the period of the great Moghuls, Shâh Jahân and Aurangzeb. Shâh Jahân and Aurangzeb granted recognition to the order as one of the official orders of the empire (Rizvi 1983).

After Muhammad Gawth of Gwalior, the order was continued by Shaykh Wajih al-Dîn Gujarati (the fifth predecessor) (d. 1018/1609) who succeeded in promoting the Shattariyyah order throughout the Indian subcontinent (Rizvi 1983: 166). Its method of contemplation, which shows similarity with yogic practices, and the eccentric behaviour of its master, were important factors in the Shattariyyah's development in India. Furthermore, through Shaykh Wajih al-Din Gujarati's successor, Sultan Arifin Sibghat Allah b. Ruh Allah and Shaykh Ahmad al-Nashawi, the order spread to Mecca and Medina (Rizvi 1983). In the 17th century these two holy cities emerged as sanctuaries of various Sufi orders and became great centres of diffusion. It was through this line that Ahmad Qushashi, the immediate predecessor of Indonesian Shattariyyah, obtained his *silsilah*.

Even though some scholars have classified the Shattariyyah as a minor order in India (Rizvi 1983), it emerged as an important order in the Indonesian archipelago during the 17th century, particularly in Sumatra. Its followers became key players in local social transformations further afield. The king of Buton in Eastern Indonesia, for example, adopted the symbolism of the Seven Levels of Being to impose a hierarchical social order within his realm (Ikram 2001). In Ulakan, Minangkabau, the Shattariyyah imbued rebels with spiritual powers in their struggle against the Dutch (Steenbrink 1984). The same situation was also found in Java, where Shaykh Abdul Muhyi provided the prominent rebel Shaykh Yusuf of Sulawesi with accommodation and political sanctuary. Abdul Muhyi's followers also took up arms against the Dutch (Kraus 1995).

D. The Shattariyyah *Silsilah* in Indonesia

I shall now outline the setting of the 17th century and the introduction of the Shattariyyah in Indonesia. In this period, Sufism and the *tarekat* were dominated by the North Sumatran school which followed the philosophy of Iban al-Arabi (d.1240) and was led by Hamzah Fansuri of Aceh. This was attacked as pantheistic in a great controversy by contemporary opponents such as Nûr al-Dîn al-Raniri (Johns 1965).

However, both Hamzah and his opponents often quoted Ibn al-'Arabî's pantheistic teaching regarding the nature of creation: that there is no separation between inner and outer worlds. Agreement was never reached on exactly how God manifests Himself in the world. Hamzah Fansuri's work explains that the phenomenal world is the external manifestation (*tajallî*) of the Ultimate Reality. In Hamzah Fansuri we read

> La ilaha il-Allah itu kesudahan kata
> Tauhid marifat semata-mata
> Hapuskan hendak sekalian perkara
> Hamba dan Tuhan tiada berbeda (Alisjahbana 1961: 76)

> La ilaha il-Allah is the final word
> The way, nought but the Unity of God
> Banish other matters from within your heart
> Servant and Lord are not apart.

The poem in its entirety expounds a system which is generally designated by the term 'The Unity of Being' (*wahdat al-wujûd*). In Hamzah Fansuri's view, the world is an outpouring of God's love. Borrowing Anne-Marie Schimmel's image, the relation between Creator and creation is like that between water and ice, the same essence, a unity, but evident in different modes of manifestation (Schimmel 1994, 1986).

Hamzah's follower, Shams al-Dîn of Pasai (d. 1630) developed this idea but for the first time in Sumatran Sufi practice, he adopted the concept of the 'Seven Levels of Being' from *al-Tuhfah al-Mursala ila ruh al-nabi,* or *The Gift Addressed to the Spirit of the Prophet*. Johns, in his critical textual edition of the *Tuhfah*, argues that the understanding of the 'Seven Levels of Being' in the Sumatran Sufi's work is more systematic than that expounded by Shams al-Din's predecessors (Johns 1965). The 'Seven Levels of Being' is a cosmology which explains the relation between the Absolute and the relative. The concept resembles that of Ibn al-'Arabî in thso far as the relative is an outward manifestation of the Absolute (al-Attas 1966). The main advantage of Ibn al-'Arabî's concept, which was adopted by Shattriyyah, is that the notion of levels supplies a metaphor which appears to solve the philosophical problems of the relation between the Absolute and the relative, or the One and many-ness.

However, such a solution can and does only appear on a metaphorical level. The difficulty with it for scripturalist or legalist is that mystical expressions applying unconventional metaphors such as 'I am God', or 'Servant and Lord are not apart' are simply unacceptable (Schimmel 1994).

Thus, the 'Seven Levels of Being' had to be interpreted in different ways. Certain Sumatran Sufis, such as Shams al-Dîn al-Samatrânî, interpreted the doctrine in the above heterodox terms but Nûr al-Dîn al-Raniri of Gujerat and 'Abd al-Raûf al-Singkel comprehended it in other more orthodox ways.

Nûr al-Dîn al-Raniri, like Hamzah, applied the metaphor of light and its shadow (*zill*) to describe the relationship between God and His creation. According to him, the world is God's shadow ('*wujud makhluk itu terang dan benderang yang jadi ia daripada nur wujud Allah*') (Christomy 1986:64). Both Hamzah and al-Raniri subscribe to the same assumption about reality. In their terms, reality is the shadow of the Ultimate. The big differences between them lie in their interpretation of 'shadow'. For Hamzah, the shadow is the logical consequence of the light. It is not created but projected. On the other hand, al-Raniri assumes that the shadow is *created* by the Ultimate.

In this 'catechismus' al-Raniri asserts that

> Jika demikianlah ditamsilkan segala ahli Sufi akan Haq Ta'la dengan makhluk, bahwasanya wujud Haq Ta'la itu sekali-kali tiada wujud Allah. Seperti kata jâbib al-Insân al-Kâmâl....Maka jika ada engkau itu Haq Ta'la, maka tiada engkau itu engkau, tetapi Haq Ta'la itu engkau, maka tiadalah Haq Ta'la itu Haq Ta'la tetapi engkau itu engkau jua. Maka nyata daripada kata ini sekali-kali wujud Haq Ta'la itu tiada jadi wujud makhluk dan wujud makhluk itu sekali-kali tiada jadi wujud wujüd (Hill al-Zill, see also Christomy 1986: 64).

> If the Sufi compares Haq Ta'la with human beings, indeed there is no parallel between wujud Haq Ta'la and God. This is explained by the master of al-Insân al-Kâmil...If you have the quality of Haq Ta'la you will not exist as men, but you will become the Haq Ta'la. Haq Ta'la is Haq Ta'la but you are man (not Him). The meaning of this word is that wujud Haq Ta'la is never embodied in mankind and mankind is not the manifestation of wujud Haq Ta'la.

According to al-Raniri the ultimate reality, the *wujud Haq Ta'la* has never become manifest in mankind, nor has creation, or the *wujud makhlûq*, ever become manifest in the divine ultimate reality.

> Bahwasanya Hakikat Allah itu sekali-kali tiada harus dikata akan dia berpindah kepada hakikat makhluk itu dan hakikat makhluk itu sekali-kali tiada harus dikata akan dia berpindah kepada hakikat Allah. (Hilll al-Zill)

> Now of the Essence (Allah) it should not be said that it is embodied in creation and of creation it should never be said that it is embodied in the Essence (Allah).

These differences escalated into an open polemic and political friction among the patrons of the respective masters, dividing even the Acehnese sultans among themselves, with their respective supporters. This conflict between the followers of Nûr al-Dîn al-Raniri and Hamzah Fansuri is well known. Al-Raniri argued that Sultan Iskandar Muda (ruled 1607-1636) should make a decree, or *fatwâ* against Hamzah and Shams al-Dîn regarding the *wahdat al-wujûd*. It was forthcoming. Al-Raniri tried to modify Ibn al-'Arabî's teaching to a more orthodox accommodation. However, his position was perhaps more political than mystical. He was ready to support any palace policies which were in accord with orthodoxy. For instance, he advised that all old manuscripts which did not carry at their head the habitual formulaic opening of Islam: 'In the Name of God, the Beneficent, the Merciful…' should be burned. He also persuaded the Sultan to ban the teaching of the *wahdat al-wujud*. However, after his royal patron died, al-Raniri ran into political difficulties. The next Sultan, Iskandar al-Thani (ruled 1636-1641) held views different from those of al-Raniri and as a consequence al-Raniri's position deteriorated. He fled back to Gujarat. The more moderate *qâdî*, 'Abd al-Raûf al-Singkel was appointed in his place.

Those responsible for a domestication of Ibn 'Arabî's teaching in Indonesia were the Meccan masters al-Qushashi and al-Kurânî, and their pupil 'Abd al-Raûf Singkel. Al-Qushashi was famous as a leader of Jawi students from the Indonesian archipelago in Mecca during the 17th century. He had links with a number of mystical orders but in Indonesia he was best known as a Shattariyyah master. He obtained his *silsilah* from Sibghat Allâh and was moreover a close friend of the writer of the above-mentioned *Tuhfah*, Muhammad Ibn Fadl Allâh al-Burhânpûrî. Both were students of the popular Indian master of the Shattariyyah, Wajîh al-Dîn of Gwalior. Al- Qushashi made a deliberate choice to teach Shattariyyah mysticism to his Jawi students. Through his discipline the metaphysical doctrines of the *martabat tujuh* were transmitted to Indonesia as part of heterodoxy, becoming the trademark of the Shattariyyah. In other words, the speculative view on the process of creation was adjusted to the legalistic view fo the *fuqaha* (Bruinessen 1994:1-23).

Among al-Qushâshî's students was 'Abd al-Raûf al-Singkel who in turn was the master of Shaykh Abdul Muhyi of Safarwadi. 'Abd al-Raûf differed in several respects from his colleagues in Aceh. He did not condemn his predecessors as heretics, or *kâfir billah*, as al-Raniri had not hesitated to do. 'Abd al-Raûf's response to the quarrel between al-Raniri and Hamzah's followers was moderate. He probably was not called upon to make a statement regarding Hamzah's teaching for the royal court because, according to him, it is not encumbent upon any Muslim to name another Muslim as an unbeliever, or *kâfir*. 'It is dangerous to accuse another of *kufr*, of unbelief. If you do so and it is true, why waste words on it, and if it is untrue, the accusation will turn back upon yourself"

(Johns 1965: 60). It must be taken into account, however, that these tendencies occurred as part of a general shift in the archipelago in the 17th century for legalists and mystics to be reconciled.

In sum, 17th century Indonesia was characterised by various mystical contests as a result of international infusions of *tarekat* brought back from Mecca by returned pilgrims. The emergence and decline of a certain order was much influenced, for example, by the fluctuating tendency to combine Sufism with Islamic law, *sharî'ah*. Thus, the attempt was made for every pantheistic element in *tarekat*, including in Shattariyyah, to be reshaped in accordance with more orthodox features.

E. The Shattariyyah *Silsilah* in West Java

There is evidence that the Shattariyyah *silsilah* in Java follows two main lines. The first can be traced back to Cirebon on the north coast. According to Muhaimin (1995:333-336) the Cirebon chain reaches back to Shaykh Ahmad bin Qaras al-Sanawî. Al-Sanawi was the father of al-Qushâshî who taught Abdul Muhyi's teacher, 'Abd al-Raûf al-Singkel. Shaykh Ahmad bin Qaras al-Sanawî in turn taught Shaykh 'Âlam al-Rabbânî who in turn taught Shaykh Hatib Qabat al-Islam who in turn taught Shaykh 'Abd al-Waqâb who in turn taught Shaykh Imam Tarbiyi who in turn taught Tuan Shaykh 'Abd Allâh bin 'Abd al-Qahhâr who in turn taught Tuan Haji Muhammad Mu'tasin who in turn taught Shaykh Imam Qâdir Îmân Hidâyat bin Yahyâ who in turn taught Sayyid Shaykh Muhammad Arifudin who in turn taught Raden Muhammad Nûr Allâh Habîb al-Dîn *ingkang apilenggih ing Nagari Cirebon, Kanoman ing Dalem kaprabonan*, ("who sat on the *kanoman* or junior throne of Cirebon") (Muhaimin 1995:333).

The second tradition, attributed to Shaykh Abdul Muhyi of Safarwadi, is a more popular one, at least in West Java, than the Cirebon tradition. This is a clear indication that Pamijahan was an important place in Java for the transmission of the Shattariyyah. This present study focuses on the Pamijahan branch.

F. Shaykh Abdul Muhyi

A number manuscripts, local narratives, and Dutch reports (de Haan 1910:462) provide convincing evidence of Abdul Muhyi's role in spreading the Shattariyyah order in West Java. However, the sources are not reliable regarding when and how exactly he learned the Shattariyyah method in Aceh and Mecca, or when he returned to Gresik in Central Java, and why he moved from there to West Java (refer to Chapter 4).

> The Prophet Muhammad
> Imam Ali
> Amir al-Muminin Husein
> Zainal al-abdidin

Imam Muhammad Baqir
Ruhaniyah Imam Jafar al-Sadiq
Shaykh Ruhainyah Sultan al-Arifin: Shaykh Abdu Yazid al-Bastami
Shaykh Muhammad al-Magribi
Shaykh Arabi Yazid al-Isqhi
Shaykh al_muzafar Turki al-Tusi
Qutub Abu al-hasan al-Kharqani
Shaykh Hudaqly
Shaykh Muhammad Ashiq
Shaykh Muhammad Arif
Shaykh Abd Allah Shattari
Imam Qadi Shattari
Shaykh Hidayat Allah Sarmat
Shaykh Haji Hudur
Shaykh Muhammad al-Gawth
Shaykh Wajih al-din Alwi
Sultan Arifin Sayyid Sifat Allah
Ahmad al-Qushashi b. Muhammad Madani . Ahmad al-Nashawi
Shaykh Abd al-Rauf
Shaykh Abdul Muhyi

Figure 16. The Spiritual Genealogy (*silsilah*) of Tarekat Shattariyyah at Pamijahan

Rinkes was the first European scholar to concern himself with the Shattariyyah in Java. In 1909, while finishing his dissertation on 'Abd al-Raûf of Singkel, Rinkes travelled to Java (Rinkes 1909). His mission was to trace the Shattariyyah order and investigate the nature of the sacred sites associated with the *wali sanga,* the nine saints who reputedly first propagated Islam there. The journey resulted in a series of articles collectively titled *De Heiligen van Java* (The Saints of Java) which appeared in the *Tijdschrift van het Bataviaasch Genootschap van Kunsten en Wetenschappen* (Journal of the Batavia Society for Arts and Sciences) between 1910 and 1913.[2] Even though he faced some difficulties in ascertaining certain historical data, his studies do provide insights into the concept of the *wali sanga* in contemporary Java. Now, in traditional Javanese historiography, Shaykh Abdul Muhyi is never identified as one of the *wali sanga*, living as he did at least one century after them. It is curious then that Rinkes' studies open with a description of the tomb of Shaykh Abdul Muhyi, the founder of the Shattariyyah in West Java. Rinkes gives us no clue as to why he took up the episode of Shaykh Abdul Muhyi first. In his further failure to provide clues about when and how the Shattariyyah came to Pamijahan, Rinkes overlooks one of the most important aspects of any account of the order's relationship to its shrines, the written evidence.

There are few written sources referring to the existence of Shaykh Abdul Muhyi. The oldest manuscript found in Pamijahan only states his genealogy. Nor is there any dating associated with him in this chronicle. Kraus (1995), the only contemporary scholar to pay attention to the figure of Abdul Muhyi, examines the existence of the Shaykh from a primarily historical point of view. Based on his research employing Dutch sources, Kraus concludes:

> The first cluster of Indonesian ulama we know about, the wali songo, stand between myth and history. The next group, the famous Acehnese scholars and mystics, Hamzah Fansuri, Shamsuddin of Pasai, ar-Raniri, and Abdur Ra'uf, as well as the Maccasarese Shaykh Yusuf are historical persons..... Abdul Muhyi of Pamijahan somehow stood between these two groups. We know that he was a student of Abdur Ra'uf, but we have no written evidence of his thought and we had no historical proof of his existence. (Krauss, 1995:28).

Krauss relies on secondary sources in claiming that Shaykh Abdul Muhyi must have lived during the period of 'Abd al-Raûf, Shaykh Yusûf and the local Sundanese figure of the Bupati of Sukapura (see Chapter 4). Even accepting Krauss' arguments, we still need additional sources to bring this figure "down to earth". In other words, as long as the original works written by Abdul Muhyi himself have not been found, he stands as half-myth and half-history. Nevertheless, Krauss speculates that the Shaykh lived between 1640 and 1715. In support of this he refers to Dutch sources which identify the Shaykh as a "hajj from Carang" and friend of the famous rebel, Shaykh Yusuf (1626–1699).[3] Krauss further claims that Shaykh Yusuf wrote a manuscript dedicated to Shaykh Abdul Muhyi. Finally, he cites sources from a local authority in Tasikmalaya (Sukapura) mentioning the Shaykh's existence. So given these facts, Shaykh Abdul Muhyi emerges as a real man, but one clouded by the absence of works clearly in his own hand.

It is interesting to note that Krauss assumes that every *wali* like the Shaykh must have bequeathed written material yet to be located. Of course, we should receive this statement with care, since various factors influence the tradition of writing in Java. A collection of manuscripts can disappear not only because of adverse political factors but also because of mere climatic conditions.

According to villagers of Pamijahan, there are external factors why original works written by their ancestor cannot be found. In the 17th century many *kiai* came home from the *hâjj* and were unable to set up their own lodges in urban areas. Some of them retreated to remote areas of the countryside. Colonial control of the *hâjj* network was very strong, particularly after Dutch troops were able to capture the northern port sultanates of Banten and Cirebon and later most of the interior of the Priangan. Some *kiai*, including Shaykh Abdul Muhyi, were recognized as supporters of rebellion. In such circumstances, it is feasible that

Abdul Muhyi might have transmitted his teachings not through written texts, as did Hamzah Fansuri and Nûr al-Dîn al-Raniri but through practical exemplary behaviour. It is important to consider Abdul Muhyi's teaching method within traditional institutions such as those in which *ulama* and *ajengan* deliver their teachings through oral discourse and practical applications. (Dhofier 1980:55) It is also easily possible to imagine how very difficult it must have been for Abdul Muhyi to introduce his teachings in a written form in the remote and backward setting of Pamijahan in the 17th and 18th centuries.

Certain areas of the interior of West Java have experienced long periods of war and rebellion. A great number of cultural artefacts were destroyed or taken away to other places. During the 1960s for example, when Islamic separatism threatened the Tasikmalaya area, a number of Hindu relics and other pre-Islamic artefacts were deliberately destroyed. Many statues in West Java lost their important identifying points of iconography such as heads or hands. One of my informants in the field recited similar stories regarding various artefacts associated with Shaykh Abdul Muhyi. According to him, in the period close to the *wali*'s lifetime not only manuscripts, amulets and magically charged daggers (*kris*) were lost but a sacred mosque containing various manuscripts relating to the Shaykh was also burned.

We should also consider that there were periods when the Shattariyyah teachings were probably abandoned by adherents under pressure from the spread of other popular *tarekat* such as the Naqshbandiyyah, Qâdiriyyah, Tîjâniyyah and Idrîsiyyah. Mama Ajengan Satibi, a descendant of Shaykh Abdul Muhyi explained to me that he had manuscripts conveying the Shaykh's teaching which he had never read, because he was not a follower of the Shattariyyah, the very Sufi order introduced to area by his ancestor.

Written materials can decay in a short time due to the unfriendly tropical climate, while the method of collection and storage of manuscripts by villagers leaves much to be desired. Accordingly, the apparent lack of the Shaykh's own works does not necessarily put his existence into question.

I found almost thirty manuscripts from various places in Java recognising Abdul Muhyi as a Shattariyyah master (see Chapter 3). Most of these manuscripts had been copied by his followers. According to the family of the Shaykh in Pamijahan, his pupils often made copies of mystical works after he had initiated them as disciples. These pupils also put their own names in the *silsilah* after the master's name. This custom is consistently mentioned in Shattariyyah manuscripts dedicated to the Shaykh. In fact, according to the villagers, a Shattariyyah manuscript which does not provide a *silsilah* in its opening is not to be recognized as genuine.

G. The Successors

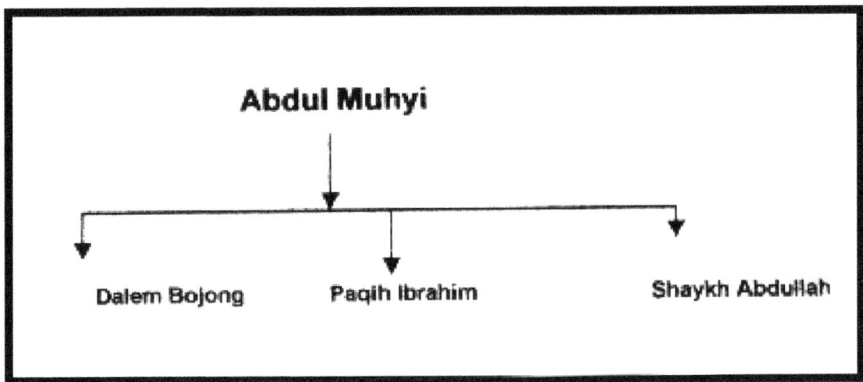

Figure 17. Shaykh Abdul Muhyi's direct successors

Abdul Muhyi's successors were very important in transforming Pamijahan into a centre of the Shattariyyah in the Priangan of West Java. From there the order spread to other regions of Java. Most Shattariyyah manuscripts from Pamijahan agree that after Abdul Muhyi died the Shattariyyah was spread by his sons by his first wife. Their names were Shaykh *Haji* Abdullah, *Sembah Dalem* Bojong and *Emas* Paqih Ibrahim. A note on each of them is necessary here.

a. Paqih Ibrahim[4]

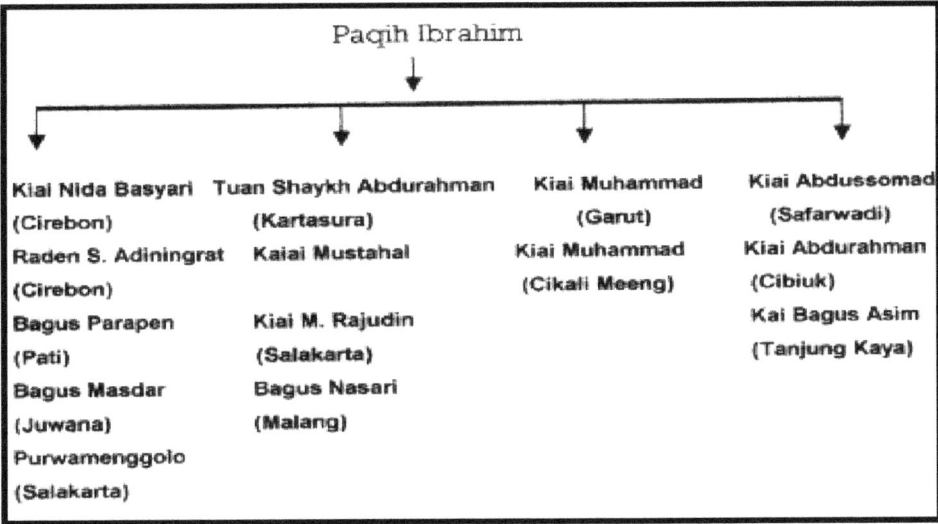

Figure 18. Paqih Ibrahim's descendants

There is no known source in Pamijahan regarding Paqih Ibrahim's life. The *Babad Tanah Jawi* indicates that there was a *penghulu* from Karang who taught Islam in Kartasura (personal communication, Professor Merle Ricklefs, 1997).

This might have been Paqih Ibrahim. Rinkes (1996) however doubts this possibility but does not provide reasons for his doubt. However, if we trace back the *silsilah* of the Shattariyyah from Central and East Java we often come across mention of a son of Abdul Muhyi named Paqih Ibrahim. There is evidence that he settled in the north coast area and there propagated the Shattariyyah. Local narratives in Pamijahan also note that, unlike Abdul Muhyi's other sons, only Paqih Ibrahim lies buried outside the village. As suggested above, it is possible that during his lifetime he made contact with Kartasura. The Shattariyyah manuscripts from Kartasura (Leiden Cod. Or. 7486b, and Cod. Or. 7446) support this possibility. In these manuscripts Paqih Ibrahim delivered Shattariyyah initiation to one Tuan Shaykh 'Abd al-Rahmân from Kartasura, who in turn taught Kiai Muar Ibnu Syahid, who in turn taught Kiai Muar Ibn Syahid or Kiai Mustahal, who in turn taught Kiai Muhammad Rajudin from Salakarta Adiningrat, who taught Bagus Nasari Malang, who finally taught Purwamenggolo from Pamukan, Salakarta Adiningrat. Furthermore, some manuscripts indicate that Emas Paqih Ibrahim not only had followers from his own village and neighbouring villages but also from as far away as Cirebon and Garut. Indeed, according to Ricklefs (p.c. 1997), Paqih Ibrahim was reported to have collaborated with rebels in the court of Kartasura and then was exiled to Jakarta.

b. Haji Abdullah

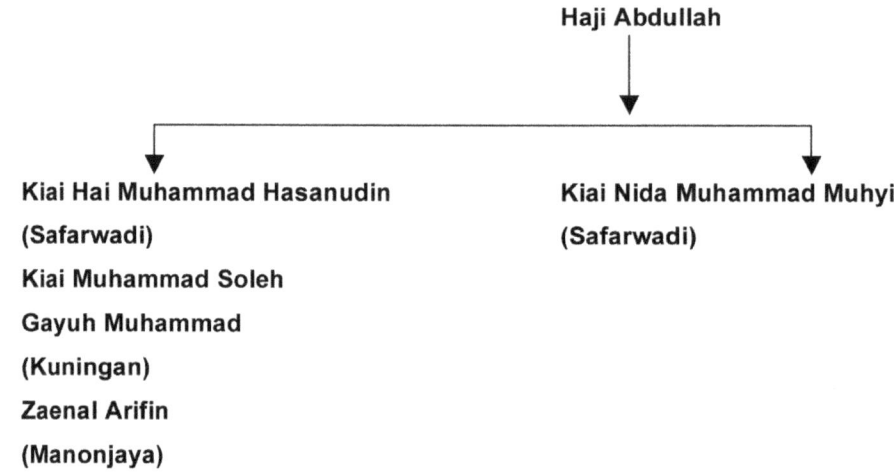

Figure 19. Haji Abdullah's descendants

Most manuscripts which I found in Pamijahan during my field work narrate Haji Abdullah's *silsilah*. Through his line, the Shattariyyah *silsilah* is linked to the *Penghulu* of Bandung, who in turn taught Haji Abdullah bin Abdul Malik who lived at Pulau Rusa in Trengganu, who then taught Lebai Bidin son of Ahmad, an Acehnese (see also Al-Attas 1963, 29).

c. Dalem Bojong

Another of Abdul Muhyi's sons, Dalem Bojong, had followers mainly from his own village, Nagara, in Sukapura, from Mandala, and from Bandung, and Garut. The current followers of the Shattariyyah in the village of Machmud in Bandung connect their *silsilah* to Dalem Bojong. According to a manuscript from Pamijahan (discussed below) Dalem Bojong provided the authorisation, or *ijazah* of the order to Kiai Mas Hijaya from whom Kiai Mas Haji Abdul Daud in turn obtained authorisation. After that Kiai Mas Haji Abdul Daud of Pamijahan taught Mas Haji Hanan who later authorised Muhammad Akna of Pamijahan. Beben Muhammad Dabas, Muhammad Akna's son, has now taken up his family's Shattariyyah tradition and is perpetuating it in Pamijahan (see below).

It is important to note here that besides these three famous sons of Abdul Muhyi who are recognised, after Abdul Muhyi himself, as initial propagators of Shattariyyah, there is another name which is also significant. Ekadjati explains that in a manuscript found in Limus Tilu, Garut, there is reported to be another son who propagated Shattariyyah, a certain Kiai Haji Abdul Muhyidin. The appearance of his name contradicts information in Rinkes' study and in local narratives, none of which mentions that Abdul Muhyi had a son named Kiai Haji Abdul Muhyidin. If the name is correct, then in full it should read Kiai Haji Mas Nida (Muhammad) Abdul Muhyi or Kiai Bagus Muhammad Abdul Muhyidin, who, according to the Pamijahan manuscripts, was the son of Dalem Bojong and a grandson of Shaykh Abdul Muhyi. Local manuscripts also state:

> ….lan iya iku amuruk maring Shaykh Hajji Abdul Muhyi / ing karang desane lan ing Safawardi padukuhane lan / iya iku amuruk iya maring Kang Putra Shaykh Hajji 'Abd / al-lah hing Karang desane lan ing Safawardi padukuhane lan / iya iku amuruk ia maring Kang Putu Kiahi Mas Nida Muhammad Abdul Muhyi ing Karang desane lan ing Safawardi padukuhane …

> ….and he taught Shaykh Hajji Abdul Muhyi / in the village of Safawardi, Karang, and he in turn taught his son, Shaykh Hajji Abd / al-lah in the village of Safawardi, Karang and / he in turn taught Abdul Muhyi's grandson, Kiahi Mas Nida Muhammad Abdul Muhyi in the village of Safawardi, Karang and in Safarwadi….

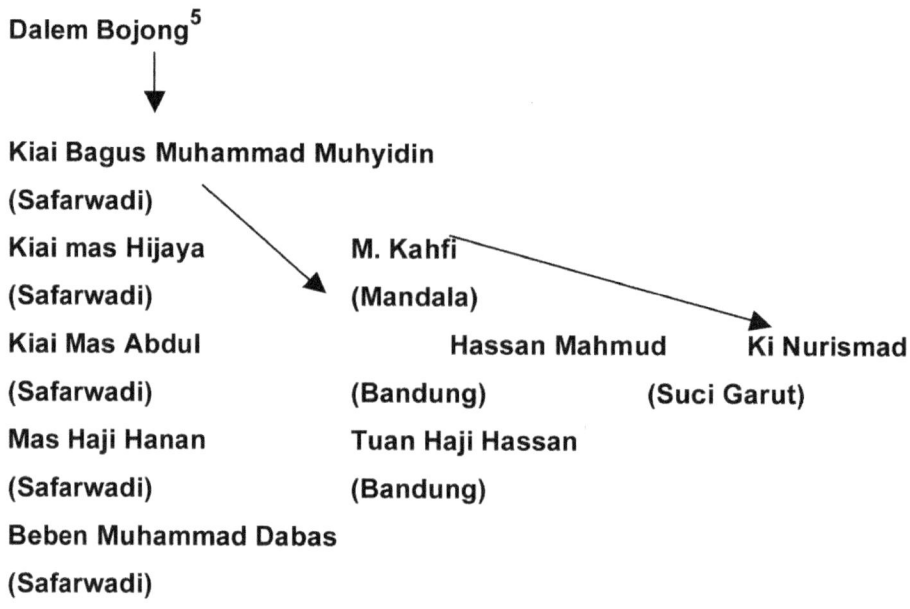

Figure 20. Dalem Bojong's[5] descendants

d. Beben Muhammad Dabas

Beben Muhammad Dabas is the current leader of the Shattariyyah in Pamijahan. He derived his Shattariyyah *silsilah* from his father, Haji Muhammad Akna, who was known by villagers as a practitioner of the Shattariyyah. He told me: "My father, Muhammad Akna, died in 1982. He said to me that I should carry on the Shattariyyah in this village." Before he was initiated by his father, Beben spent time in a *pasantren* school in Pekalongan on the north coast of Central Java. His family was surprised by his ability to study and to lead a *tarekat* because the Beben they knew as a child had been a naughty boy. After spending time in the *pasantren,* he returned to Pamijahan and established a new Shattariyyah chapter, registering his association with the Attourney General of Tasikmalaya on April 4, 1991.

Some prominent members of Shaykh Abdul Muhyi's family consider Beben Muhammad Dabas to be too young to be the leader of the Shattariyyah in the village. The most prominent custodian of Pamijahan and the owner of several Shattariyyah manuscripts, Ajengan Endang expressed an opinion representative of such attitudes. He explained that theoretically it is very difficult to obtain an *ijâzah* in the Shattariyyah order because its teaching is the *wali*'s own and can be fully comprehended only by those of *wali*-like stature. Thus, says Ajengan Endang, there are only a few people in contemporary West Java able to practise the Shattariyyah properly. For his part, Beben himself seems to reject such criticism. In his view, as long as one has the true *niat,* or intention to learn the Shattariyyah, one can receive an *ijazah* from a master. It does not matter if the conferrer or the recipient of the *ijazah* is still young.

Beben's' *silsilah*, which he obtained from his father, is legitimate, not only from the requirements of the *tarekat* but also from the government's point of view. His full claims to legitimacy, however, are more complex than this.

By hereditary privilege, Beben is connected to his father, once recognised as the foremost local figure in the practice of Shattariyyah. Beben has also made use of a manuscript, apparently collected by his family, to confirm his status as a legitimate master. In this manuscript, he has added his own name to the Shattariyyah *silsilah*. Evidently, he did this after a period of study under one Ajengan Sukawangi of Singaparna, the *murshid* or most authoritative Shattariyyah master in the district, who initiated him into the order and bestowed the *ijazah* on him. It should be carefully noted, however, that the way Beben Muhammad Dabas inserted his name into the *silsilah* after that of his father is ambiguous. Traditionally, he should have listed his name after that of Ajengan Sukawangi, his initiator into the Shattariyyah practice.

To recapitulate, Beben argues that his father *bequeathed* him the Shattariyyah, and that it is by virtue of this fact that it is legitimate for him to continue the tradition. He also made the Shattariyyah oath of allegiance to the order, *talqin* before the Ajengan Sukawangi in the traditional way. Finally, Beben has listed his *tarekat* officially in the office of the Attorney General and this is the third source of his legitimation.

Official, "political" recognition of Dabas' *tarekat* community has come from the local Attorney General's office (*kejaksaan*) in Tasikmalaya. It is somewhat odd that a Sufi *tarekat* should be registered with the government, as if it were a *kebatinan*, or spiritualist group. In a certificate given by the *Sekretariat Umum Team PAKEM*, Beben Muhammad Dabas is recognised as the leader, *pimpinan* of the group. The main objective of his group, which is written on the certificate, is to develop Islamic instruction through the teaching of right religion, *tauhid* in order to gain personal peace in this world and in the hereafter (*'mengembangkan ajaran Islam melalui ajaran Tauhid demi tercapainya bahagia dunia dan akherat''*). The government certificate of authorisation also states that the source of the *tarekat* is "teaching based on Al-Qurân, Hadîth, Ijmâ' ulama and Qiyâs" – all orthodox principles. Perhaps the most important feature of the certificate can be seen under its Point 6, in which it confirms the history of the order. The brief history goes as follows:

> "Sejarah singkatnya, bahwa saya menerima ajaran tarekat ini dari ayahanda bernama Muhammad Akna dan Beliau menerima ajaran ini dari Mas H. Hanan ke-29. Beliau dan K. Mas H. Abdul Daud ke-28 Beliau dari K. Mas Hijaya ke-27. Beliau dari Shaykh Abdulloh dan Bagus

Muhammad Abdul Muhyidin Pamijahan ke-26. Beliau dari Shaykh Haji Abdul Muhyi Safarwadi Pamijahan ke-25. Dari Shaykh Hamzah Pansuri Singgil ke-24. Dari Shaykh Abdur Rouf ke-23. Dari Shaykh Ahmad bin Muhammad Madinah (Shaykh Qossin) ke-22. Dari Shaykh Abi Muwahib Abdullah Ahmad ke-21. Dari Shaykh Sibgatullah ke-20. Dari Shaykh Wajihudin al-Alnawi ke-19. Dari Shaykh Muhammad Gaos dan putra Khotimudin ke-18. Dari Shaykh Husuri ke-17. Dari Shaykh Hidayatulloh Sarmat ke-16. Dari Shaykh qodi Satori ke-15. Dari Shaykh Abdullah Shatori ke-14. Dari Shaykh A'rif ke-13. Dari Shaykh Muhammad Asik ke-12. Dari Shaykh Maula Nahari ke-11. Dari Shaykh Hasana Harqoni ke-10. Dari Shaykh Rumli Tari tusi ke-9. Dari Shaykh Qutub Mudofar ke-8. Dari Shaykh Arobi Yazidi istri ke-7. Dari Shaykh Muhammad Magribi ke-6. Dari Shaykh Abdi Yazid Bustami ke-5. Jafarus Sodiq ke-4. Dari Shaykh Imam Muhammad Bakir ke-3. Dari Shaykh Jenal Abidin ke-2. Hasan Husen R.A. dan dari Sayidin Ali bin Abi Tholib K. W. beliau dari K. Nabi Muhammad S.A.W.

Beben's blood relationship with the *wali* through his father, his *silsilah*, and government approval for his group act as significant proofs to some villagers that Beben Muhammad Dabas is indeed a legitimate Shattariyyah leader.

H. Conclusion

The Shattariyyah emerged as part of an expansion worldwide of Sufi orders in the 17th century. A dynamic network of various important orders characterises this period. In Indonesia, the order gained followers not only in Sumatra but also in Java. Shaykh Abdul Muhyi emerged as a prominent figure in Java after 'Abd al-Raûf al-Singkel. It is through his *silsilah* that followers in various places in Central and East Java also derive their intellectual chain.

The Shattariyyah *tarekat*, like any other *tarekat*, experienced fluctuations in its development. In Pamijahan and in other parts of Java, Shattariyyah followers were overwhelmed by other, later *tarekat*. These fluctuations have often been a consequence of the influences absorbed by pilgrims while undertaking the *hâjj*.

Beben Muhammad Dabas claims that his Shattariyyah still survives in the village of Pamijahan, and therefore the *silsilah* of the Shattariyyah in Pamijahan constitutes a true *silsilah*. The contemporary Pamijahanese see this *tarekat* genealogy not only in terms of Sufism but also as an instrument of legitimation for all the families in Pamijahan who claim to be related to Abdul Muhyi. All Pamijahanese claim that they have inherited the characteristics of Abdul Muhyi's Sufism. Thus, the *silsilah* is not only used to legitimate Beben Muhammad Dabas' Sufi group but also serves as an embedded identity for the Pamijahanese.

The various *silsilah* also come forth as a major means of continuing the cult of the *wali*. People believe that by reciting a particular formulaic chant, which is dedicated to the names listed in the *silsilah*, they will obtain their saint's blessing, *barakah*.

What I have outlined above locates Pamijahan as an important place - and the events of its history as important events - in the story of Sufism in Indonesia, particularly in West Java. It also provides a simple but telling example of the fact that, as Azra (1995) has described so effectively, examining the genealogy of a Sufi order helps to reveal the network of clerics and *ulama* scholars behind the Sufi phenomenon.

ENDNOTES

[1] For a comprehensive study of this transmission, see Azra 1994

[2] Rinkes' articles have recently been collected and translated into English under the title *The Nine Saints of Java* (Rinkes 1996)

[3] In an article on Shaykh Yusuf, G.W.J. Drewes refers to a passage in the *Babad Cerbon* indicating that Yusuf sought refuge from the Dutch in the village of Karang (probably modern Pamijahan) around the time that Shaykh Abdul Muhyi is thought to have been living there. (Drewes 83-84).

[4] For other sources on Paqih Ibrahim see also mss. Cod. Or. 7486b, 7446, 7455, and 7443 in Leiden University Library

[5] See also Mss. 793b, 7433, 7486, 7455, 7397b in Leiden Library,

Chapter 7: Grasping the Wali's Teaching

> Be sure you accept correctly the meaning of the One and the mirror. Understand this in its proper sense. Do not accept it in a mistaken [way]. Understand these metaphors. And the meaning of 'return'. Do not [claim yourself] to become God (Tuhfa, Johns 1965)

A. Introduction

In the previous chapters, three different types of narratives functioning in the village have been identified: the narrative of the ancestors, the narratives of space, and the body of narratives relating to Sufi *silsilah*. While the previous chapter discussed the tradition behind the *silsilah* of the Shattariyyah order, this chapter will discuss the teaching of the Wali, Shaykh Abdul Muhyi.

In the village, what it is called the 'teaching' of the Wali is not as clear as we might imagine. Various spiritual teachings in the village are often ascribed to Shaykh Abdul Muhyi. These are scattered and may range from only a proverb dealing with the Shaykh to the whole metaphysical doctrine of Shattariyyah or Qadiriyyah-Naqshabandiyyah. The distance from the Wali to contemporary Pamijahan has created a fuzzy perception of what should be properly called the Wali's teaching. Furthermore, there is the question of whether the teaching of Shaykh Abdul Muhyi can be designated as a single doctrine, such as that of the Shattariyyah, or as a combination of various mystical teachings.

It is possible for a Sufi to be initiated into various orders. In the 17th century, for instance, the master of Shaykh Abdul Muhyi, Abd al-Rauf al-Singkel, was reported to have had more than two *ijazah* or Sufi accreditations (Riddell 1984; Fathurhman 1999; Azra 2001). Abd al-Rauf's master, al-Qushashi, was also a member of various *tarekat* in Mecca. In fact, most *tarekat* do allow their followers to embrace more than one order. There are of course exceptions, but they are not dominant. For example, the *tarekat* Tijaniyyah forbids its followers to become members of other orders (Muhaimin 1995:336). However, in the case of Shaykh Abdul Muhyi, the ambiguity of his teaching is partly caused by the fact that no manuscript has been found in the village, or in any library, that is written directly by him. Most manuscripts giving us a clue to his existence appear to have been written by his followers in later periods (E. Kosim 1974; Rinkes 1909; Krauss 1995).

On the other hand, as I mentioned in Chapters 3 and 7 (see also Christomy 2002), there is significant evidence that Shaykh Abdul Muhyi initiated many followers from Java into the Shattariyyah, or, at least, *silsilah* through his name even reach as far as Trengganu, Malang, Surakarta, Cirebon and various small villages in West Java.

The number of manuscripts in the library of Leiden University in The Netherlands is more than thirty. Therefore, it is not surprising that a number of scholars have questioned the role of Shaykh Abdul Muhyi in originating or delivering his teaching. For example, Krauss (1995) set out to clarify Muhyi's historical identity. Even before Krauss wrote his article, in 1974 important preliminary research had been conducted by a team of historians from the University of Padjajaran. (Kosim 1974)

It is important here to recall their findings. The research focused on the advance of Islam into the interior of the highlands of Sunda. One of their discoveries that is important here is their identification of the Wali's teaching. According to Kosim (E Kossim 1974)

> Dalam hubungan ini ternyata Tarekat Shaykh Abdul Muhyi termasuk dalam Tarekat Shattariyyah. Keterangan yang menjelaskan bahwa Shaykh Abdul Muhyi menganut Tarekat Shattariyyah, bersumber dari Kitab Shaykh Nursada dari Sumedang Kulon sebagai murid kelima. Kitab ini ditulis pada tahun 1842. Sebaiknya kita harus mengambil sumber langsung dari kitab yang ditulis oleh Shaykh Abdul Muhyi sendiri, tetapi sayang bahwa sampai kini kami belum mendapatkannya. Yang tersebar di Jawa Barat kebanyakan adalah ajaran Shaykh Abdul Muhyi yang dituliskan oleh murid-muridnya yang diangkat sebagai Khalifah atau pengganti-penggantinya. (p. 129)

> In relation to this (what has been discussed above), the tarekat of Shaykh Abdul Muhyi comes under the Shattariyyah order. The evidence that he followed the Shattariyyah is based on the Kitab Shaykh Nursada from West Sumedang who was a fifth generation student (of Shaykh Abdul Muhyi). The book was written in 1842. Naturally we should take as our source the writings of Shaykh Abdul Muhyi himself, but unfortunately, up to the present time, none has been found. What we do have circulating in West Java are mainly the teachings of Shaykh Abdul Muhyi written by those of his students, promoted to the rank of Khalifah (Deputy) or of their successors.

Proceeding from a philological framework, it is difficult to identify manuscripts that are directly written by the Wali. Alifya Santrie (1987: 107-113), however, has tried to speculate that the name of Shaykh Muhyidin in the manuscript of the Shattariyyah is none other than Shaykh Abdul Muhyi. Now, my evidence from the village and the Shattariyyah manuscripts suggests that Shaykh Muhyidin is the grandson of Shaykh Abdul Muhyi. In one of his findings, Kosim (1974: 1), states that the teaching of Shaykh Abdul Muhyi is a combination of

Shattariyyah doctrine and the *kabuyutan* teachings of the pre-Islamic period, such as were used by the Wali Sanga to attract local Javanese to Islam.

> Doa-doa yang diajarkan Tarekat Shaykh Abdul Muhyi sering menggunakan percampuran doa antara "ajaran kabuyutan" dan ajaran Islam. Adapun yang dimaksud dengan ajaran kabuyutan ini meliputi ajaran kabuyutan Sumedang, Cirebon, Karang Kamulyan dan beberapa tempat lain dari Jawa Barat. Doa kabuyutan terdiri dari susunan kalimat yang sulit difahami. Mungkin ini yang disebut sebagai 'jangjawokan". Doa-doa ini meliputi hampir seluruh keperluan kehidupan yang pokok, antara lain: pertanian, hubungan seksuil, penolak dan penyembuh penyakit, perdagangan, kekebalan supaya tidak mempan akan peluru atau senjata tajam. (p. 137)

> The prayers taught by the tarekat of Shaykh Abdul Muhyi often employ a mixture of those from kabuyutan or the 'teachings of the ancestors' and from Islam. What is meant by the 'teachings of the ancestors' here includes the sources from the ancient centres of Sumedang, Cirebon, Karang Kamulyan and a number of other places in West Java. Their prayers are couched in words difficult to understand. Perhaps they come under the term 'jangjawokan'. These prayers cover almost every basic need in life, including farming, sexual relations, the prevention and the curing of disease, trade and the state of invincibility whereby one cannot be touched by bullets or sharp weapons.

Even if speculation about Abdul Muhyi's fusion of two traditions can be verified, there are still problems concerning the evidence to hand. The University of Padjadjaran's team explored what had been learned by an owner of manuscripts in Sumedang, Shaykh Nursada. This figure is identified as a fifth generation student of Shaykh Abdul Muhyi, based on the *silsilah* of the Shattariyyah. One manuscript of Shaykh Nursada, the *Kitab Shaykh Nursada* written in 1842, (Kosim 1974) not only contain Shattariyyah teachings derived from Shaykh Abdul Muhyi but also other mystical teachings and mantra from the sources called kabuyutan. The argument still needs to be explored. According to the Kitab Shaykh Nursada, the Shattariyyah followers of Muhyi learned kabuyutan from different sources. The team speculates that the kabuyutan teaching could also have been followed by Shaykh Abdul Muhyi.

The team argues, "

> Kalau Sheykh Nursada di sini dijelaskan mendapat Ilmu Kawaliannya dari Sunan Gunung Jati. Apabila pada urutan silsilah guru di atasnya disebutkan dari Shaykh Abdul Muhyi, maka dapatlah ditarik kesimpulan bahwa ajaran Shaykh Abdul Muhyi pun bersumber dari Sunan Gunung Jati. Memang kalau kita hanya menggunakan fakta di atas sukar untuk

mencari keguruan antara Shaykh Hamzah Fansuri Singkil dengan Sunan Gunung Jati, atau hubungan antara Shaykh Abdul Muhyi dengan Sunan Gunung Jati. Tetapi kalau kita telaah lebih lanjut ajarannya yang bercampurkan doa-doa "kabuyutan Cirebon", jelas di sini ada pengaruh yang kuat dari ajaran Ilmu Kawalian yang hidup di Jawa Barat. Ajaran ini meliputi pandangan politik atau pun hal-hal yang menyangkut pada masalah pertanian, perdagangan dan gerakan mengebalkan diri.

Regarding Shaykh Nursada, it is explained that he received his Wali teachings from Sunun Gunung Jati. If the order of the silsilah of the teachers goes back to Shaykh Abdul Muhyi, we may draw the conclusion that his teaching also derives from Sunan Gunung Jati. Of course, if we restrict ourselves to the facts above, it is difficult to find a student-teacher relationship between Shaykh Hamzah of Singkil and Sunan Gunung Jati, or a relationship between Shaykh Abdul Muhyi and Sunan Gunung Jati. But if we examine more closely the teachings with their admixture of 'kabuyutan of Cirebon', is it clear that there is a strong influence from the teachings of the walis' knowledge which is still alive in West Java. These teachings embrace political vision and even things pertaining to farming, trading and the movement to make oneself invincible to weapons.

We need additional evidence as to whether Shaykh Abdul Muhyi actually taught the teachings of the ancients (*ajaran kabuyutan*). The researcher from the University of Padjadjaran attempted to establish a relationship between the teaching of Shaykh Abdul Muhyi and that of Sunan Gunung Jati; and between the Islam which came to Pamijahan and the Islam propagated by the missionaries of Gunung Jati, who often used *ajaran kabuyutan*.

In contemporary Pamijahan there are indications that any spiritual teachings other than *fiqh*, or jurisprudence, and those of the *tarekat* Shattariyyah are also attributed to Shaykh Abdul Muhyi. However, if we follow Vow (1980) and Azra (2001), the *sanad* in legalistic teaching and the *silsilah* in Sufism can be used as historical evidence behind the *ulama* and the Sufi networks respectively. Of course, we have to allow higher priority to the Shattariyyah *silsilah* for describing Muhyi and his teaching. Nevertheless, it is imprudent to exclude materials other than the Shattariyyah teachings found in contemporary Pamijahan as unrelated to Muhyi's teaching. Hence, my position is to look at all material, not in the spirit of finding historical evidence but rather to find the best description of how people orchestrate all of the symbolic materials available in their culture to make meaning of their contemporary lives.

I will therefore first describe in general terms the meaning of the teaching of the *Kitab Wali*. I will then discuss other variants that are believed to be part of the Wali's teaching. The discussion will focus on the doctrine of creation. This doctrine is the starting point of the mystical journey for the Sufi but it is also the most crucial point of debate between legalists and Sufis. While Sufis hold the view that it is possible to travel into the inner world of Reality, the legalist holds that this view is unprecedented in Islamic tradition. I will not discuss here the conflict between these groups. Rather I will attempt to unveil the most basic metaphysical doctrine of Shattariyyah and its meaning in society. It is difficult to describe a Sufi order without first determining its metaphysical doctrine, since this has significant implications for theorising the distance between the Creator and His creation.

In Sunda, the doctrine is clearly adopted from Abd al-Rauf's work (Azra 2001; Johns 1955 and 1965; Rinkes 1910). Yet the manuscripts from Pamijahan and neighbouring areas in the Priangan rarely refer explicitly to particular works of Abd al-Rauf, such as the *Dakaik al-Huruf* (cf. Johns 1955). This tradition can be traced back to Ibn Fadhilla's teaching expounded in the *Tuhfa al-Mursala*. (: 1965:8)

Johns (1965) states that the *Tuhfa* is the most significant source whereby Shattariyyah followers in Java comprehend the concept of the seven grades of being. Johns also gives an interesting commentary regarding the circumstances of the composition of the *Tuhfa*. He states that the manuscript recording Ibn Fadhilla's work was written in the Grand Mosque in Tegal Arum by a 'famous religious affairs officer' (Johns 1965:23). Unfortunately, the scribe did not reveal his name. Thus although we do not have hard facts here, as I mentioned earlier, the local story of Pamijahan places Shaykh Abdul Muhyi's son, Paqih Ibrahim in Tegal (cf. Rinkes 1910). Furthermore, in the texts it is reported that he taught relatives of the Sultan of Cirebon and the Sultan of Surakarta who continued their studies on Shattariyyah in Mecca. From my discussion of the *silsilah* in Chapter 6, there are many indications that Muhyi's followers penetrated these regions (Rinkes 1910; see also Christomy 2001). To some extent this possibility was also indicated by Rinkes when he wrote about Abd al-Rauf's teaching in Java (1910).

There is room for us to speculate that Abdul Muhyi, or his followers, copied Ibn Fadhilla's works and distributed their versions of them along the north coast of Java (personal communication M.A. Ricklefs 1997). Johns does mention a relationship between Shaykh Abdul Muhyi and the scribe of the Javanese *Tuhfa*. It is also possible that one of Muhyi's sons, Paqih Ibrahim, who according to local lore settled in Tegal, had links with the *Tuhfa*. Furthermore, according to a Shattariyyah *silsilah* that is affiliated with the village of Safarwadi or Pamijahan, Paqih Ibrahim initiated Kiai Nida Basyari from Cirebon, Tuan Shaykh Abdurrahman from Kartasura, and Kiai Muhammad from Suci Garut (Christomy 2001, see also Chapter 6). Until the present day, the family of Paqih Ibrahim makes a yearly visitation to the shrines of Pamijahan.

These notions remind us that the history of Shattariyyah in Indonesia, particularly in Java, remains obscure. This is illustrated by the process of transmission of the *Martabat Tujuh* in Java in which, according to Johns (1965), the Javanese showed themselves to be more interested in practical matters and applications of the doctrines rather than in theoretical speculation. Here I will present a general outline of Shattariyyah doctrine as it appears in the manuscripts associated with Shaykh Abdul Muhyi. My general comments on the contents will follow. It is also my major theme that the manuscripts of the Shattariyyah, like the manuscripts of the Pamijahan *Babad*s, provide significant space for the defining of identity and strengthening the latent power of *barakah*.

B. Origins of Shattariyyah Teaching

The Shattariyyah order, including texts it inspired like the *al-Tuhfa al-mursala ila ruh al-nabi* or: *The Gift addressed to the Spirit of the Prophet* (Johns 1965: 218) was domesticated in Mecca. It has been shown that the 'wild' tendencies and the pantheistic character of the Shattariyyah were 'tamed' by 'neo-Sufis' and legalists such as al-Qushashi (Azra 1995: 246; Johns 1965: 218). The mystical speculations of Ibn Arabi, as passed on by Fadhillah, are interpreted in more a moderate form. As a result, the original doctrine of five grades of Ibn Arabi, as interpreted in Indian Shattariyyah, is modified into seven mystical realities under the hand of al-Qushashi, an Arabic scholar of great influence on Indonesian scholars in the 17th century (Christomy 2001: 41; Azra 1995: 246). According to no less than five manuscripts in Pamijahan, and to some thirty in holdings in Jakarta and Leiden, Abdul Muhyi owed his mystical linkages to the line of al-Qushashi. In other words, the Indian variant of Shattariyyah Sufism come by way of the very heart of Islamic culture, Mecca itself, and only later spread to the islands of the Indonesian archipelago.

The main question with which I am concerned at all times relates to the status of these mystical materials within the local culture of Pamijahan. As has been mentioned above, all tangible and intangible signs are orchestrated towards maintaining and strengthening the blessing, the *barakah*. We have to draw first on the main teaching indicated by the Book of the Wali.

C. *Martabat Tujuh* or The Seven Grades

The most important mystical principle in Shattariyyah is the description of Being. The Creator and the created are conceived of as realities that need to be deeply understood properly by all Sufis. If one is unable to comprehend these relations, one will fail to be a Sufi. In the grand narrative of Sufism, the ontological status of Being in the Muslim world has become a serious debate between Sufi and those of legalist inclination. (Johns 1975: 252) At one level, both sides agree that God is the owner of reality and they also agree that the Reality is God (*al-Haq*). But the discussion proliferates on how the material world (*dunya*) is to be conceived. In the *Tuhfa al Mursala ila ruh al-nabi* or *The Gift addressed to the Spirit of the Prophet* (Johns 1965), the scribe warns of the possibility of misinterpreting the relationship between inner and outer being,

> Den kena dera nampani / tegesing paesan tunggal / den sami wruh ing tjiptane / sampun kaliru ing tampa / den wikan ing sasmita / miwah ing tegesing wangsul / ajwa andadi Pangeran / (Tuhfa, Johns 1965)

> Be sure you accept correctly / the meaning of One and the mirror, / understand this in its propers sense, / do not accept it in a mistaken [way] / understand these metaphors / and the meaning of 'return' / do not [claim yourself] to become God./

The most crucial point is found in the third level which is called the level of Fixed Prototypes (*a'yan thabit*). According to the *Tuhfa*, "The Fixed Prototypes then are neither created nor uncreated since they have no exterior [existence]". In Pamijahan this level is known as *martabat katilu* or the third level, The Blue Print of Being in the inner World.

The pantheistic Sufism as subscribed to by Hamzah Fansuri or al-Samartani theoretically rejects a dichotomy between The Source of Light and the light. Even though Shattariyyah teaching derives from the same source as Hamzah's teaching, in fact, the main figure in Shattariyyah, Abd al-Rauf, in his work *Tanbih al-Masyi*, states that "The world is like a shadow, it is not an essence... so that according to this teaching men are the shadow of the True Reality, or the shadow of His Shadow". This why some scholars see Abd al-Rauf as a moderate figure compared to other figures from the school of *wahdat al-wujud* in the archipelago, also inspired by Ibn Arabi, such as Hamzah al-Fansuri .

Being or Reality is hierarchically conceived in seven basic levels; and if we look carefully into the manuscripts of Shattariyyah from Pamijahan, these seven levels can be grouped into two segments. The first three levels describe the inner dimensions, or batin, while the other four are devoted to the outer, or lahir.

1. *Ahadiyah* or The Level of Oneness:

In reading the manuscripts of the Shattariyyah, we are often confronted with series of icons, indexes and symbols in written or graphic modes. This elaborate signification system is most likely designed for the general reader so that there can be no misconception arising from the reading process. The Shattariyyah teaching unveils the relation between the inner and outer being by using a schematic diagram consist of seven circles. Each circle is ranked from an empty circle to lesser circles crisscrossed by horizontal as well as vertical lines. Each circle conceptualises a nature of beings.

According to this view God is initially manifest in the first level of Being. This consists of (1) the grade of emptiness (*ahadiyah*), then (2) the stage of first individuation (*wahdat*), followed by (3) the second grade of individuation where God manifests His Name (*wahidiyat*). Secondly God creates *alam* or worlds/realms consisting of (4) the world of spirit (*alam arwah*), (5) the world of ideas or prototypes (*alam mithal*), (6) the world of form (*alam ajsam*), and (7) the world of Perfect Man (*alam insan kamil*).

Unlike the *Tuhfa* (Johns 1965), the scribes of the Pamijahan manuscripts have deliberately deployed various schematic diagrams. These diagrams may not originally have been part of Shaykh Abdul Muhyi's *silsilah*, but the number of them generously extends the manuscript.

The following illustrates how Beben's manuscript or *The Book of the Wali* draws on iconic images in order to clarify its mystical view of reality.

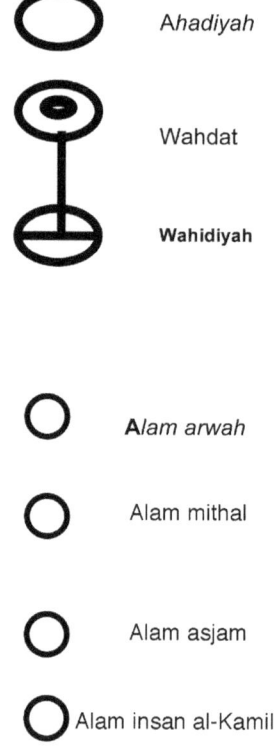

Figure 22. The concept of the Seven Grades of Being in 'iconic' mode

The first circle is conceived as the level of emptiness (*ahadiyah*). According to Pamijahan's Shattariyah patron Beben Muhammad Dabas, our faculty of thinking is incapable comprehending this level. Most Shattariyyah manuscripts found in Pamijahan which mention Abdul Muhyi's genealogy explain this stage with the phrase: 'at the time of the state of emptiness...' (*tatkala awang-awang uwung-uwung*). This metaphor is also popular in the Javanese context. The well-known Javanese poet from mid 19th century, Ronggowarsito, in his mystical work the *Wirid Hidayat Jati*, uses the same expression (Simuh 1987: 67). The Pamijahanese too use a circle to schematise this concept. To quote a metaphor given by Beben Muhammad Dabas, Reality is like a blank sheet of white paper (*sapertos kertas kosong*).

> Bismillah al-rahman al-rahim, punika martabat Allah Taala tatkala ing dalem gaib kang karihin cinaritaken tatkala awang-awang uwung-uwung bumi langit durung ana
>
> *In the name of God the Beneficient, the Merciful, this is the state of Allah in the time of emptiness when the world had not been created.*

The manuscript then quotes the Hadith in which the Prophet instructed his followers not to attempt to figure out the reality of the Essence but only to comprehend His creations or signs. It is through signs that humans can understand the Creator. At this level, God exists as the absolute reality. The manuscripts even teach that at this stage God has not revealed His name. Hence, the only appropriate attribute for Him is oneness (*ahadiyah*). The Pamijahanese Sufis call this the 'ultimate form' (*zat kang mutlaq*) and the 'ultimate reality' (*wujud mutlaq*). God can only be conceptualised as non-determination (*la taayun*), non extant (*ghaibul guyub*), the inner-self reality (*kunhi zat*), and self non-extant (*gaib al-huwiyat*).

> Yakni ahadiyah eta martabat zat latayun ngarana, ghaibul guyub eta ngarana, jeung kunhi zat eta ngarana, jeung gaib al-huwiyat eta ngarana, jeung gaib eta ngarana, jeung wujud mutlak eta ngarana, jeung dat mutlak eta ngarana wujüd mahd, eta ngarana anu wajib hurip Allah Ta'ala, eta mohal mati huripna sajeroning hurip badan anu sajati, maka jadi lah urang huripna kalawan huriping Allah, nyata mungguh dina urang martabat akhadiyat. (Beben's manuscript)
>
> Ahadiyah is the level of non determination (zat la taayun), it is non-extant (ghaibul guyub), and it is the innermost essence (kunhi zat), and it is non extant (ghaib al-huwiyat) and it is the absolute existence (wujud mutlak), and it is the absolute essence (zat mutlaq). This absolute being (wujud mahd) must exist. This is Allah, Allah will not die in His absolutness, our life depends on HIS existence. This martabat resides in us.

2. *Wahdat* or Individuation

If God does not create anything within the first level, in the second level, according to the teaching, He creates His own attributes. According to the texts, God then reveals His attributes for the first time. In this stage, He reflects His existence as the first 'manifestation', like a source of light, for the first time illuminating his qualities. This manifestation is called *wahdat*. This level is symbolised by a dot within a circle, which means that there is an attribute to the Oneness (*martabat sifat*). However, it is still a non-existential attribute (*ta'ayun awal*) within the Hiddenness of God. (Johns 1965: 42-43) In other words, the ultimate source has created a light, but the light has not been reflected. This level mediates between the Ultimate Reality and His later manifestation as will be seen at a later stage. The empty circle that appears in the first stage is now dotted. It illustrates that a point in the circle functions as a medium between the Absolute and Otherness in His hiddenness. It is linked to the next stage of creation called *wahidiyat*. This is the reflection of the light.

In regard to this stage, the Pamijahan manuscript explains:

> Yakni wahdat eta martabat sifat naqtu gaib eta ngarana taayun awal eta ngarana, jeung su'un zat eta ngarana jeung hakikat Muhammadiyah ngarana, anapon anu kanggo dina naqtu ghib eta opat perkara nyaeta wujüd 'ilmu nur Syuhüd, ari wujüd eta ibarat dat ari ilmu eta ibarat sifat ari nur eta ibarat asma ari suhüd eta ibarat afal eta kalawan kersaning Allah, eta martabat wahdat mungguh di urang.

> Wahdat is His attribute which is called (naqtu gaib).. It is also called the first individuation (tayun awal), it is also called the predisposition (su'un zat), the essence of Muhammad (hakikat Muhammad). The naqtu gaib can be divided into four: existence (wujud), knowledge (ilmu), light (nur), and sight (syuhud). Wujud is the name for the reality (zat), ilmu is the name for attribute, the light is His name, (syuhud) is the sight of him on behalf of God's will. This level resides in us.

This level of individuation can be explained in four modes of attribution (*naqtu ghaib*), namely (1) His existence, (2) His knowledge, (3) His light (*nur*), and (4) His sight (*shuhud*). These four modes of manifestation are also known as the four non-existential attributes or *batin*. Regarding this concept clearly both heterodox and orthodox hold the same positions. For instance, what Al-Attas (1970) describes in his outline of Hamzah Fansuri's teaching on the concept of self-divine manifestation parallels the *Kitab Wali*. "The first degree of determination is fourfold: Knowledge (*ilm*), Existence (*wujud*), Vision or Presence (*shuhud*) and Light (*nur*)." At this level, God exists (*maujud*) in His hiddenness which is also called the fixed prototype (*ayan thabita*). The fixed prototype is known in various potential states of being - such as possible non-being, possible reality, possible pure being, possible Light of Muhammad, Light, vision, first individuation, attributes of preexistence, pure spirit, and divine spirit.

The prototype of the Prophet Muhammad conceived in this level is well recognised among the Sufi. (Schimmel 1994) Beben's manuscript explains:

> "Satuhune Allah Taala itu andadeken ing bumi lan langit iku asal saking kang cahaya haqiqat Muhammadiyah lan ingaranan malih nur Allah lan ingarana malih cahaya iku ta'ayun awal arane lang ingaran malih nur Muhammad lan ingaranan malih bahru al-hayat lan ingaranan malih ruh Rabbani lang ingarnan ruh qudddus lan malih ingaranan naqtu ghaib…jujuluk hakekat saking sakehing mumkinat ikut kabeh tatkala lagi tetep ing dalem a'yan tsabitah."

> Truly, Almighty God reflects Himself in the earth and the sky in the form of His light, called the Light of Muhammad which is also called the Light of God, or the First Light, or the Light of Muhammad, or the Reflection of Life, or the Spirit of the Lord, or the Holy Essence, or the Four Inner Beings… their names are the Essence of Possible Realities – all still within the Primal Light..

This crucial point is mystical understanding as stated by Beben Muhammad Dabas. The Light of God is reflected in a blueprint of the light of Muhammad.

3. Wahidiyat

If we follow the Shattariyyah levels of being schema from top to bottom, the circle is firstly empty, secondly dotted, and thirdly lined. These are the circles as drawn in *The Book of the Wali*. According to this system, after God revealed His knowledge at the second level, He reflected his knowledge (light) to become the blueprint of His knowledge (*ayan thabitah*). These particular manifestations appear in the inner circle.

> Yakni wahidiyat eta martabat asma jeung af-al ta-yun tsani eta ngarana a'yan tsabitah eta ngarana al-ruh ruhyi, ari hurip eta hurip urang kanyatahan hakikat na manusa kabeh, anu wajib kersa Allah eta mohal lamun henteu keresa nafas kanyatahan karep maka jadilah urang eta karep kalawan kersana Allah nyaeta martabat wahidiyat mungguh di urang.

> Wahidiyat is the level of His name and the second determination (af'al ta'yun tsani), it is called a'yan tsabitah, it is called the spirit, this is the spirit of mankind whose existence depends on Allah. This grade of Known and the Fixed Prototype (wahidiyat) resides in us.

Some Shattariyyah manuscripts also characterise this level as that in which the name of God (*asma Allah*) manifests itself in the inner world (*batin*). It is also conceptualised as the blueprint of the universe (*wahidiyat iku iya iku hakikat kita kabe*). Sometimes the author describes this state by making an analogy with a shadow play (*wayang*) performance (cf. Johns 1965). From this perspective, Being is called *tayun tsani*. It reveals itself because the relation between the possessor of the light and its shadow is similar to that between the lamp and the shadow (*wawayangan*) of puppets in the shadow theatre.

In the manuscripts, a circle in the third level has a horizontal and vertical line, meaning that there is a multiple manifestation in one, or unity in multiplicity. Compared to the previous level or *wahdat* which a dotted circle, this circle has been occupied by more complex representation. To illustrate this level, it is important to refer to an iconic sign given by the manuscripts.

In other words, these three points reflect the multiplicity when the first reality (*uwung-uwung awang-awang*) which is only known by The Knower has been transformed into Knowledge (*ilm*) and its manifestation, or has been known (*malum*) by Him. This level (thirdness), together with firstness and secondness are conceived by the manuscripts as the Inner Being.

This gives justification for the Sufi to theorise that under certain conditions a human being (specifically the Prophet Muhammad) can ascend to these levels as seen in the miracle of the Isra Miraj, and in certain instances, some Sufis are believed to have such a capability.

The mystery for Sufis lies in the question whether the outer world is part of the inner world. In Malay Sufism, the relationship between the inner and outer is revealed by the linkages between: the seed and the sprout, the ice and the water, the sun and the sunshine, and other such analogies. For devotees of *wujudiyah*, in essence there is no difference between outer (*lahir*) and inner (*batin*) since the reality is One. However, moderate Sufis who still find substantial differences between 'seed' and 'sprout' or 'ice' and 'water' reject such metaphors. Abd al-Rauf al-Singkili, for example, the pupil of al-Qushashi and the Master of Shaykh Abdul Muhyi, in fact put his position in moderate terms. However, he did not condemn the *wujudiyah* followers as unbelivers (*kafir*) as did Nur al-din al-Raniri.

Beben's manuscript further clarifies the first three stages. According to his manuscript the level of emptiness is called He or The Ultimate Reality (*zat*). The second level is called His Attribute, the attribute (*sifat*) of He that is Allah. The third level is called His Name (*asma*) that is 'the most merciful'. The manuscripts also describe these three stages in three circles. Elsewhere the manuscripts elaborate the link between three levels as the relationship between the Uniqueness, the attribute of the Uniqueness, and the name of Uniqueness.

We will now see how the teaching relates the inner world to the outer world. The four next stages are part of the outer world.

4. Alam Arwah

The realm of spirit, *alam arwah*, is perceived as an outward manifestation of His attributes. As seen in the metaphor of 'sun and sunshine', the spirit is a generic element that is similar to the 'reflected generic light'. In other words, for the Sufi, this is the actualisation of the 'blueprint' of reality that is manifest in the outer world (*zahir, lahir*). This is a created light which is generated from the third stage, *wahidiyah*.

The light that is reflected in the outer reality is often referred to as the name for the Prophet Muhammad's spirit. It is also identified as the form of the world, *wujud alam*. A dilemma raised by pantheists, such as the followers of *wujudiyah*, regarding the relation between Essence and World, is initially solved in this stage by Shattariyyah interpretation. According to Shattariyyah, the 'sprout' and 'seed' exist because the owner of the seed deliberately provides an atmosphere in which the 'seed' will bloom. God with his power produced His light. Thus, the light is a created light, and if the light is created then man could not be a creator.

According to the manuscript, this is the level of reality where the world depends on the light of the sight of God, *nur suhud*. If we return to the metaphor of light, this level is the reflection of light which is 'switched on' by the Ultimate Owner of the light.

> Yakni alam arwah eta ngaran nyawa Muhammad rahamani padana ngaran nyawa Muhammad, wujüd alam, nur suhüd anu wajib kawasa Allah eta mohal apes anggahota kahananing qudrat maka jadilah urang kawasa kalawan pangawasaning Allah Ta'ala nyaeta tegese alam arwah mungguh di urang.

> The stage of spirit, alam arah, is called as a name for the spirit of the beloved Muhammad. It is also called the created 'being', wujud alam, and the light of his Sight, nur suhud, which depends on Allah. Our reality comes into existence due to His power and sight and the level of spirit, arwah, resides in us.

Furthermore, as a generic light, the spirit is not yet shaped to express its ultimate destiny. It is the universal spirit before it is transformed into other forms. In philosophical terms, it might be called the purest substance. The spirit manifests itself when God says: "Be!" and something becomes (*Kun fa yakun*. Qur'an 2:117). Beyond this point, spirit is classified into various universal types as evidenced in the fifth stage, the *alam mitsal*.

5. Alam Mitsal

In literary terms, *mitsal* is an image. Thus, *alam mitsal* describes the imagination of the pure spirit that appeared in the previous level. Beben, the owner of the manuscript and a Sufi, says that at this level the spirit of *alam arwah* has received a destiny, *anarima pandum*, and has a form. This stage is illustrated by the circle which is separated from the first three levels. The text states that Allah transforms pure spirit, *nyawa rahmani*, into four kinds of spirit: a vegetable spirit (*nyawa nabati*), an animal spirit (*nyawa hewani*), a corporeal spirit (*nyawa jasmani*), and a spiritual spirit (*nyawa rohani*).

> Yakni alam mitsal eta ngarana sifat Muhammad rahmani eta ngaran nyawana Muhammad nyaeta kawitan [ngabagikeun] Allah Taala eta kana nyawana rahmani jadina opat. Kahiji nyawana nabati kadua nyawana khewani, katilu nyawana jasmani, kaopat nyawana rohani anu wajib [mikarsa] Allah Taala eta mohal kahananing sama maka jadilah urang eta mikarsa kalawan sama ing Allah Taala nyaeta alam misal mungguh dina urang.

> The alam mitsal designates the attributes of Muhammad the merciful, this is name of the spirit of Muhammad. This is the first time God modifies the spirit into four. The first is the vegetable (nabati) spirit, the second is the animal (hewani) spirit, the third is the bodily (jasmani) spirit, and the fourth is the spiritual (rohani) spirit. These spirits resides in us.

This level describes the four spirits who become the essence of the manifested spirits and body in the world or *alam ajsam* in the next level.

6. Alam Ajsam

The Shattariyyah texts reveal that the next stage is the materialization of these substances into matter (*ajsam*). For the first time, spirit manifests itself in the phenomenal world, jasad nu wadag.

> Yakni alam ajsam eta jujuluk jasad Muhammad nyaeta kawitan ngadamel jasad nu wadag, alam ajsam ngarana, basirun nu wajib ningali Allah Taala eta mohal lolong panon kahanning basa maka jadi lah urang eta aningali kalawan paningaling Allah Taala, nyaeta teges na alam ajsam mungguh di urang.

> The material world is designated to the body of Muhammad. That is when God for the first time created the phenomenal creation through His Sight. The Creator has perfect sight. The Sight makes the creation which we are able to see. Thus, this level, ajsam, resides in us.

The teachings describe this stage in detail. They state that after one hundred thousand years Allah mixed four spirits, the *nabati, hewani, jasmani*, and *rohani* or *jauhar*) into the *ruhiyah*:

> Maka tatkala uwus mangkono iku, antarane saketi limang laksa tahun cinampuraken dadi sawiji, maka dadi jasad alus, maka iku ingaranan rühiyyah arane kang dendoiharken jasad alus, kang kasap iya iku jasad kang anarima dosa lang kang anarima pecah-pecah lan kang anarima balung busuk lan kang anarima pancaindra kang dohir kang batin iya ikulah alam ajsam arane (The Limus Tilu Manuscript).

> When it appeared, around one billion five hundred years later, the essence of nabati, hewani,. Jasmanim and jauhar were mixed into one called ruhiyah. Ruhiyah is the new substance which accepts destiny and must recognize its own sin, which must decay and accept the five senses It is called an invisible and visible substances.

After God created the substances He declared into existence a particular attribute, *sama*, so that the substances could hear God when He declared, "I am the God of mankind, am I not?" Then each spirit, *ruhiyah*, stood up and recited *Al-hamdu li l-lah Rabbi l-alamini* (Praise be to God, Lord of the Universe) and recognized that Allah is the only God of mankind (*hamba*). After that, the substances declared that they would obey God. Then, according to this teaching, God asked His creations or substances to confirm again His command. After that the substances knelt and recited greetings (*salam*).

After God created them then He ordered angels to place birds and plants on earth. The first creation on the earth was seed (*waturi*). The birds took the seeds. God then created *jinn* from fire and placed them in the world. However, the *jinn* devastated the earth because they were able to assume human form. God then ordered angels to remove *jinn* from the earth and put them in the seventh hell

The substances had to acknowledge this process of creation. At that time, God told them that everything in the world was created for you, *jauhar*. Ruhyia (Muhammad) declared, "No other God but you must be obeyed, and I (Muhammad) am your servant".

7. Insan Kamil

After the four substances took this oath God ordered the angels to mix them (water, earth, fire, wind) into spirit. This was the creation of man, called *insan kamil* or the primordial perfect man.

> Yakni alam insan kamil eta nyaeta ngaran sampurnaning Muhammad nyaeta kawitan Allah Ta'ala ngadamel manusa kalawan manusa insan kamil, [kalam bakona] nu wajib ngandika jeung wajib [langgeng]. Allah Taala eta mohal pireu lisan kahananing kalam, maka jadilah urang angucap kalawan pangucaping Allah nyaeta tegese insan kamil mungguh di urang. (Manuscipt D)

> Alam insan kamil is the attribute of the perfect Muhammad, in which God for the first time created mankind from the blueprint of Muhammad's perfection. Allah has unlimited spell, so that we are also able to speak. We speak because of Him, thus perfect attributes arose in us.

This is the last stage of creation when the prototype of mankind manifests itself in the world. So all of mankind has the same source, that is, the perfect spirit of Muhammad. Manuscripts from Limus Tilu describe this concept in detail. They say that God put the created spirit or the relative spirit called *ruh idafi* into the first man, Adam. For the Sufi, Adam is not the first man. Adam's spirit is part of the spirit of Muhammad, His reflection, who recited the Confession, the *shahadat*. According to the text, the spirit, *ruh idafi*, entered different parts of Adam.

The *ruh idafi* which penetrated Adam's tailbone or coccyx is called the *jauhar manikem* (substance). The *ruh idafi* which penetrated Adam's face is called the perfect substance. The latter is the source of the perfect unchanging spirit and the first is the spirit that was capable of being shaped to different destinies. According to this teaching, the two spirits were taken by angels and spread across the earth to become the prototype of various races. Later these prototypes were taken again and were ordered by God to recognise the perfect substance.

Furthermore, the Limus Tilu Manuscript explains that this substance spread into to the air and was scattered over the world, *a'yan kharijiyah*, and had to be acquainted with the prophethood (*nurbuwat rasulullah*) in Adam's face. The way a substance accepted the *nurbuwat rasulullah* varied. Thus according to this teaching, the spirits received different destinies and character depending on the way they saw *nurbuwat rasullah* on Adam's face. For example, a substance that only sees the shadow of Adam will have a short life in the world. A substance who sees Adam's feet will be a representative.

Every creation or *jauhar manikem* recognises Adam. Only Qabal and Muqabal reject Adam's existence. Qabal adan Muqabal are the evils and *jinn* who claim that their substance is superior to Adam's who was made from water, wind, fire, and earth.

The teaching then describes that Adam wanted a friend, a woman. At that time, *ruhiya* had never been divided into gender categories. So God created woman from the left rib of Adam, or the *tulang sulbi*.

D. Conclusion

In 1998, I presented a paper on Shaykh Abdul Muhyi's teaching in a symposium held by the Masyarakat Naskah, the Indonesian Manuscript Society, in Jakarta. I mentioned in a simple way a specimen of a manuscript of the Shattariyyah order found in Pamijahan. After my presentation, a man approached me. He suggested in all seriousness that it was better not to discuss the subject of the teaching in public. Two years later, in 2000, the Masyarakat Naskah held another symposium, this time in Padang, West Sumatra. On this occasion I presented a paper titled 'The function of manuscripts in West Java: the case of Shattariyyah'. Again, I was warned by the same person, who apparently was a member of Masyarakat Naskah and a follower of the Shattariyyah. He advised me that the manuscripts being studied had a spiritual energy that would cause difficulties for those who touch and read them without a master's guidance. Because all

Shattariyyah manuscripts are passed on through a chain of linkages to the past (*silsilah*) and initiation (*baiah*), an unauthorised person is unlikely to be able to access their true meaning. This Sufi even advised me not to physically touch the manuscript for six months, until I had completed a series of monthly rituals suggested by him.

The ritual looked simple enough. After *magrib* prayers at 6 p.m., I had to recite a particular prayer, *doa*, and remain sitting quietly for about an hour until the *isya* prayer at 7 p.m. I had to do this without being disturbed, so I had to lock myself in my bedroom, he said. The same suggestion, but in a more moderate form, was given by a senior lecturer in my faculty at the University of Indonesia, who also is evidently a follower of Shattariyyah. She holds a PhD in Javanese philology and works on mystical manuscripts. Unlike the first person, my colleague gave me a simple warning not to talk about any particular letter or character in the manuscripts. The point was that the Shattariyyah theorises Being by using various iconic signs: characters, images, and schemas.

In order to find further guidance, I went to the *pesantren* of Cipasung which is near my hometown of Tasikmalaya and which is the largest in West Java. There I consulted a prominent 'mystical scholar', an *ahli hikmah*. He has family links with Ajengan Ruhiyat, the leader of the *pesantren* and one of the most prominent legal scholars of the Nahdatul Ulama in Java. The Nahdatul Ulama has declared a *fatwa* listing the 'accepted *tarekat*s' or *tarekat mutabarak*, in NU circles. The Shattariyyah is one of these. I asked various questions regarding my experiences with the Shattariyyah manuscripts and reporting my encounters with the Shattariyyah adherents in Jakarta and Padang. He explained to me that I had an opportunity to *neplak* or to make a close description of the manuscript material, but not to make any public interpretation, or *ngahartosan*, of it.

Beben Muhammad Dabas of Pamijahan (see Chapter 8) was of the same opinion. However, he did not agree with the man who had ordered me to make ritual preparations before reading the manuscripts. Beben invited me to his assembly, *zawiya*, and narrated all the basic teachings of Shattariyyah. He read the mansucripts aloud while I made notes, and later he allowed me to make a complete set of photocopies of his manuscripts. He said that anyone with a general knowledge of the teachings of Ibn Arabi would easily comprehend the Shattariyyah's teaching.

Pak Undang, one of Beben's best friends, a young scholar who had graduated from the Bandung branch of the State Institute of Islamic Studies (IAIN) gave me a more scholarly explanation. He said that what had been described to me by Beben was a sophisticated mystical explanation of the relation between Creator and creation. It was a view of *via causalitatis, via eminentiae,* and via *negationis* (cf. Schimmel 1994: 21). According to Pak Undang, for the non-Sufi, it is easier normatively to comprehend the basic doctrine of Islam, or the *syahada*, "there is no God but Allah". He states that in a non-Sufi or legalistic or *syari'a* view, the word 'God' designates a general domain of meanings. It can be applied to any conceptualisation of The Divine. God, by definition, should be Unique and his Uniqueness is found in His name. In fact, while there might be more than one conceptualisation of The Divine, all are only Allah, the God of the Muslims. The expression "He is Allah" should then be differentiated from other teleological concepts. He is The Most Powerful who creates everything from nothing, *teu aya janten aya*. Because Allah is The Most Powerful, He is everywhere and cannot be conceptualised in terms of human spatial concepts. He cannot be comprehended by our intellect, yet He is also closer to us than our jugular veins (Qur'an 50:16). According to Pak Undang, the Shattariyyah provides a moderate interpretation of that mystery. In a simple way, the teaching tries to illustrate that everything is He (Schimmel 1994; 1986); everything is from the Light; but the world is a created light.

After giving me this short course in the Shattariyyah, Beben then explained that there is room to comprehend this relationship beyond the terms of the *syari'a*. The Sufi tries to do this under guidance. I had, he said, to be initiated first in order to receive the true teachings of the Shattariyyah.

Chapter 8: Tapping A Blessing in The House of A Young Sufi

"You of mysterious gentleness, grant me your mysterious gentleness. O Gentle One." (Khataman al-Tarekat al-Shattariyyah/Beben)

A. Introduction

Anthropologists, who have studied the concept of 'precedence' in Austronesia argue that the appearance of genealogies among common descent groups can be traced to particular 'cognate' metaphors that rely on 'botanic' icons and spatial arrangements. (Bellwod 1996; Fox 1997:8) Along the same lines, Parmentier (1987), who uses Peircean semiotics, illustrates the 'schematic' features of similar metaphoric icons in the Belauan Islands. Canberran anthropologists, as well as Pelras and Parmentier, draw attention to the function of metaphors in social action. Various 'iconic metaphors' linked to the concept of 'precedence' and to the implication of spatial arrangements and other materialised symbols, were found orchestrated in the Austronesian societies that they study.

In Pamijahan, instead of a botanic icon, a cognate concept is employed, which represents iconically the four 'sides' of the tomb and also the four imagined cultural spaces, or *pongpok* (see Chapters 5 and 9). The process of 'remembering origins' through metaphor is also found not only in the eastern parts of Indonesia but also in the western Indonesia, as suggested by Sakai in her study on Gumai People of Sumatera where Muslim influence is strong. (Sakai 1997) The Gumai point of origin within social hierarchy is represented by a ritual space.

Drawing on these studies, I examine here the use of genealogy in the process of a 'refurbishment' of the Sufi order in Pamijahan and its location in the village culture from the perspective of traditional narratives. This examination focuses on two crucial points in the village: the first is the personal narratives recited by the leader of the Order; the second is the narrative of the 'keepers of the key' or *kuncen*. I attempt to argue that the blessing of the Wali is negotiated through various 'doors' of the narratives. Furthermore, the availability of materials from the past and of memory of the past,[1] manuscripts and oral accounts in the hands of the Sufis may be used for contestation of precedence through the authority of meaning.(see also Fox 1996:131)

B. Holding the Line, Grasping the Blessing

In Pamijahan the two lines of transmission through heredity and through the Sufi order produce two different lines of authority in the symbolic world. If the key keepers, or *kuncen* mostly derive their legitimacy through family genealogy (Fox 2002), the Sufi leaders gain their authority from their linkages, called *silsilah*, to the founders of the order, as well as through hereditary links with the Wali. (Azra 2001 and 1995;Trimingham, 1998; Vow 1980)

Usually site custodians or *kuncen* who do not have links to the Sufi *silsilah*, cannot be Sufi leaders. On the other hand, theoretically, a village person without close links with Shaykh Abdul Muhyi's line still has the chance to be leader of a mystical congregation if he has been initiated and has received a license, or *ijazah*, as well as a Sufi *silsilah*. In Pamijahan, all the custodians have genealogical links with the Wali, but not all of them are the followers of the Shattariyyah order or the Wali's Sufi tradition. Traditionally, the role of the custodians in Pamijahan, as was stated by some elders to me, is not only to maintain the Shrine but also to 'manage' the rituals of veneration of the saint within the Sufi order, or *tarekat*. In previous generations, the elders said, the principal custodian, who was called the *Panembahan*, was also the propagator of Sufism. This accords with the information given in the *Kitab Wali* where some prominent people in the past in the valley of Safarwadi were also an important transmitters of the Wali's *tarekat* teaching.

In spite of this, the situation is now slightly different from the period of the early custoedians. The decline of Sufism in the village has had an influence on the psychology of the local people. Some villagers even believe that the *barakah* granted to them is not stable. It can be lower at one time or higher at another time, depending on the daily conduct of the village. Hence, the Wali's descendants, through the role of custodianship, make unremitting efforts to preserve the flow of *barakah* into their village. Besides meeting all of the obligations of *ibadah*, they also have to carry out additional prayers suggested by tradition. More than that, they have to comport themselves properly as the Wali's descendants whose obligation it is to serve pilgrims, or *nu ziarah*, and to embrace the *tarekat* as devotees of the Way.

To be the descendants of the Wali is to be able to behave as required by the grand narratives of the village. However, the great influx of pilgrims in recent times has influenced the development of the role of the custodians. But at the same time, there is a feeling, particularly among the young Sufis, that the villagers have abandoned the main teaching of their ancestor, the Wali. The custodians concentrate mostly on local pilgrimage where they are the most significant actors in the rituals. All the village ceremonies as well as practices associated with pilgrimage have to be carried out under their authority. Apart from their management role, there are some vital rites associated with the Sufi traditions required of them.

Generally, however, the custodianship and the Order seem to have different authorities: one in the hands of *kuncen*, the other in the hands of the Sufi leader. These two traditional institutions play significant roles in drawing the Wali's *barakah* into the village.

Saint veneration, *tarekat*, and *ziarah* are all hallmarks of popular Sufism. Therefore, it is important to outline briefly Trimingham's extensive discussion of the evolution of Sufi orders in the wider world of Islam from a socio-historical perspective. According to Trimingham, Sufi practices in the Moslem world can be classified into three stages: the stage of the individual Sufi, the stage of association, and the stage of organisation, or the *taifa* phase. Each stage, as Trimingham explains, depends upon the relation between the leader and followers, upon a syllabus or curricula, and on the regulations applied. In other words, the first stage is that of the lonely Sufi, the second stage is that of the Sufi gathering or association; the third stage is the Sufi organisation with its tight regulations and recruitment. Furthermore, another point made by Trimingham (1998) is his abstraction of the relation between the third stage of Sufism and the cult of saints, as well as pilgrimages. He states:

> "The complete integration of saint-veneration with the orders chracterizes this stage. The taifa exists to transmit the holy emanation, the barakah of its founder; the mystical tradition is secondary. ... Another aspect of this stage is that it provides a means of embracing within Islam all the extra-mural aspects of popular religion—belief in barakah, materialised in the form of touch, amulets, charms, and other mechanical means of protection and insurance (Trimingham 1998, 88)

Thus *tarekat* and *ziarah* practice are 'fully blended with the saint-cult' (ibid); they are in the same domain of meaning; the belief in *wilaya* (or consecration), or sainthood. The *tarekat* is highly dependent on the *wilaya* (Gilsenan 1973). In some cases, this role of charisma cannot be delegated through hereditary linkages. As in the case of Beben Muhammad Dabas of Pamijahan (see below), the line of the *silsilah* could, of course, be transferred through hereditary linkages, but the quality of sainthood cannot pass through this line. Accordingly, the *tarekat* can survive without the existence of a leader who has the spiritual quality of a Wali. After the Shaykh dies, the *tarekat* is perpetuated by his pulis (*murid*) initiated in the Path. However, the *tarekat* will be halted if it is incapable recruiting new novices who will be trained to be advanced Sufis and who in turn will preserve the *silsilah*.

Therefore the *tarekat* is vulnerable to the loss of linkages or to decease, if the Shaykh or the leader cannot transfer the line to younger followers. In the case of Safarwadi, the Shattariyyah Order is currently being 'renewed' by a young Sufi while the prominent elder members of the Wali's family tend to concentrate on pilgrimage activities.

The decline of the Shattariyyah Order in Safarwadi is partly influenced by the current absence of a Shaykh al-Mursid, a Master of Masters. The immediately past master of the Pamijahan congrgation has passed away and his successor is seen as too young to be a master. Furthermore, the circumstances, or the difficulty, in comprehending Sufi instruction, on the one hand, and in paying due attention to activities around the pilgrimage on the other, have contributed to the reduced condition of the Shattariyyah congregation. What is more, the expansion of other wealthy Sufi orders from outside the village has reduced the role of the *tarekat* of the Wali. The largest contemporary Sufi order in West Java, and probably in Indoneisa, the *Tarekat* Qadiriyyah-Nashabandiyyah, has vast resources which prove to be a magnet and have the potential power to initiate new novices in huge numbers. This is due to the charisma of the order's local leader Abah Anom of Surialaya, Tasikmalaya. (Zulkifli 1994: 85) In this case, small orders like the Shattariyyah have difficulty in attracting other followers who might have already embraced other orders with better buildings, good political connections, and beautiful annual festivals.

It is important to see then what has happen to the Shattariyyah Order when the Tijaniyah order surpassed it in Cirebon, as has been illustrated by Muhaimin. (1995:336) He states that, "The Tijaniyah relies on simple rites relative to other *torikoh* (orders), yet promises its adherents high spiritual efficacy and merit, together with its friendly attitude towards worldly life rather that the ascetic tendency usually exhibited by other Sufi orders". (Muhaimin 1995: 346)

I found in Pamijahan that the problem is not only the difficulty of the instruction but also the availability of the tutors who are capable of initiating novices. In regard to this situation, a prominent elder learned in legal texts (*ahli fikih*) who had studied in the various popular *pesantren* in West and Central Java said to me, in more metaphorical terms, "It is not compulsory for the son of a Bupati to be a Bupati, for the son of a *kiai* to be a *kiai*." He then smiled simply and gave me his interpretation of this, that it is not compulsory for the familiy of the Shaykh to be the followers of the Shattariyyah Order. It could also mean that it is not compulsory for the villagers to follow the Wali's mysticism.

However, if this is the case, what are we to make of contradictory views posed by the grand narratives that are found in oral transmission and the manuscripts of the ancestors regarding *tali paranti*, or custom? Which of the narratives of the Saint, theoretically, should be followed by all villagers? That of his mystical journey? Which narrative is or is not compulsory, and which one can or cannot be modified? Who is or is not appropriately in charge of the management of the *barakah*? These are crucial questions, not only for me as an outsider who needs to make abstractions in order to seek a better understanding of the culture, but also for the locals who are grappling with the meanings of their customs and narratives.

Accordingly, what I would like to present here is the serious effort undertaken by a young Sufi to renew the Shattariyyah Order in Pamijahan. In 17th century Sunda the Path of the Shattariyyah was important; Shaykh Abdul Muhyi was the foremost propagator of the Shattariyyah of his period. Now when a young

Sufi wants to 'refurbish' the Way of the Wali, obstacles soon appear in the eyes of the young Sufi and he realise the delicacy of the problem. He and his followers have to face other elders who in fact believe that the Shattariyyah is deceased or dying and who are satisfied with their pragmatic role as the guardian of the Wali's signs. Beben Muhammad Dabas, the Sufi, however has a different view of the way *barakah* should be tapped.

C. The *Zawiya*

The Shattariyyah Order is perceived as a domain of ancient mysticism that many villagers believe is difficult to practise. Historically, the Shattariyyah came earlier than other currently popular orders in the regency of Tasikmalaya such as the Tijaniyah, Idrissiya, or Qadiriyyah-Naqshanbandiyyah. Some elders and prominent custodians are of the view that Sufi practices have been in decline for a long period. I learned that the villagers believe that it is complicated to participate in the Wali's *tarekat*. There are even villagers who think that the Order has disappeared from contemporary Pamijahan, since there is no true Shattariyyah successor who can transmit the Way to the younger generation. A leading custodian told me that, in other places in Java, he had met real disciples of the Wali's teaching who still practised it and initiated new followers. Despite this, the custodisan asserted that the Shattariyyah tradition was defunct in Pamijahan. Later I was to discover that this was his way of warning me that, whatever Shattariyyah practices I might still come to witness in Pamijahan, they were, in his judgement, not authentic.

By September of 1996, I had spent three months in the field without being able to confirm a single piece information given by Rinkes (1910) regarding the existence of the Shattariyyah order in Pamijahan. Then, early one afternoon, before the *shalat ashar* prayer, someone approached me and informed me that he had what I was looking for. That night at about 10.00 p.m. he invited me to his house and showed me a manuscript written in *pegon*, the Arabic letters used in some circumstances to write the Sundanese and Javanese languages. He said that this was the Wali's teaching. This was my first contact with Shattariyyah material in Pamijahan. My informant confessed to me that he was actually unable to comprehend the contents of the manuscript. He had simply collected it as an artefact because of its value as part of ancestral heritage, its *kakantun karuhun* value. He also stated that in his village there was not a single person who could continue to translate the Sufi practices of the ancestors. At that time I had almost come to the conclusion that what had been described by Rinkes (1910), Lombard (1996: 136--138) and Krauss (Lombard 1996), and in several manuscripts as well was, in fact, difficult to verify in the field. My hopes rose.

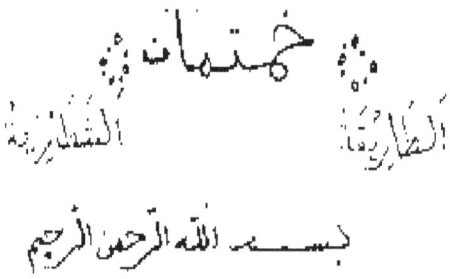

Figure 23. The first line of the first page of *Khataman al-tariqa al-Shattariyya*

It was later in Batu Ngijing, where I had been collecting data on the population, that while awaiting the *zuhur* or noon prayer in a small hut that had been erected from coconut trees for the cigarette smokers, I was approached for the second time regarding the Shattariyya order by a young man who had graduated from the State Institute for Islamic Studies (*IAIN*). He informed me in a low voice that the same night after the *Isya* prayer, about 9.30 p.m, I was invited to come to Beben's Muhammad Dabas' house. It was my policy never to reject any invitation related to my fieldwork, or to any social activities, so naturally I accepted.

Late that night, after I had waited for an hour, I met the young Sufi master. He came out onto the verandah of his and invited me to accompany him to his Sufi assembly place, or *zawiya*. He said modestly that he had a few 'stories' about Shattariyyah. He then admitted to me that he was a true follower of the Shattariyyah in the village, and without claiming more, that he was a regular leader of the Shattariyyah congregational meetings. In his *zawiya* he went to a cupboard and took out some papers. These documents were a manuscript, and a certificate given by the government, approving his activities as the leader of Shattariyyah congregation. He drew my attention to the *silsilah*, or genealogy of the masters. Furthermore, he said that Sunday afternoon was the time for the Shattariyyah congregation to conduct assemblies.

The Shattariyyah *zawiya* assembly, or communal *dikir*, is mainly performed in Beben Muhammad Dabas' residence. This *zawiya* hall is located within the smoking territory (see Chapter 4). The shrines-and-*zawiya* configuration is typically part of the transformation of the Sufi order into more popular practices. (Eickelman 1990; Gellner 1969; Trimingham 1998) Beside the *zawiya* there runs a small creek that marks the boundary between the most sacred territory (the non-smoking area) and the less sacred area (the smoking area). However, both areas are still located within the *kaca-kaca*, or the sacred border gateway, thus still inside the sacred territory of Kampung Pamijahan. The *zawiya* is about 100 metres from the gate to the north, about 200 meters from the sacred mosque, 500 metres from the Shrine and 700 meters from the Safarwadi cave.

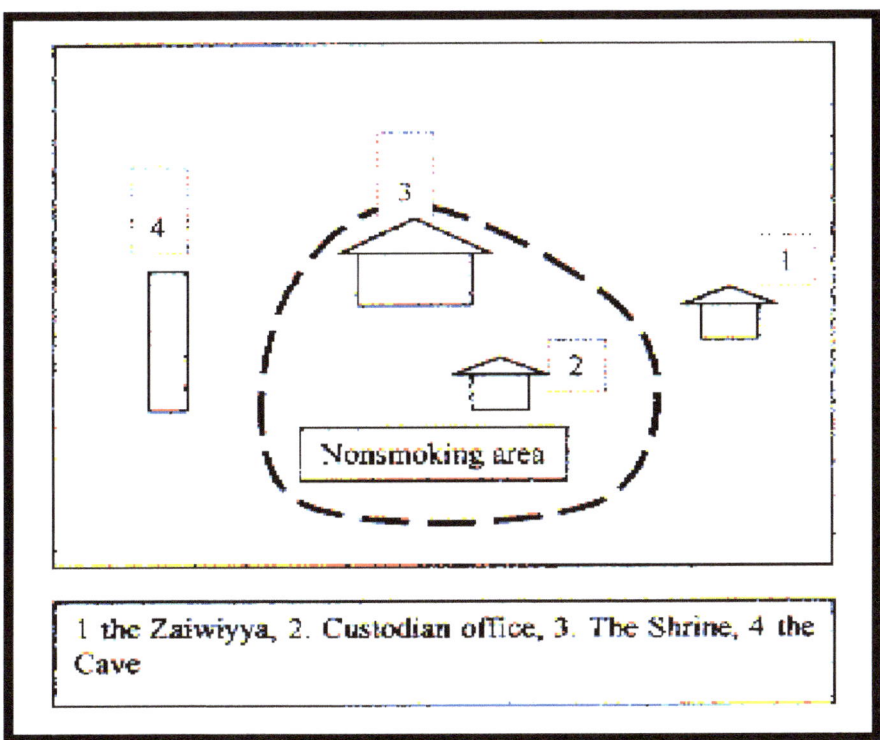

Figure 24. The *zawiya* and the most sacred space of Pamijahan

This location of Beben Muhammad Dabas's *zawiya* is a strategic one because pilgrims have to pass it before coming to the sacred mosque, the shrine or the cave. I believe that the *zawiya*, located as it is between the gate and the mosque, the shrine, and the cave, is the result of making the most of available land, while considering the feelings of the custodians and their families.

The *zawiya* has been built right behind Beben's house, amidst groups of houses belonging to the Wali's family from different lines of descent, or *pongpok*. Mainly young people occupy the area, or families who do not have rights of residential privilege, or who do not have enough land, to build their houses in the central territory or in the non-smoking area of the village. There is a clear demarcation in social level for the families who live close to the sacred mosque and inside the smoking territory. Their proximity to the heart of the sacred artefacts directly reflects their genealogical closeness to the Wali. However, the site of Beben's residence and his *zawiya* do not mean that he does not have any linkages to the inner territory. His mother still lives in the area of the centre, in the non-smoking area itself. Beben also keeps a small gift shop on the path close to the shrine. Furthermore, he is given a shift of 24 hours a week in the custodian's office as one of the custodians in charge. This is due to the fact that he has the right to this role as one of the prominent members of the third side, the *pongpok tilu* (see also Chapter 9). In other words, Beben retains fruitful access to the symbols of the centre.

However, in the eyes of other older custodians at the symbolic centre, the combination of the Sufi institution which he runs and his service as a member of the custodial staff, is 'too much', 'too heavy', and has come too early in Beben's life. Beben, for his part, does not have any argument about their reservations. He is just respectful of these issues. His position in the village, as he always stated in our interviews, is simply to carry on or "*hanya menjalani.*" Behind his humble explanation there is also latent symbolic power being negotiated. Beben, and other groups who create new options for tapping the *barakah* are in fact trying for, to borrow Fox's terminology, precedence (1996:131). Beben is only one of the custodial staff and he is in charge just once a week. Also, he does not come from the first side, the *pongpok hiji*, so it is difficult for him to be dominant in the sacred administration (*pakuncenan*). By erecting his *zawiya* and renewing the Sufi congregation (*tarekat*) of the Wali he is able to tap *barakah* through different sources. Shattariyyah is the oldest *tarekat* in the village. In popular perception, no-one masters this mysticism any longer; yet Beben has deliberately set out to access this symbolic past.

Indeed, in the *zawiya* symbolic power is derived differently from the symbolic power of the pilgrimage rituals. During the pilgrimage, villagers play the role of the hosts in the Wali's house and serve the pilgrims as well as possible. In the *zawiya*, on the other hand, Beben and his devotees access the blessing as 'the humble disciples' (*murid*) of the Wali and other mystical masters listed in the genealogy. We shall see this in the ritual of *khataman*.

The disciples take part in a mystical congregation every Sunday night. Unlike other larger *zawiya* in other places in the Tasikmalaya region, such as at Surialaya, Beben's *zawiya* is small and is not equipped with a boarding house. Most of the followers come from villages around Pamijahan. To the north of the *zawiya*, there is the third biggest mosque in the village, where some old manuscripts were previously preserved.

Beben Muhammad Dabas — at the time of my fieldwork he was 37 years old — derived his mystical linkages from his father, Haji Muhammad Akna, who was known by other villagers as an individual who practised the Shattariyyah. Beben told me, "My father, Muhammad Akna, died in 1982. He said to me that I had to carry on the Shattariyyah in this village."

Before his father initiated him, Beben spent time in a *pesantren* in Pekalongan, North Java. In village culture, most young Pamijahanese have to spend a period in a *pesantren* when they reach fourteen or after they finish primary school (*Sekolah Dasar*). However, only a few people in Beben's generation attended secular schools. He is one of a few young Pamijahanese who went to a secular school, junior high school, in Karangnunggal. After that, he continued his study at a senior high school (*Sekolah Menengah Atas*). As his family and neighbours related, during his time at high school Beben showed no sign that he would become a Sufi. The villagers even saw him as a 'bad boy' because he was often involved in fighting with gangs from a nearby area. His parents, mindful of the moral fibre of his family, then sent him to a traditional Islamic boarding school. He also spent time at other *pesantren* in Central and West Java.

Later, Beben's family was surprised at his ability to study Sufism because they knew that he had been a rather naughty boy. After spending time in the *pesantren*, he returned to Pamijahan, establishing the Shattariyyah *Tarekat* congregation on April 4, 1991.

D. The Communal Congregation

In Beben's *zawiya,* blessings can be solicited through two types of practices: individual observance and a large weekly communal ritual called *tabarukan*. *Tabarukan* is the most important and highly influential of gatherings. It has structural as well as contextual elements. I will illustrate how meaning is structured in the three of the most important parts of *tabarukan*: the *khataman*, the *dikir* and the initiation of novices into the order. The *khataman* ritual involves the sending of 'presents' or *hadiyah* to the ancestors, Sufi masters, martyrs, the close relatives or *karabat* of the Prophet, and to the Prophet Muhammad himself. *Khataman* is a weekly congregation where the members of the Order gather and share religious experience. It takes the form of a recitation of verses from the Qur'an and the collective uttering of formulaic mystical chants. Although some elders in the village regard Beben as too young to be a leader of a *tarekat* association in the village, he claims that he has been able to persuade seven hundred people to join his association. Most of them come from Pamijahan and neighbouring areas. The greatest numbers of his followers derive their links to ancestral lines through Muhammad Akna, Beben's father, and theses linkages are associated with the *Pongpok Tilu*. But there are also many others who are not linked to his father's ancestral lines. It is in this ritual that Beben demonstrates his ability to lead a congregation.

In the ritual of the *khataman*, the adherents are directed by certain explicit and implicit texts to particular interpretations. I will demonstrate presently how such texts are delivered.

I observed hundreds of people arriving at the *zawiya* at 5.30 p.m. on a Sunday afternoon. They came mostly from villages far from Pamijahan, some of them not connected by road and still without electricity. To reach Pamijahan, they had to trek through hilly forests and valleys on foot, in some cases for up to three hours. In the face of such difficulties, they often try to come early to Pamijahan. Some of them would not set out for home until the following morning, or others would return home in groups after midnight. They bring their own food. For them travelling from their villages to Beben's house in Pamijahan is very demanding. Some of them accept it as a kind of sacred journey. Going to Muhyi's village and following his teaching, for them, is an expression of respect and devotion to Shaykh Abdul Muhyi.

The *khataman* of the Shattariyyah is actually open to any one interested in mystical congregation. The vast majority of participants range from thirty to seventy years in age. Only rarely did I come across followers still in their twenties. There are more men than women, yet women number almost 45 per cent. Families or couples usually come together. The vast majority of the participants are farmers, plus some member of custodial families.

The participants fall into three broad categories. The first are the 'true' followers of Shattariyyah who have acquired their teaching from Muhammad Akna (Beben's father) as acknowledged by everybody. On one night of the *khataman* ritual, Beben introduced me to the 'true' devotees of Shattariyyah in the village. One of them was called Mang Jamhari. He had been initiated by Beben's father. He explained:

> I, Mang Haji Qadir Asna, Mang Jamhari, threw myself into the mystical journey and now continue the 'work' that we have had from your father, who said this: "Now, Mad, my young brother, life is uncertain, and if I should depart this world, my youngest child should succeed me…"
>
> It is our hope that what he said will come true. Not long after that, he left us. He was about eighty at the time. I, Kang Isa, and the father of Kang Unang, were all close friends. We went along (to the initiation into the Shattariyyah) and slept two nights in the mosque. We were wrapped in white cotton shrouds, and even if we were bitten by something, we had to stay still. Our heads faced north (as in Islamic burial) and if something touched us we were not allowed to move. For almost three hours nobody came near us. We were afraid, something moved the floor mat, then someone appeared, then my father said, "Come, on." Then we were bathed by him. I was the first…

The second category comprises the elders of Pamijahan who have the esteem of the younger generation like Beben. Although they were never formally initiated, or had *bai'ah*, they respect and support Beben's activities. They often say that all of the *tarekat* are good as long as they can be classified as 'legitimated' (*muktabarah*) orders. The third category of participants are Beben's followers who have been formally initiated into the Shattariyyah. From the Sufi perspective, the structural relation of teacher (*guru*) and pupil (*murid*) can only be applied to this third group. They have been initiated directly by Beben. The followers often call him 'Ajengan', a Sundanese term for an Islamic scholar similar to the term *kiai* in Javanese. To a certain extent, the first and second groups exist as counsellors and patrons for his activities.

Beben opens the ritual by giving his introduction. The respect of the participants towards Beben is evident. In a low voice and with confidence, he always delivers the reasons why they have to perform the ritual. He affirms that the *khataman* of the Shattariyyah is an effort to find *barakah* and to cleanse the heart.

On one occasion, I tried to ask Beben what he meant by an 'unclean heart'. For him, this meant any intention not based on *ikhlas* or on a true devotion to God. *Ikhlas* is a compulsory condition for serving God or doing devotions (*ibadah*). There is no *ibadah* without intention, and there is no true intention without absolute devotion *ikhlas*. *Ikhlas* is doing something prescribed without reservation because of belief in God's commands.

He continued that people who come to the shrine of the Wali because of worldly desires may have an unclean heart. For instance, the pilgrims should not ask the Wali to give them a good position in the government, huge profits in their trading or success in school. They should come to the shrine in order to remember that eventually they also will die. They have to be mindful of their relationship with God. The shrine is one of the best places for such contemplation since it is the Wali's place. Most of the senior custodians also share this rhetoric about the cleanliness of the heart. It has also become the most common explanation in the village to describe pious activities in relation to the Wali. Even so, Beben often criticises villager pilgrims who do not understand the real meaning of the pilgrimage.

According to Beben, the spirit is like a vehicle or a knife. We have to maintain the gears of a vehicle in order to keep them sharp. If we do not cleanse our heart regularly, as we cleanse a knife, mud will cover it. Dirt that has covered our compassion for a long time is difficult to scrub off. Everyone can prove his or her sparkling heart, which not only belongs to the Shaykh of the Order but also to commoners. Beben said: "We have access to the Wali's blessings (*barakah*). We have access also to cleanliness if we want it."

Beben's introduction to the *khataman* was not only addressed to his followers but also to me, since I had previously asked him about his legitimacy. He also desired to address other custodians who, behind his back, often criticize his legitimacy in the *tarekat*. As I understand it, Beben believes that he too has the right to channel *barakah* as long as his heart is clean and pure. He has often stated this clearly on different occasions.

One of the ways to obtain a pure heart is to have awareness of the human position as humble men before the Creator. The followers also have to be aware of their knowledge which is derived for the greater part from their ancestors, their master and their Prophet. Consequently, the first part of the ritual is to acknowledge the humbleness of those gathered and to address the entire company of *gurus* in their mystical linkage. A text of the *khataman* follows below, copied from Beben's own handwriting. It was written in Arabic and Sundanese. Note the repeated use of the Opening chapter of the Qur'an, Surah 1, *Al-Fatiha*.

The Liturgy of the Khataman performed in the Zawiya of Beben Muhammad Dabas, Pamijahan

Khataman al-tariqah al-Shattariyyah

IN THE NAME OF ALLAH, THE MERCIFUL, THE COMPASSIONATE

To the Elect Prophet Muhammad, Peace and Prayers of Allah be upon him and upon his house and all his companions. Let us recite Al-Fatiha for them.

(2)

Then to the souls of his fathers and brother prophets, messengers, closest angels, martyrs and holy people, and to the souls of our father Adam, our mother Eve and their posterity until the Day of Judgement. Let us recite Al-Fatiha for them.

(3)

Then the souls of our masters, followers and Imams Abu-Bakr, Umar, Uthman, Ali and the other Companions (sahabat), relatives (karabat) and their followers until the Judgment day. Let us recite Al-Fatiha for them.

(3) Then to the souls of the learned imams (al mujtahidin) and their imitators in faith, wise scholars (al ulama) and faithful readers, and to the souls of interpreters (al-mufasirin) and speakers and all religious mediators, and to the souls of every holy Muslim man and woman from east to west and from the right to the left of the earth. Let us recite Al-Fatiha for them.

(4)

Then to the souls of the Shattariyyah community and all those on the righteous path, especially the honourable Shaykh Abdallah Shattari, Shaykh Qadi Shattari, Shaykh Mulla Tertousi, Shaykh Mawla Nahari, Shaykh Abd al-Rauf bin Ali, Shaykh Haji Abdul Muhyi (friend of God in Sifar al-Wadi), Shaykh Abd Allah, Shaykh Bagus Muhammad Nida Muhyiddin, Shaykh Abu-Daud and their ancestors, descendants, relatives and followers. Let us recite Al-Fatiha for them.

(5)

Then, especially to the souls of the honourable Mas Haji, Mama Haji Hanan and Mohamed Akna. Let us recite Al-Fatiha for them.

(6)

Then to the souls of our fathers and your fathers, our elders and your elders, our dead and your dead, those who have done good to us and have rights on us, those who have advised and sought advice and imitated us in supplicating for goodness. Let us recite Al-Fatiha for them.

(7)

Then to the souls of all believing Muslim men and women, both alive and dead, from the east to the west and from the left to the right of the earth, from generation to generation, from Adam's creation until the Day of Judgement. Let us recite Al-Fatiha for them.

(8)

When Allah's help and victory come, and you see men embrace His religion in multitudes, celebrate the praise of your Lord and seek His pardon. He is ever disposed to mercy. Please recite inna anjalna and the qulhu. Have We not lifted up and expanded your heart and relieved you of the burden which weighed down your back? Have We not given you high renown? Every hardship is followed by ease. When you have finished resume your toil, and seek your Lord with all fervour. Say: "Allah is One, the Eternal God. He begot none, nor was He begotten. None is equal to Him." (Qur'an Surah 112, Al-Ikhlas)

Then please form an Intention (niyat).

In my prayer upon the Prophet, may the prayers and peace of Allah be upon him, I have willed to obey Your order, to believe in Your Prophet, to love him and yearn for him and glorify Your power. With Your favour and kindness, accept my prayer and clear the obscurity of my heart, and make me one of your worthy believers.

O God, pray upon our lord Muhammad, the illiterate Prophet, and upon his House and all his Companions.

Let us recite the shalawat.

O God, Your full prayers and complete peace be upon our lord Muhammad through whom our troubles will be settled, our hour relieved, our needs fulfilled, our desires achieved, and our final hour gratified. His holy face will turn clouds into rain. Bless his House and Companions every moment, as many times as the number of everything known to you.

(9)

To the soul of Shaykh Abdul-Muhyi, our master, elder and lord Kangjeng Shayh Haji Abdul Muhyi, friend of God in Safr al-Wadi, Pamijahan, may Allah sanctify him. Let's recite Al-Fatiha for him.

Please recite: O God, You alone will fulfil our needs (recite 7 times). Lift up our station in life (recite 7 times). Repel our disasters (recite 7 times). Resolve our problems (recite 7 times). Answer our call (recite 7 times). Heal our diseases and ailments (recite 7 times). O Most Merciful (recite 7 times).

In the name of Allah, praise be to Allah. Allah alone will eliminate evil (recite 3 times).

In the name of Allah, praise be to Allah. Allah alone will bring goodness (recite 3 times).

In the name of Allah, praise be to Allah. Every grace you have comes from Allah alone (recite 3 times).

In the name of Allah, praise be to Allah. Every good thing comes from Allah alone (recite 3 times).

In the name of Allah, praise be to Allah. Every grace comes from Allah alone (recite 3 times).

In the name of Allah, praise be to Allah. There is no power but through Allah (recite 3 times).

In the name of Allah, praise be to Allah. There is no might or power but through Allah, the Supreme, the Great (recite 3 times).

Praises and thanks to Allah, and there is no God but Allah. There is no might or power but through Allah, the Supreme, the Great (recite 3 times).

O Powerful, I have grown stronger with your power. O Powerful, I seek my strength in You and in Your Messenger (recite 3 times).

O Living and Eternal, there is no God but You. You enlighten the life of the heart and of the mind (recite 3 times).

Living and Eternal, there is no God but You. Have mercy on me, You Most Merciful (recite 3 times).

You, of mysterious gentleness, grant me your mysterious gentleness (recite 3 times).

O Gentle (recite ya latif 1641 times).

I seek the pardon of Allah, the Merciful and Compassionate (recite 3 times).

O Lord, may Your prayer and peace be upon Muhammad, his House and Companions (recite 3 times).

O Lord, open my mind with knowledge (recite 3 times).

O Lord, I seek you and your favour. Grant me your love and knowledge (recite one time).

I have willed to come closer to Allah. The best confession of faith is that there is no God but Allah.

Allah, there is no God but Him, the Living, the Eternal (please try to recite this dikir at least 100 times and at most 300 times).

Allah, there is no God but Him, the Living, the Everpresent. (After completing the dikir, let us close with with a supplication (doa).

Allah, there is no god but Him, the Worshipped. Before we recite the shadat rassul (Muhammad, the Messenger of Allah) we have to recite a supplication (doa). Allah is truly present. There is no God but Allah. Muhammad is the Messenger of Allah. May the prayers and peace of Allah be upon him.

Let us recite a doa.

O Lord, o gentle, o gentle, o gentle whose goodness has touched the people of Heaven and of the earth. We beseech you, by your mysterious gentleness. You have spoken and what you have spoken is the truth. Allah is kind to his people. He provides for whoever He wishes because He is Almighty and All-Powerful. We beseech You o Lord, by Your Might and Power, to help and support us in all our words, actions, conditions and graces, and to protect us from every evil, castigation and calamity that we have deserved through our inadvertence and our guilt, for You are Forgiving and Merciful. You have spoken, and what You have spoken is the truth. You forgive many people. O Lord, by virtue of whom you have forgiven and who have turned to You, I implore You to direct me and to hide me in your mysterious gentleness, for You are Almighty. May the prayers and peace of Allah be upon our master Muhammad, his House and Companions, and thanks to Allah, Lord of all. Amen.

Al-Fatiha

Signature & Seal

Al-Faqeer

(Beben Muhammad Dabas)

Board of Education Pamijahan, 16 June 1997

E. The *Baiah* Session

Initiation, or *baiah*, is crucial in Sufi practice. The ritual brings new disciples to the world of inner space. Accordingly, they need special guidance from the master otherwise the journey on the long path will lead to confusion and even, quite literally, to the destruction of the soul and mind of the pupils. Sufism, as stated by Beben, is like a journey up a steeply sloping riverbank or Safarwadi (*safar al wadi*) - a term also used by the villagers to refer to the sacred place founded by the Wali. The path has internal obstacles that gradually become harder as one proceeds to the objective of Sufism. The *baiah* of the Shattariyyah provides an initial map and direction for the mystic 'travellers'. It is also a license to practise within the order.

As seen previously, the *Kitab Wali* reveals five important themes: (1) the *silsilah*, (2) the *ijazah*, (3) *dikir*, (4) the types of novice (*murid*), and (5) the metaphysical doctrine specific to the Shattariyyah. It was surprising to me that since the manuscripts of the Shattariyyah are preserved in the hands of other custodians and some village elders, only a few have mastered all of these five elements of the *Kitab Wali*. One of them is Beben.

Even though Beben often talks about his activities modestly, as a simple *taburakan* gathering, that is 'to seek *barakah* with *barakah*', the method and the goal are full of blessing. The gathering is a way to tap the blessing of the Wali and the *tabarukan* itself is a recitation, which it is believed has been internally touched by the blessings of the masters whose names are recited in the *tabarukan*. In fact, he also applies a standard procedure that is also found in other established orders: the *baiah*, or initiation. He requires this ritual of new disciples who desire to make the mystical journey under his guidance.

What Beben applies has been known for centuries. Traditionally, the orders in popular mysticism have three levels of devotees. These are the *shaykh* or the master, the *wakil* or *khalifah*, who is the representative of the founding master, and the *murid* or students. (Trimingham 1998: 170-179) It is the case that Beben acts as the one with the authority to initiate new Shattariyyah followers. During my field work I observed such a ritual initiation, *baiah*, or as it is sometimes called, *talqin* in the Shattariyyah mode. However, Beben confesses that he is not a Shaykh of the Order with the quality of *murshid* (a true master) of the Order. Rather he is a humble man who simply wants to perpetuate the heritage of the ancestor, *kakantun karuhun* (see Chapter 3). In Beben's case, his rituals and the adherents he claims, are only a small part of a mystical association. It is not an organisation. Beben realises that a Sufi brotherhood needs a powerful master, or a *shaykh al-murshid*. In spite of this, the perpetuation of the *Kitab Wali* is crucial for him and he feels he does not need to wait until one of the Wali's family in the village becomes a *murshid*. In his own words, "we are now learning the *kakantun karuhun*," or we are still practising the ancestor's teaching "*Urang mah nuju diajar ngamalkeun kakantun karuhun*". (personal communication, Beben 1997) Through his discourse, in fact, Beben is able to take on a small part of the role of the *murshid* in order to initiate his new adherents.

Baiah then is the 'vow of allegiance'. A *murid* approaches the Shaykh of the order asking him to pass on his knowledge about the inner world. According to Trimingham (1998:14) in the early period of Sufism, initiation was very difficult to acquire because at that time the Sufi was not a teacher with followers but a lonely ascetic in search of a personal knowledge of the inner world. Later, when Sufism emerged with a larger range of social organisation, some orders, in fact deliberately sought followers, often competing with one another and vying about their qualities. Some of the orders designed an exclusive method to find new followers by proposing the condition that their new members quit all previous linkages. As we know, it is just as common that the seeker can affiliate with various orders as much as he desires. However, Muhaimin (1995:342) in his study of Cirebon found that the Tijaniyyah order, in fact, applied a restriction on new devotees requiring them to cut their affiliation with any previous order. For Muhaimim, this requirement is part of the competition between orders.

Beben does not require his new followers to forsake any previous order if they want to affiliate with the Shattariyyah under his tutelage. Often, in his sermons, in front of his followers, he states that all Sufi orders, by nature, are the same. They provide us with proper guidance for seeking a way to the inner world. Thus, in Beben's terms, one is permitted to affiliate with any method of guidance, as long as it is able to lead to the inner world. At the time of my fieldwork Beben himself was in fact in the process of setting up a new branch of the Qadiriyyah-Naqshabandiyyah Order of Surialaya, which is the largest order in West Java and probably in Indonesia at the moment.

Organising mystical associations means the establishment of certain rules. Later, these become the characteristic of the order. One of the important rules is found in the *baiah*. According to one Shattariyyah follower from Cirebon who made a *ziarah* pilgrimage to the shrine of Shaykh Abdul Muhyi, and whom, coincidently, I met during my fieldwork, was initiated into the order after fasting for a period of seven days. On initiation, he also had to provide a cone of fragrant, festive rice and accompaniments (*nasi tumpeng*), a length of white cotton cloth, a *samak* or woven grass mat, as well as perfume of different kinds.

However, in Pamijahan, Beben makes no such requirements. The *baiah* often takes place at the night after Beben has conducted the mystical congregation with his followers. I observed four married couples who asked Beben to initiate them into the Wali's *tarekat*. Instead of asking the novices to bring materials of various kinds, he only asked them to clean their bodies in ritual ablution (*wudu*) in the mosque which stands not far away from his house. The new members then gathered in a small, dark room. They stood solemnly facing Beben. They were asked to hold Beben's hands. After that, Beben requested them to follow his words, line by line. He recited the following:

> Saya berlindung kepada Allah dari godaan syaitan yang terkutuk. Sesungguhnya mereka janjikan kepadanya adalah apa yang mereka janjikan kepada Allah, tangan Allah ada di atas mereka. Maka barang siapa mengingkari sesuatu ia mengingkari dirinya sendiri, dan barang siapa yang menyempurnakan janji yang telah diikat dengan Allah, maka Allah akan memberinya pertolongan yang besar.

> I take refuge in Allah from the promptings of Satan the accursed. What these persons here pledge is their pledge to Allah, and His hand is upon them. So whoever denies something, he denies it for himself, and whoever fulfils a promise which he has made before Allah, then Allah will grant him all assistance.

The new *murid* should realise that *baiah* is meant to establish an important allegiance. Should he neglect his vows, access to the mystical journey under the leader's guidance will be denied. Conversely, he will reap the benefits if he meets his commitments. After this, Beben instructed the pupils to make other allegiances. The next recitation connects them formally with the linkage of the predecessors of Shattariyyah, or the *silsilah*. Beben rehearsed the statement and the followers recited it. The testimonial said:

> I willingly take Allah as my God, I embrace the religion of Islam, I acknowledge Muhammad as my Prophet, I believe the words of the Qur'an, I bow in the direction of the Ka'bah, I follow the Shaykh (Abdul Muhyi), I accept his teachings and his pronouncements, I embrace the poverty of the Friends of the Prophet, may they be with me and gather all of us up safely from wickedness.

The theme of loyalty and humilty were uppermost in this ceremony. Next, the guru and the *murid* recited together the following supplication:

> I repent and beg forgiveness of Allah the Almighty, there is no God but He, he is all-Living and Eternal. Oh God, greetings and peace be upon our lord Prophet Muhammad, his Family and his Companions.

Then the guru and the *murid*s also recited the creed of Islam three times: 'There is no god but Allah', after which the new followers pronounced a recitation of the Shattariyyah 100 times. After that, the *baiah* session was closed with this final supplication:

> Before the Prophet Muhammad (upon Him be peace), his Family, Companions, all things come from God. (Recitation of Al-Fatiha.)

> Before the family of the silsilah, their forebears, their descendants, their leaders, all things come from God. (Recitation of Al-Fatiha.)

> To the soul of my teacher..., to his forebears, his descendants, his leadership and all things which come from God. (Recitation of Al-Fatiha.)

Only then were the new members fully recognised by the *guru* as disciples of Shattariyyah. They had the right to recite the *dikir* of the Shattariyyah and the obligation to follow the Shattariyyah mystical journey.

F. The Shattariyyah *Dikir*

The Shattariyyah teaching is close to the interpretation of Ibn al-Arabi's ideas on the relation between the inner world, or *batin,* and outer world, or *lahir*. Theoretically, the Shattariyyah agrees that the external world is the manifestation of the internal world. However, as I discussed in Chapter 6, the Shattariyyah tries to solve the problem of *batin* and *lahir* by proposing the modality taken to come close to God. His knowledge and power make everything that exists and is revealed. The external world is part of the inner world, but nevertheless, they argue, the outer world exists only by God's Grace. Thus, the external world is dependent upon God.

Hence, the objective of the Shattariyyah is to 'enter the inner world' and finally to 'approach' the Ultimate through the practice of cleansing the heart. 'To approach the Ultimate' is the most moderate interpretation for the Wujudiyyah teaching. For the followers of Wujudiyyah such as Hamzah al-Fansuri, the Unity of Being is conceivable. The master of the Shattariyyah in 17th century Sumatra, Abd al-Rauf, to the contrary, stated that "the essence of the world is something other than al-Haq. (see Faturahman, 2001) This means that the Shattariyyah takes a slightly different position to the Wujudiyyah doctrine, which had been part of the previous Shattariyyah practice in India. The Pamijahan Shattariyyah is similar to Sumatran Shattariyyah in terms of its 'softness' or moderateness vis-à-vis the Wujudiyyah. The implication of the doctrine can be found in the practice of mystical chant (*dikir*). For Wujudiyyah, *dikir* is a method to find Unity, but for the Shattariyyah in Pamijahan it is to witness His Glory, or *nyaksikeun,* with a pure of heart.

The followers of the Shattariyyah, like other Sufis, believe that if the heart is dirty it will generate dirty deeds in return. Because the heart is scrubbed clean by the Light, it can render the inner world in which the mystic can 'come close' to Allah. (Trimingham 1998: 201-203; Faturahman 1999; Beben's manuscipts) To comprehend the relation between the *lahir* and the *batin*, the Shattariyyah develop their own method, which is slightly different to other *tarekat* in Tasikmalaya.

The Shattariyyah followers have to practice their personal *dikir* every time after finishing each of the five daily obligatory prayers, or *shalat lima waktu*, and they also have to take part in communal *dikir* such as the *tabarukan* sessions guided by Beben. The *dikir* is complicated, since it is recognised as a special means for the journey into the inner world.

Manuscripts of the Shattariyyah, as also quoted by Beben in his explanations to me, mention that the *dikir* can be divided into two general classes based on its methods. The first is a mental *dikir*, that is a *dikir* 'spoken' silently in the heart. The second is *dikir* spoken out loud. The mental *dikir* adopts Indian Sufi practices by applying breath control similar to that of Yoga. The practice centres on the phrase 'there is no God but Allah', or *la ilaha illa Allah*, and the practice symbolically represents the process of the inhalation of the name of Allah and exhalation of sins. This process is clearly explained in the manuscripts. According to Beben, the mental *dikir* controls the recitation of *la ilaha* by following the rhythm of breathing. *La ilaha* is a statement of negation meaning 'there is no...' The disciples should exhale the breath while mentally declaring the negation. After that, the *murid* should inhale and pronounce *illa Allah* or 'but Allah' mentally. This *dikir* should be practiced over and over by the novice. The function of the *dikir* is to bring the *murid* to the realisation that there is only One Reality, or *al-Haq*.

A second type of mental *dikir* is to recite 'He' or *Hu*. The believers have to concentrate on the word 'He' which refers to 'He is Allah'. If the novice has mastered these first and the second recitations, he then proceeds to the third *dikir* called *dikir l-lah*, "Allah –Allah", and continue with *Allah Hu* or 'Allah is He' finishing with *Hu Hu* or "He He". These latter two are considered for advanced learners. The same recitation could be pronounced aloud, a practice called *dikir al-zahri*. There is an even more advanced *dikir*, which can only be acquired personally from the master, and should be undertaken only under strict guidance.

What should be noted here is that the *dikir*, whether performed personally or communally, has various meanings for the villagers. From the framework of *ibadah*, the followers do not hesitate to regard the congregations, *tabarukan*, or *khataman*, as a form of servce to God within a Sufi framework. From a different perspective, I found that other doors to the blessing, *barakah*, are being opened to the villagers. If the pilgrims from outside Pamijahan have to spend a lot of energy and money to become the guests of the Wali (see Chapter 9), it does not mean that the villagers only receive *barakah* from their role as the host of the pilgrims, or *nampi tamu*. They also can 'tap' the blessing from the mystical congregations, as they do in *tabarukan* sessions. Even Beben tends to give special status to his activity 'to seek *barakah* with *barakah*'. The rituals of the *khataman*, *tabarukan* and *dikir* themselves are already radiated by the blessing because the text and recitation used have been touched by the holy masters enumerated in the *silsilah*, and for this reason the *barakah* that may be tapped is doubled. More than that, Beben also indicates that it is his association's objective to make the inner journey and to find good in God's sight. In short, it seems to me that the Wali's blessing not only flows into the village through pilgrimage and the custodianship, but also through the Sufi Order.

G. Conclusion: Telling Stories, Taking Precedence

The main metaphor in Pamijahan is related to the 'cognate expression' called *pongpok*. The *pongpok* is an imagined rectangular symbolic space providing the villagers with a way of locating their affiliations based on ancestral linkages. This is slightly different from the common metaphors in Austronesia that use various distinctive 'botanic metaphors' (Fox, 1997:8). The implications of this ideology of *karuhun* are found in the spatial order and hierarchical concept of symbolic interactions where the first side is the place of the primary family in the order. By virtue of this position, the family is then a primary group in society. The phenomenon is framed as 'the creation of precedence' that is "a priority in time but also a priority of position, rank or status" (Fox 1996: 9; Bellwood 1996: 25). This symbolic structure is maintained and ritualized in day-to-day activity. However, there is a space to negotiate this frame.

To comprehend the issue clearly, I will quote verbatim the narrative below, which was spoken to me by Beben Muhammad Dabas one night after he had finished leading the *Khataman* of the Shattariyyah and initiating new disciples. It was my first encounter with the Shattariyyah group in mid-November 1997 and I had been just three months in Pamijahan. Beben explained to me his *perjalanan,* or journey, in Sufism and his reading of the villagers' opinions. For the purpose of analysis, I will make some annotations (cf. Parmentier 1994: 86-88) in order to identify the modalities used in the narrative.

Beben's narrative, even though simple and short, in fact, displays the features that Peirce calls, 'iconic', 'indicial', and 'symbolic'. These three modalities are related to the modes of representation in reference to its 'object'. These signs mediate the past to the present. Thus, I have to frame these modalities in a third category called linguistic markers or 'glossing', 'references', and 'pragmatics'. (Parmentier 1987)

Beben's Narrative

[1] When we're face to face they treat us well, but behind my back... I don't know what the problem is.

[2] Actually, they're the majority and they all babble. They're unprincipled,

[3] Sometimes ... sometimes they say the Shattariyyah in Pamijahan is finished, but even Mama Haji Kosim himself recognises us.

[4] I asked Pak Abdu if I could study with him. But he refused, because Muhammad Akna, my father, could carry it on (the teaching of the Shattariyyah).

[5] When I married I began to 'study'. My intention then was the spiritual sincerity that I have now. Indeed, I feel firm in the 'journey' although

in reality I'm still only learning. But it's a genuine journey and I'm optimistic.

[6] Society at large has accepted us.

[7] And now it has become known outside the village that I'm one of the heirs of the tarekat. I'm just a beginner, not an adept.

[8] A while ago we were only 400, now we're up to 700.

[9] And there are even a number of young people coming in, they're mad keen, from the Western part of the village, saying they want to join us, just to witness a khataman here.

[10] From the Kaum, West Pamijahan and Warung Antay. And yet Wa Haji's from the Kaum, and so is Haji Endang. But, thank God, there are older ones among them who keep on coming.

[11] What I perform for them in the special big meetings is tauhid (the doctrine of Islam), but in my own terms and according to my own character. If I discuss tauhid, there is nothing to be hidden and I do not depart from the Law (shari'a).

[12] The Law is explained here based on the Essence, over there it is based on the Law. Here it's based on the ma'rifa, or Knowledge, so there is new meaning here for the novice.

[13] I show and I explain these things only after they have taken initiation.

[14] As for the explanation of the tarekat, even though the book is displayed to them, they cannot comprehend its contents.

[15] Sometimes when they ask, they're not ready for the answers. But they still want to know, so the way begins to open for them.

[16] Why do others 'blockade' us with what they say and do, as if we do not exist here.

[17] As if the Shattariyyah were only in Cirebon, or anywhere, they never mention the one in Pamijahan. Well, we know their agenda.

[18] There seem to be no external obstacles, but obstacles of other kinds… I'm positive about the future.

[19] The reason is that the people of Pamijahan feel rather embarrassed by the fact that they are part of the community of the sacred site of Pamijahan, they are very aware of this.

[20] They don't know what to do – should we really dance on the grave? We claim to be the people of Pamijahan, but we cannot make the 'journey'.

[21] Because there are young people around, we plant our seeds in this generation. They only turned thirty yesterday, but they're initiated. It was done in the mosque.

[22] There are some people who are interested in the spiritual dimension; if they try to put it into words, it will not come out right.

[23] Sometimes their hearts accept my existence, but if they recognise me their pride gets in the way. Beben is just a young sprout... Sometimes if the target is not God Himself, it is really difficult, resentments arise.

[24] Logically and literally it is possible, but the reality... is that they go and join up with outsiders.

[25] People dare to try to take my followers away.

[26] But that becomes an impetus for me, people are just like that. If they can say that there is no tarekat here, if they can deny it, why haven't they wiped us out?

Beben's narrative above, of course, should not be treated as the most representative example of negotiating the Wali's signs in the context of 'precedence'. (cf. Fox 1996; Bellwood 1996) However, since I observed a lot of materialized signs relating to his speech, I regard his narratives as an example of negotiating the signs of *karuhun*, the signs of the 'sides' of the tomb. Beben has 'travelled' to a symbolic territory while other prominent families have preferred to stay in the area of safely at the centre of the pilgrimage blessing site. Beben has not only moved to the more condensed mystical territory but has also literally build his *zawiya* outside the most sacred territory. (cf. Bellwood 1996:25-26)

Beben tries to present himself as a humble young man. This is not because of some individual psychological burden but rather socio-cultural factors. By socio-cultural factors, I mean the totality of the system of symbolic patterns of interaction that influence people's behaviour. The fact is that, at that time of my talk with him, Beben was 37 years old and relatively young compared to other prominent members of the guild of custodians, and some elders believe that to enter Sufism properly one should reach at least the age of forty. An elder explained to me that Sufism is not an easy way of life. One should be able to reduce involvement in worldly life gradually. The age of forty is a good time to start.

One prominent custodian informed me that one day a young politician came from Bandung who had family links with the Wali. He asked to be initiated into the Shattariyyah Order. The custodian replied to the young man "as long as you are still in active in a political party and still under the age of forty, then you won't be able to perform the mystical journey." This is evidence that there is an agreement of opinion among the elders and prominent *kuncen* that the Way, or *tarekat*, is not for ordinary people. However, the young Sufi Beben does not accept this condition.

As seen in the excerpt above, Beben is displaying three important signs. The first is the sign referring to someone's speech. In his narrative he recited what others have said about his activity. It should be noted that Beben did not refer to particular names [1, 3, 23]. His narrative also mentions 'the ongoing speech event' [7-15] and a 'pragmatic' meaning derived from 11, 12, 13 and 23. He did not only evaluate 'signs in the past' and make a discourse of history [4], but he also dared to show to outsiders, like me, that he is one of the points in the continuum of history. To do this, he also demonstrated his ability to recite some pragmatic patterns from tradition, [11, 12, 13, 14], which explicitly enhance his position as a young Sufi.

Figure 25. Beben Muhammad Dabas (left) leads communal prayer

From the illustration above, it is becoming clear that a 'convention' or *tali paranti* is being negotiated. For Beben and his followers, to negotiate the 'convention' is to 'play' with two kinds of narratives. Adopting what Parmentier refers to as 'the sign of history' and 'the sign in history', the first narrative is 'the narrative *of* Sufism', and the second is 'the narrative *in* Sufism'. The young Sufi master has to collect all the narrative in history to hand. In my view, this young Sufi is one of the best collectors of Shattariyyah manuscripts in the Valley. He has a complete version of a Shattariyyah text. A manuscript of the Shattariyyah itself is an icon of history. It presents to the believer as a sign from the past. Indeed, Beben's father, as seen in Chapter 6, is part of the historical narrative.

The *silsilah*, the main key word in the narrative of Sufism, 'resides' in Beben's *zawiya*. This is 'a sign in history'. However, the young traveller also has to broadcast the narration of his journey *perjalanan* or *tarekah*. This is a 'materialization' of the past in his contemporariness. It is a kind of tapping of *barakah* from the margin of the village. It is not derived from the custodianship. It is not only that his *zawiya* is located on the border between the sacred and the profane, but also because his followers come from the young generation and a group who are distant from the primarily family in the *kapongpokan*. There is a situation where the custodianship and the Sufi Order are interested in the symbol but interpret it through different routes. The custodians are primarily taken from the leading figures in a *pongpok* which has a clear *kokocoran* or line of descent. Beben himself is one of the staff of custodians representing the *pongpok tilu*, or third side. However, the *pongpok hiji*, where the leader of the custodians is from, seems to take precedence in term of *ziarah*.

Such regimentary meanings have stimulated the young 'traveller' to create and find a different 'institutional' meaning through a different door of the symbolic sources of veneration of the *Wali*: namely the institution of Sufism. Just as the custodians mediate pilgrimages, so the Sufi leader or, at least, the representative of the Order, manages the mystical organisation in the Valley of Safarwadi. This is slightly different from the case discussed by Trimingham (1998) where the management of the sacred sites is likely to be attached to the Sufi institution.

In the past, as suggested by the senior custodian, a custodian should belong to two legitimate traditions. He should get access to the custodianship as well as to the mystical congregation. However, in contemporary Pamijahan, he confessed, many custodians have not read, nor do they practise, the Book of the Wali properly. He said that some of them are not even acquainted with the nature of the Wali's mysticism. This lack of knowledge and practice of Sufism among the custodians is now being perceived as one of the main factors in the decline of *barakah* in the village. It is important here to rephrase what Hefner called "the consequence of a distribution of cultural knowledge" in societies in which "everyone does not rethink tradition" in each generation. Indeed, for many people it need not even be the object of much intellectual concern. (Hefner 1985: 9-18): The knowledge of the past and present are in fact scattered. In other words, there is a distribution of knowledge of the past based on cultural and social categories.[2]

From these two narratives, thus, we learn that the scattered past is brought to the scattered present. The main themes of the narratives lie in the process of comprehending that scatteredness. What is happening in Pamijahan now affirms a dynamic relation between the symbolic past, the present, and the agency of the social interaction, which, in Hefner's phrase, is called 'cultural reproduction'. (Heffner 1985) In Safarwadi, this not only involves liturgy, which is derived from the sacred narratives, but also social interaction, which secures the transformation of knowledge (ibid).

Some villagers see rebuilding this *tarekat* as obedience, but others see it as the expression of local affairs. In fact, for Beben, there is no question regarding his legitimacy because he inherited the teaching from his father, a true Shattariyyah follower in Pamijahan.³ Thus it is possible for an institution to create a new intermediary space outside the institution of the custodianship, but the custodians see such an institution as tapping the blessing "not through the right 'door'". On the other hand, what happens in Pamijahan also reminds me of what Gellner (1969), Eickelman (1976) and Gilsenan (1973) describe about the relation between the Sufi orders and social dynamics. The *igguramen* of North Africa must exercise various strategies in order to maintain their position in the loci of *barakah*. This is due to the fact that when saints blessing increases, the blessing has to be be distributed. Gellner signifies that the saintly lineage roles increase better by acting as the mouthpiece of the God. However, Gellner found that the saint's *barakah* might decrease if they were incapable of performing their functions and they had to leave the central territory of the *barakah* (Gellner 1969: 70-80). Thus, for Gellener, there are two kinds of holy men: an effective and ineffective saint (ibid).

It is my argument in this volume that the strategies implemented by the villagers in order to pull blessing to their social activities involve various narratives sources and strategies. Now, in Islam a strategy should be confirmed by Scripture or otherwise it is not regarded as *ibadah*. *Ibadah* in Islam, as always suggested by the custodians, has double edges: the vertical as well as the horizontal. In the former, the followers perform very highly structured rituals prescribed in the five pillars of Islam. On one hand, the meaning of these rituals is addressed to God Himself. On the other hand, the meaning of *ibadah* is related to good conduct that is primarily addressed to men. Yet, the relation between the vertical line and horizontal lines is similar to the two sides of a coin. In the language of the custodians, to serve the pilgrims is a horizontal ritual; the chance for conducting a good deed for the pilgrim guests. But at the same time it is also understood as ritual in the vertical mode; to provide pilgrims with shelter and to guide them properly through the pilgimrage experience, will bring a reward from God. Thus, supposedly, all conduct is performed in order to activate the vertical axis as well as the horizontal one. The inseparableness of *ibadah*, or ritual, and custom, or *tali paranti*, has been discussed by Muhaimin (1995) in his ethnographical notes on local Islam in Cirebon. However, Muhaimin does not discuss further the consequences of different interpretations of the same category of *ibadah* in relation to the symbolic institution (ibid, 109-149).

In the valley of Safarwadi, the translation of the Wali's *barakah*, which is mediated by various rituals, is subject to negotiation and even conflict among the participants as is seen in the rituals of Sufism. In the literature on rituals and religions, there has been considerable research on the function of ritual as the means of mediating social conflict. (Gellner, 1969: 5) The study of Javanese religion (Geertz, 1976:355) suggests that ritual is unable to mediate a conflict between two groups who actually retain the same beliefs. In Pamijahan, the potential conflict inheres in the spatial organization and in the narratives of the Wali. Since a certain group has dominated the cultural affairs of the village, however, the latent conflict can be transformed into the more symbolic exercises as found in the case of the Shattariyyah Order.

Beben realised that to tell a story of local affairs to me could give rise to problems in the future. He is not a man to make a 'revolt' in the sacred sites. Rather, he is trying to find a symbolic place in the villagers' affairs from which to publicly criticise the role of the *pakuncenan* while still remaining part of this traditional institution. His affiliation with the third of the 'sides' or *pongpok*, not the first, renders him, to some extent, vulnerable in the guild of custodians (*pakuncenan*) where the first *pongpok* appears to dominate the assembly. This is a simple example of how 'the ideology of the founder' functions in social action (Parmentier 1987). The study mainly questions the role of a 'founding ideology' in relation to 'hierarchy', and 'equality'. Even though studies mention that there are various modalities applied in the field studied, the common discourse of the founder ideology is apparent.

If we consider that a particular culture is constituted from various sign functions (Geertz, 1973: 29-30) then we have to put the *'khataman*, indeed the whole Shattariyyah Order of Pamijahan, as one of the most important signs in the valley 'signifying order'. As has been illustrated above, the Sufi congregation, the leader of Shattariyyah, the followers, the space or *zawiya* and the liturgical text are all displayed in the residence of Beben Muhammad Dabas. The sheer numbers of disciples, who mainly come from the neighbouring areas of Pamijahan, significantly indicate how important these signs are in the valley of Safarwadi.

However, some villagers are unaware of the potency of Sufism while others have fruitful access to the pilgrimage. Sometimes it is also not a matter of awareness but rather a matter of choice. For instance, whether to perpetuate the *Wali's* Order or to serve the pilgrims and maintain the shrines, the choice, in fact, is not easy, particularly when the web of *'tali paranti'*, or tradition and custom, must approve it. Accordingly, there is an important phenomenon that should be explored further in order to comprehend the 'semiotic' process involving various groups in society that claim to be of a legitimate chain and have access to the blessing of the Wali. The question here is why and how the 'signs of the past' are negotiated.

ENDNOTES

[1] See, Jun Jing (1996) for an illustration of social memory used at the sacred territory in Dachuan village.

[2] There are parallels here with the case of the Dachuan people who have to utilize all the memories of suffering as a consequence of the impact of communist policy on their customs, for the sake of a good present (Jun Jing 1996). In the Dachuan case, the elders ritualize all their narrative memory for the young generation. However, the younger cohort also come up with their own strategies as some have been educated in secular schools and have obtained more worldly goods then the custodian of narratives.

[3] Ewing (1997) deploys a psychoanalytic approach to the Shaykh's discourse.

Chapter 9: Pilgrimage at Pamijahan: Practice and Narrative

> Now concerning the purpose of pilgrimage, it is to create a 'bridge' by which we connect our wishes to God's Emissary, or to the Prophet, or to all the Friends of God, in order to obtain a result which is granted by our Lord God. (Risalah Adab al-jairin).

A. Introduction

Ziarah, or pilgrimage, is the most sublime and intense symbolic interaction in the valley of Safarwadi or Pamijahan. Both the 'signs of the past' and the 'signs in the past' are mixed, modified, and 'broadcast'. In previous chapters, I draw attention to the significance of ancestral signs in the lives of the villagers. Now, I will look at these representations from the perspective of outsiders, as well as villagers, as they make devotional visits to the shrine of the wali.

Pilgrimage in the Muslim world appears in two significant modes. The first is the sacred journey to Mecca in the days of Dhu' l-hijja, the twelfth lunar month, which is made incumbent on the faithful by Scripture (Qur'an 2:286; 3:97). It is the fifth of the Five Pillars after the profession of faith (*syahadah*), the five daily ritual prayers (*shalat*), the fast (*saum*) in the month of Ramadhan, and almsgiving (*zakat*). The Five Pillars of Islam stand as a sturdy framework supporting the whole range of complicated ritual actions, collectively called *ibadah*, that are incumbent upon Muslims. The basic criterion for determining whether a particular devotional act, or act of *ibadah,* can be defined as serving God, is the intention of that act, called *niat* or, in Pamijahan, *niat ibadah*. Thus, any form of devotional ritual would be meaningless if not performed in the service of God with pure *niat*. The Five Pillars of Islam function as a mnemonic device to translate all Islamic prescriptions into action.[1]

However, there are also *ibadah* which are not clearly stated in the Five Pillars, but are the result of interpretations of certain traditional recollections of the sayings and deeds (*hadith*) of the Prophet Muhammad or even the result of local understanding regarding these traditions and the scriptures. *Ibadah* at this level is to some extent still recognised as accepted ritual when it has the approval of religious scholars, or *ulama*. In the anthropology of Islam in Indonesia, such secondary practices are collectively classified as a 'little tradition', (Eickelman 1990; Eickelman 1976: 4) designating them as beloging to a more popular discourse. In this perspective pilgrimage to the tomb of the wali is regarded as forming part of the 'little tradition' (see also Jamhari 2000).

The *hajj*, or pilgrimage to Mecca, is compulsory for those who are able to supply their travelling expenses, are in good health, and can provide sufficient food and money for their family left at home. It is not compulsory for the poor or the sick. The pilgrimage to Mecca is deeply rooted in the narrative of the prophet Ibrahim. According to Islamic tradition, Ibrahim and his son Ismail were ordered by God to build the Ka'bah, the house of worship now standing in the centre of the Baitul-Haram mosque in Mecca. From that time the Ka'bah, in the Qur'an called *Al-Bait* or 'The House', became a place of pilgrimage. Later, through the Qur'an, pilgrimage to the Ka'bah was prescribed and perpetuated by the Prophet Muhammad and his followers for all time.

> "Remember, We made the House a place of assembly for men, and a place of safety; and take ye the Station of Abraham as a place of prayer; and We convenanted with Ibrahim and Isma'il that they should sanctify My House for those who compass it round, or use it as a retreat, or bow, or prostrate themselves (therein in prayer)." (Qur'an 2:125)[2]

The visit to Al-Bait has inspired some Muslims throughout the Islamic world to copy the structure of the *hajj* in making visits to the sacred sites of holy men, or *wali*. So at the very least, for some Indonesian Muslims, to go to Pamijahan, and to other local pilgrimage sites, is to perform a preliminary pilgrimage before they go to Mecca.

There has been some debate on the status of local *ziarah* in the framework of *ibadah*. The practice influenced by belief in the existence of wali or similar holy figures who can be accessed after their death, and this has been subject to controversy among Muslim scholars. Nevertheless, *ziarah* still plays an important role in daily practice.

Examining the practices around pilgrimage in Pamijahan enables us not only to recognise the importance of this act for participants (Fox 2002; Quinn 2002; Taylor 1999) but also to highlight the way narrative is used as an expressive medium for various purposes. Pamijahan has become the third most popular pilgrimage destination in West Java after Cirebon and Banten. Pilgrims from Java and Sumatra come to this sacred village bringing with them a variety of motivations and devotional intentions (*niat*). They trust that Shaykh Abdul Muhyi's site is a location for everyone who wants to seek blessing (*barokah*). According to the villagers, Shaykh Abdul Muhyi's blessings have transformed Pamijahan from a poor area to the most prosperous rural community in the district of Bantar Kalong. For Pamijahanese, then, the wali's blessings, or *barokah*, adhere to their village. In turn, they have responded to such blessings by setting up various social and religious institutions such as the guild of custodians (*pakuncenan*), a sufi community, and a traditional Islamic school (*pesantren*). In their accounts, these institutions are an expression of gratitude (*syukur*) because

God has given good fortune to the community through the person of Shaykh Abdul Muhyi.

For this reason, Shaykh Abdul Muhyi's tomb in Pamijahan is recognised as a most sanctified place. The tomb custodians maintain that they never solicit people to come to Pamijahan, yet the number of pilgrims coming to the village increases significantly every year.[3] This veneration has spread to other neighbouring tombs, or *makom*,[4] which are historically also related to Shaykh Abdul Muhyi; namely Makom Khatib Muwahid in Panyalahan, Makom Shaykh Abdul Kohar in Pandawa, Makom Sacaparana in Bengkok, and Makom Yudanagara in Pamijahan. These blessed tombs are popular pilgrimage destinations after Abdul Muhyi's grave and the sacred cave, Guha Safarwadi.

To comprehend this practice, it is important to outline the main narratives related to pilgrimage in Pamijahan. The first is to be found in the Manual of Pilgrimage or *Risalah Adab al-jairin*,[5] a printed material written by some previous custodians and the second is an oral account delivered by the custodian. Both of these narrative sources give the significant grounds used by villagers and visitors to perform the pilgrimage successfully. Pilgrimage to the tomb of Abdul Muhyi is prescribed and mediated through these narratives. I will illustrate this by focussing on the three most essential elements of pilgrimage as found in the narratives: ideology, the participants and the sequence of rituals.

Mediation or Approach

The *Risalah Adab al-jairin* mentions explicitly the concept of mediation, or *wasilah,* that is central in pilgrimage. *Wasilah* is derived from the Arabic meaning "to reach", or "to come to", "a means", and "a connection". In the Qur'an the term appears in two *ayat*: Surah al-Maidah 35, and Surah al-Isra 75. For some Islamic scholars the meaning of *wasilah* in the Qu'ran is to perform *ibadah* (worship) as prescribed in *syari'ah*. But *wasilah* can have other meanings. It can mean a place in paradise, as recited in the Prophetic Traditions, or Hadith. *Wasilah* can also mean to seek help from someone. This *wasilah* can be found in the *Hadith* as well. Finally, *wasilah* is a method of finding a way to God by using an absent figure. It is this practice, so common to popular Islam, that has become the focus of controversy. Persis, the *Persatuan Islam*, or Islamic Union, a reformist organization based in Bandung and active in West Java from 1926, promoted the scripturalist thinker Ibn Taimiyah and rejected *wasilah* and *tawassul* in this latter sense.[6] Nonetheless, for Pamijahanese, *tawassul*, or mediation is an attempt to build a bridge, *lantaran* in Sundanese, between human beings and God. Here the connection, the *lantaran,* is the literal translation of *tawassul*. Such a notion is also derived from interpretation of the verse in the Surah al-Maidah, which reads:

O ye who believe! Do your duty to God, Seek the means of approach unto Him, And strive with might and main in His cause that ye may prosper. (Qur'an 5: 35).

The *Adabuljairin*, the Manual of Pilgrimage, says:

The meaning of this ayat is:

"That is making a lantaran by visitation to wali who have been recognised by Allah, in short, in order to receive God's blessing through the wali's karamat, so that our intention will be mediated by them. Our wishes will be conveyed by the wali to Lord God the Most High. All of you have to perform pilgrimage to the tombs of the prophets, wali, and others pious Muslims because these men are given ability as if they were still alive in the world, so that for them there is no difference between being dead and alive. Their safaat, the help which they give us, is greater than before they died, and so they are able to jungkereng, or return to the phenomenal world just as if they were still alive... (Adabuljairin 2)

If we look carefully, there are three key words denoting the central issues in 'mediation' or 'approach'. The first, according to the villagers, is that all conduct should be based around *tawassul*. *Lantaran*, the locals' gloss on the Arabic term, is also a method or a bridge to achieve blessing from God. We humans should seek out a spiritual environment in order to perform *tawassul* rites. The purpose of pilgrimage is to bring about *tawassul* by visiting holy men, or *wali karamat*. This is explained in another part of the *Risalah Adab al-jairin*.

The purpose of pilgrimage (ziarah) is to create 'a means' (lantaran);[7] that is, a way to convey our purpose to the Rasul or to the prophets or to the wali or to pious Muslims[8] so that our wishes are granted by the Lord God. For example, we ask to strengthen our faith, or we ask (iman) for addition to our fortunes which is halal to us in service of God (ibadah), or we want to meet repayment of debts sooner, or we ask for a solution to misfortune and perplexity. These are called 'the way to convey these wishes' or tawassul.[9]

Ari maksudna ziarah nyaeta ngadamel lantaran, nyantelkeun maksud urang ka para Rasul atawa ka para Nabi atawa ka para Wali atawa ka para salihin supaya ngarah hasil diijabah ku Gusti Allah sapertos nyuhunkeun rizki anu halal kanggo ibadah, atanapi hoyong enggal ka taur hutang, atanapi nyuhunkeun hoyong leungit kasesah kabingung, etateh disebut tawasul (Adabuljairin 1)

Furthermore, the *Risalah Adab al-jairin* puts in plain words that causal effect, the *lantaran*, can be created by attaching (*nyantelkeun*) and entrusting (*nitipkeun*).[10] The metaphor of attaching and entrusting states explicitly how *ziarah* is significant. The custodian clarifies that we never delegate or *nitipkeun* to someone who cannot be trusted. Similarly, we never trust someone who is not willing to help. For the Pamijahanese, *tawassul* in this sense, is an effort to attach one's wishes to the holiness of the Shaykh. In regard to the concept of *lantaran*, the locals have a popular metaphor, as told to me by an informant one evening. *Lantaran* is a consequence of hierarchical relations as suggested by "the story of the bupati" as follows:

> "Lantaran is a kind of bridge which can bring us to our objectives. Let's say, if we want to meet a high ranking officer or Bupati, we have to follow the protocol in his office. The Bupati can receive us in his office formally or at his guest house. However, the Bupati often rejects our schedule or proposal if we have not followed the protocol, or tata krama. If on the other hand we are close to the Bupati, he will always pay attention to us. Then we don't need to follow formal protocol because he knows us."

The second crucial notion associated with *wasilah* or *tawassul*, is the manifestation of *jungkereng*. According to the Pamijahanese, a wali never spiritually dies and he is even able to become visible in the world again, or *jungkereng*, as in real life. As is suggested by the *Risalah Adab al-jairin*, the wali is able to recognise what is happening in the village and can communicate with the inhabitants or with visitors. One villager said that when electricity first came to the village, an old man in a white turban appeared in a vision and came up to him, saying that the village would face difficulties. There was a belief in Pamijahan that the close descendants of the wali should maintain 'proper' behaviour, which included not installing any electronic appliances such as televisions and radios near the sacred places.

This story is related to penetration of the village by the technology of modern entertainment such as television, VCD players, and satellite antennae. But many young people have different feelings towards tradition. When electricity came to the village, a good number of them immediately installed these devices. For the elders, this alteration in life-style was disturbing. Shaykh Abdul Muhyi, as stated by the custodians, comes to the locals whenever the village is in danger and this is what he was believed to have done when he appeared.

Because a wali never dies, he is able to give *syafaat* (Arabic: syafi) meaning 'help'. In turn, *ziarah* to the Shaykh's tomb is of significance to the villagers and visitors. Finding benefit, or *syafaat* is the third concept connected with *wasilah* in the *Risalah Adab al-jairin*.

The idea of the intermediary is widely accepted in popular belief and has been influenced by sufi traditions. In sufism, the master or the *shaykh* is supposed to mediate for his pupils' wishes. Students are urged to get the master's blessings.

From this point of view, it is not surprising if the villagers who claim to have inherited sufism from Shaykh Abdul Muhyi translate the concept of *wasilah* into the pilgrimage activities. To delegate prayer, or *nyantelkeun doa*, is 'to attach *doa* to the holiness of the master'. Accordingly, pilgrimage to Shaykh Haji Abdul Muhyi is an accepted bridge or *cukang lantaran*. The *Risalah Adab al-jairin* also claims that *ziarah* practice occurs in the Prophetic Traditions known as hadith.

> The Prophet (Kangjeng Rasul) also often made ziarah visits to tombs. This is clearly stated in the in the first chapter of the Hadith Muslim, page 8553. Kangjeng Rasulullah sala al-lahu alaihi wa sallam, at the end of the night, often makes devitonal visits Baqing[11] and delivers greetings to those who are buried there.

Thus, the Pamijahanese tend to invest the term *tawassul* or mediation with a particular meaning, that is, to formulate a means to approach God by performing pilgrimage. The Pamijahanese also perceive this practice as an acceptable bridge because the Qur'an and the *hadith* support it. Indeed the Pamijahanese seem to have found a way to synthesise a theological interpretation of the conception of the intermediaries with their own traditions.

However, for some the "stairway to the blessing" is not always clear. One needs a tutor and guidance to grasp it, and it is the tomb custodians, the custodian or "key bearers", who offer assistance and lessons to the pilgrims.

C. Custodianship

The Sundanese word *pakuncenan* is derived from custodian, "key bearer" which in turn is derived from *kunci*, "key".[12] The *pakuncenan* is the village guild of custodians. It is led by a custodian (custodian) who is elected by the members of the four main families (*pongpok*) descended from Shaykh Abdul Muhyi. At the time of writing (2002) Engku Syukrudin from *pongpok* I headed the *pakuncenan*. The task of the pakuncenan is to maintain Shaykh Abdul Muhyi's shrine and help people to perform the correct rituals at the site. The head custodian also acts as the village head. The rank and file of custodians have various roles in pilgrimage, supporting the *pakuncenan*, registering pilgrims and helping pilgrims in their rituals.

The *pakuncenan* is a relatively new institution in Pamijahan. I learned about it from my informants in the field. The first site custodian referred to as a custodian was Haji Muhammad Kosim who died in 1985. His lengthy full name gives his lineage: Haji Muhammad Kosim bin Abd. Mutholib bin Kiai Madhoip bin Kiai Uba bin Kiai Madhanan bin Nida Muhyidin bin Shaykh Abdullah putra Shaykh Haji Abdul Muhyi. Before him, Pamijahan or Safarwadi had been ed by a custodian who had the title of *Panembahan* (literally "he to whom honour is due"). Previously, besides acting as the custodian, the *panembahan* also had the authority to manage all local religious affairs, including the supervision of pilgrimage. However, around the 19th century the Dutch colonial government introduced a formal administrative apparatus centred on a mosque official called a *naib*. The institution of *panembahan* was converted into that of the *pakuncenan*, and since then the pakuncenan has administered pilgrimage, while all other religious affairs have been handled by the *naib*.

In response to these external factors, the villagers invented the guild of custodians *pakuncenan*. Folk narratives recited by one the custodian staff explain the emergence of custodianship around the middle of the nineteenth century, after visitors began to come to the site in large numbers with all their various rituals and intentions. Abdul Muhyi's descendants had the obligation to regulate events in this situation. The following is a narrative delivered by A.A. Khaerusalam, a prominent member of the Muhyi family who later wrote the book, *Sejarah Perjuangan Shaykh Abd al-Muhyi* (The History of the Struggles of Shaykh Abdul Muhyi).

> On Monday the 8th of Jumadil Awal in 1151/1730, after the subuh prayer, he returned to the One (Rab l-zat), being at the age of eighty.
>
> News of Muhyi's death circulated widely. His followers, both, those who lived close to him and those who came from distant places, made their way to Pamijahan to express their condolences.
>
> Thereafter, people always came to visit his tomb, showing their respects in various ways, such as reciting al-Qur'an (membaca al-Quran),[13] reciting the phrase 'all praise to Allah' (membaca tasbih), reciting the phrase 'God is Great' (takbir), reciting the phrase of 'the glory of God' (tahmid) and reciting the phrase 'there is no God but Allah, and Muhammad is His Messenger" (tahlil), so that the graveside resounded with their words. All the blessings of their prayers were intended for him. There were also people who hoped to seek barakah from the place in various ways; and there were people who sought barakah by conducting tawassul through the holy charisma of Muhyi in order to fulfil their wishes.
>
> Because of the great number of pilgrims who conducted ziarah at the tomb of Shaykh Haji Abdul Muhyi, Muhyi's son wondered whether such practices would disturb the power and sanctity of Muhyi and his tomb. Then the descendants of Kangjeng Shaykh gathered to discuss an appropriate way to protect and maintain their ancestor's tomb.

In a village council meeting, it was decided that the maintaining of the shrine and its surrounding area would be assigned to the four families of the wali. However, as stated in Khaerussalam's book (Khaerussalam 1992) the management of the shrine would be controlled by three clans or sides called *pongpok*. These groups mainly originated from the three sons of the wali from his first wife, Ayu

Bakta. These sons were Sembah Dalem Bojong, Shaykh Abdulloh and Media Kusuma. They also agreed to give the status of custodian to descendants of another of Muhyi's wives, Sembah Ayu Salamah. Thus, custodial rights were distributed evenly over four lines of descent. Based on this pact the shrine's management was similarly divided into four sides or *pongpok*.

> Therefore, the maintenance of Muhyi's tomb and his heritage was given to the pakuncenan which has four groups called pongpok. The first pongpok was called pongpok hiji, the main side, or pongpok pokok. The others are called pongpok dua, pongpok tilu, and pongpok opat. Pongpok is a kind of right to maintain the shrine. These four pongpok originally come from the Muhyi line. The leader of the villagers was the panembahan in previous times or the custodian today. The kuncen staff is elected from among the four pongpok. The custodian never comes from outside Muhyi's descendants. This is a testament from our ancestors that kapongpokan should be continued by his descendants or seuweu siwi.

Such arrangements later become a potential source of the conflict and resentment with descendants of Abdul Muhyi from his other wives. According to this pact, the descendants of the first wife gained more privileges over the symbolic space, particularly the centre area of Pamijahan. They also claim to be the members of the family who have stayed on the land for centuries and have never moved outside the sacred territory. On the other hand, many descendants of the other three wives left the land and some of them have never returned to Pamijahan. Soon after Pamijahan come into existence as a popular pilgrimage destination, they tried to settle again in Pamijahan and have now become a potential source of conflict with the first group. Matters have become complicated in cases where some of them gained positions in the government bureaucracy and have tried to use their positions to regain some of the symbolic signs of authority which they have lost.

It is not clear exactly when the pilgrimage to Kangjeng Shaykh became popular. However, we have a significant clue that in the eighteenth century a noble from the city of Sukapura (now Tasikmalaya) performed rituals on this site.[14] A manuscript points out that when the political elite came into dispute over internal political or personal matters,[15] they would visit the tomb of Abdul Muhyi to make oaths and vows. Such visits are believed to have had a great impact on the political figures of the time. According to *Sajarah Sukapura* (The Chronicle of Sukapura) edited by Hermansoemantri (1979, 24):

> His brother, Raden Patih, said, "I will not be satisfied until you have taken the true oath. Brothers, you must gather at Shaykh Abdul Muhyi's tomb where we will make a true oath so that our oath has power. Soon after they arrived in Pamijahan and they sat down around the tomb.

Pilgrimage at Pamijahan: Practice and Narrative

According to Sajarah Sukapura, soon after the oath was sworn one of the participants, Dalem Subamanggala, fell sick and after a short time, died. Subamanggala, according to Sajarah Sukapura, is buried in Pamijahan close to Shaykh Abdul Muhyi's tomb. Subamanggala is called Kangjeng Dalem Pamijahan, become his tomb is to be found in the southern corner of the Muhyi Shrine, covered by an umbrella (payung). It is the only tomb in the shrine which is associated with the aristocracy of Sukapura, the 'ruler of the world'.

In time, saintly linkages have legitimated custodianship. The *pongpok* groups claim to have symbolic authority over territory associated with their place at the tomb. They have followers in this "territory" both in the Desa Pamijahan and outside the Desa Pamijahan.

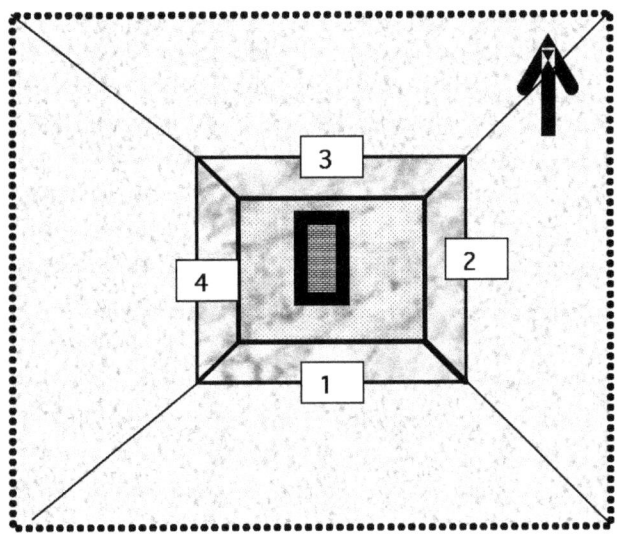

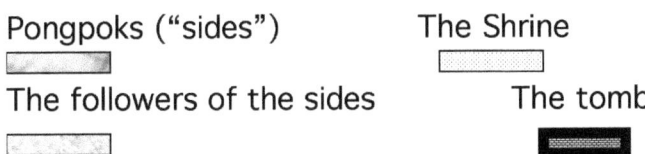

Figure 26 the Tomb and the *pongpok* Sides

Regarding this system, the custodian recites Kangjeng Shaykh's testimony that 'anyone who breaches this tradition, which has been delivered by our descent, will not gain prosperity for his family',[16]

> Saha bae anu nyisikudi kana katangtuan anu parantos diserenkeun ti luhur... aya basa kaluhur aja sirungan ongsor aja oyodan (The Kuncen)

What should be noted about the notion of place is that such a division is structured hierarchically, reflected in cardinal numbers resembling the structure of genealogy, where the oldest family occupies the most important position. The first family or *pongpok hiji* occupies the south 'side'. This 'side' is sometimes called the southern door (panto kidul). This first family's place is important because most rituals are held in this area.

According to the leader of the first group, the group is responsible for maintaining the rituals held in the area. In practice, in contemporary Pamijahan, most important rituals associated with the wali will pass this gate. Therefore, politically, the first family has a legitimate control of the important 'ritual space' (see, Fox 1997). The chief custodians always come from the first *pongpok*.

Accordingly, space in Pamijahan can be imagined ritually in a rectangular shape where each side represents a sub group derived from the wali's wives. There is also another way the Pamijahanese conceived their village. Space is also conceived in terms of closeness and the mystical journey of the ancestors. The places are interconnected by the itinerary of the mystical journey of the Shaykh on his early journey to the village. Each spot in his itinerary is crucial in the spatial concept; the cave, the mosque, the non-smoking are part of the sacred journey of the wali. Furthermore, the space is also related to the concept of (*kerabat* or *qaraba*) as has been illustrated by the arrangement of the *pongpok*. Later, some people from outside Pamijahan also follow the idea of closeness by connecting themselves to a 'side' which is relatively close to their hamlet. The leader of a 'side', hence, symbolically has followers in those ritual spaces. For example, villagers on the west side of the villager such as Padahayu, Sabeulit Cirakoneng, Pamijahan, and Parungpung mongpok to the *pongpok kulon* (West group, *pongpok tilu*) which is lead by Media Kusuma. People in the villages of Bongas, Ciwalet, Cintabodas, Cilumbu, and Cihandiwung associate themselves with *pongpok kidul* (South group, *pongpok hiji*) led by Sembah Dalem Bojong (Muhyi's son from Sembah Ayu Winangun). Shaykh Abdullah from *pongpok kaler* (North group, *pongpok dua*) has territory in the northern area such as Pandawa, Pajadun, Sangulat Saronge and Leuwinaggung; and finally Sembah Ayu Salamah has territory in *pongpok wetan* (East group, *pongpok tilu*) or the eastern part such as Lebaksiuh, Cilangkruk, Petir, Cilingga, Campaka, and Cikawung. Thus, the imagined spaces can be seen on the map below (the figure 4).

These affiliation is ritualised in shrine renovation and in yearly rituals such the commemoration of the Prophet Muhammad, muludan. The shrines are renovated and maintained not only by the kuncen and his family on each side but also by people outside Pamijahan who belong to a particular *pongpok*. At muludan they will send 'tribute' to the *pongpok* leader.

Pilgrimage at Pamijahan: Practice and Narrative

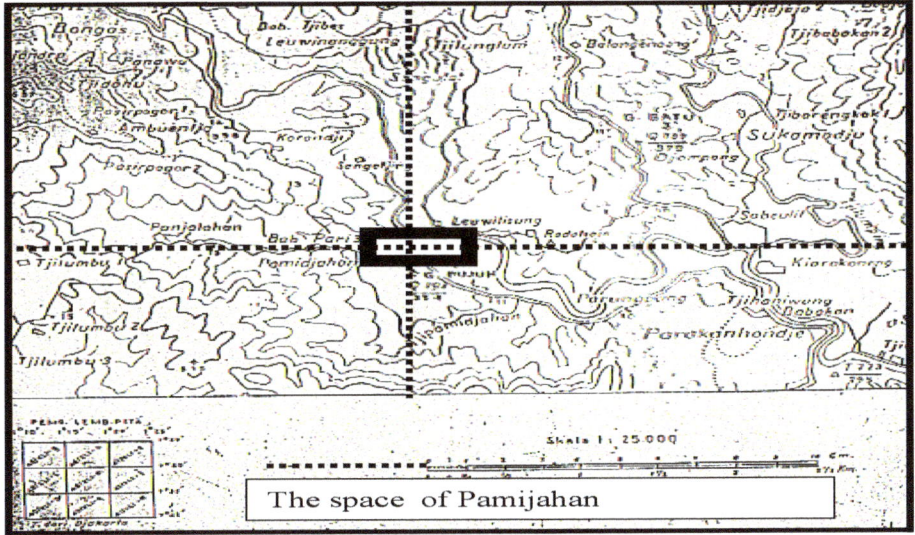

Figure 27 the space and topography of Pamijahan

During my field work, 1997-1998, I observed that a member from *pongpok* I, Pak Engku Syukrudin, had been elected as the second kuncen. He was a farmer and had some pesantren association before he was elected. Like other elected senior custodian, he uses his house as an office. He came from the primary 'side' or *pongpok* Santana.

After interviewing members of other *pongpok*, I found different attitudes regarding his election. According to my informant, the previous custodian, Mama Ajengan Kosim was better than Engku Syukrudin. My informant said Mama Ajengan Kosim had spiritual powers and so every visitor was given a gift, such as an amulet, or verval cham (*isim*), or advice (*nasihat*). Other said that Engku Syukrudin was not really appropriate for the custodian due to his lack of spiritual power. Furthermore, according to him, the son of the previous custodian, Mama Ajengan Satibi, should be the real successor or the custodian. Mama Ajengan Satibi spent his life at various Pesantren and now he teaches santri at Pasantren Karamat Safarwadi. However, Mama Ajengan Satibi had a stroke near the time of election and Engku Syukrudin was elected. As a legitimate custodian, however, he prefers not to exercise his rights to income other staff. Previously the custodian received 20 percent of the income and 80 percent was divided among the four groups; but now, the custodian no longer receives this privilege. He only acquires a share (bagian) from his *pongpok*. However, the custodian still receives additional income since he has more personal clients than other staff.

Currently, shifts are distributed the four pongpok groups so that each *pongpok* has the job for one week looking after the shrine and serving pilgrims. They occupy the custodian's house 24 hours a day. Every day, around three or four men from one *pongpok* are on duty.

The custodians on duty can be classified into three categories. The first, the leader, is called the custodian. The second are the custodian's staff (*staf* custodian), and these in turn are subdivided into those who registers pilgrims (n*u ngadaftar*) and those who conduct them to the shrine (*nu jajap ka makam* or nu *ngaziarahkeun*). The third category is that of guides to the cave of Safarwadi. These are called *nu jajap ka guha*.

A leader of a pongpok (ketua *pongpok*) acts as the head custodian during a shift. He has to ask and record visitors' identities and their intentions. He also offers guidance to guests. The majority of visitors prefer to be guided, and there are two main reasons for this. The first is that they are unable to perform their own ritual. The second is that they believe that Muhyi's family has the "license" to mediate their intention (*pamaksadan*).

While the *pongpok*'s leader registers pilgrims and collects donations, other staff, often two or three men, act as mediators in the shrine. Those who accompany the guest to the shrine are called nu jajap ka Makam. If visitors need guidance, then the custodian employs his colleagues who sits close to him. They will accompany visitors to approach Kangjeng wali's tomb while the *pongpok* leader stays in the office.

Another type of custodian is one who accompanies visitors to the sacred cave (nu jajap ka guha) after the main ritual at the tomb. The custodian who accompanies visitors to the shrine get their allowance from the leader as well as from the guest, but staff who escort pilgrims to the cave only receive money from visitors about which they have to negotiate. Visitors have to rent a pressure lamp and are expected to pay for their guidance. This group does not affiliate formally with the custodian. As a marginal group, they try to organise themselves. The organiser, who comes from *pongpok* III, regards the role of nu jajap ka guha is as important in pilgrimage practice because they guide visitors to trace the labyrinth and show its importance. They are important in transferring the tradition of these sites. When I went there for the first time, they often explained the importance of pilgrimage. They also narrated the miracle of Kangjeng Shaykh in the caves. However, the p*akuncen*an is the authoritative institution, which does not want its activity to overlap with theirs, even through former organiser said to me that this organization had merged with the pa*kuncen*an.

There are instructions in writing that every pilgrim to Muhyi's tomb should report to the custodian. In contemporary Pamijahan seems to have been interpreted in various meanings. Firstl, there are those who say that it is compulsory for the pilgrim to be guided, whether they are able to do their own ritual or not. Second, pilgrims can in fact do their own ritual as long as they are able to perform them and have been registered (*ngadaftar*). Thirdl, whether pilgrims or not are able or not to perform their own ritual, if they present money for registration (*ngadaftar*) they have the choice of being guided or not.

The economic impact of the pa*kuncen*an is tremendous. Thanks to their collective income, the custodians are able to build mosques, renovate the shrines, circumcise every Rajab, and more importantly provide a cash source for the Muhyi families. In 1996, one cusdotian told me that, in total, the custodians receive donations (sodaqoh) from the pilgrims of around one to two hundred thousand rupiah every day particularly during peak season. The pa*kuncen*an also control the money placed in the boxes which are located along the path to the shrine. In fact, this is geates than the amount given directly to the custodian at registration. One charity box (Kas Amal) can contribute at least a million rupiah a week. The boxes are put at the gate of the shrine; others are located close to the custodian house. Ajengan Endang reported that 15 percent of this income is spent on social activity, 25 percent for the pa*kuncen*an, 25 percent for the petugas, and the remaining 25 per cent for education (pendidikan or pesantren). The local government also gets benefits since they charge for every vehicle, which comes to Pamijahan.

The pakuncenan has significant authority compared to modern institutions such as the village leader. For example, the village leader always comes to the Maulid festival, which is performed by the pakuncenan. On the other hand, when the village leader performs a festival in the village hall (balai desa), the custodian does not regard it compulsory to attend. The *pakuncenan* is also able to invite the provincial governor or the local district head (*bupat*i) to his gathering, while it is difficult for the village head to do this.

D. Pilgrims

In the villagers' view, all visitors who come to Kangjeng Shaykh's tomb, whatever their motives are the guests of the holy man (*tamu Wali*). The custodian categorises pilgrims primarily based on the way they perform rituals, though their motives are also taken into account. However, it is difficult for the custodian to identify the purpose of all visitors.

Pilgrimage is mostly carried out as a personal ritual. For example, Karna, a pilgrim, confessed that he did not explicitly tell the custodian his aim. Karna ran a business in Jakarta. His was business went bankrupt and he had to make repayments to investors. However, he reported to the custodian as only 'making a visit' or 'bade *ziarah*'. Deden, another visitor, came to Pamijahan to solve his marriage problem. His wife had asked for a divorce but Ridden still loved her. He said to the custodian that he came "To find a quiet place", or milari katenangan. One staff member said to me that it is not compulsory to know explicitly what the intentions are for pilgrimage are. He believes that pilgrims generally have particular intentions, or gaduh *pamaksadan*. In some cases, pilgrims visit the shrine due to an assignment from their teacher.

There are various categories of pilgrims based on their behaviour. The first category is the ordinary visitor, or nu *ziarah* biasa. The ordinary pilgrims (nu *ziarah* biasa) are weekenders who come to Pamijahan not only for *ziarah* but also for spiritual refreshment. They come in groups of one to four luxurious buses. Pamijahan's fresh air and green scenery offer an attractive atmosphere for those who work in polluted cities such as Jakarta, Bandung, Surabaya, and other big cities of Java. They often rent houses for the night, including meals. Before returning home, they often buy various local product as souvenir gifts.

Visitors like this have become the main source of income for local residents. In the peak season, villagers are able to sell more gifts. One villager says that she gets an extra five thousand hundred rupiah a month. This amount is equal to a high school teacher's monthly salary. Moreover, villagers also get money from visitors who stay in their houses. Villagers charge them from one to five thousand rupiah a night including food. This type of visitor is in the majority of pilgrims in peak seasons such as Mulud and Rajab. They come from various places in Java. The flow of pilgrims has been influenced by the development of road networks in Tasikmalaya. Remoteness is no longer a problem since Pamijahan is now accessible to all vehicles. Moreover, Pamijahan has been set up as one of the targets of a pilgrimage network in Java by various organisers. Some organisers have linked Pamijahan with other established pilgrimage destinations such as those in Gresik, Cirebon, and Banten.

Another characteristic of nu *ziarah* biasa is that they may be able to perform rituals but they do not perform any additional ritual after the main ritual (*tawassul*). They only make a short visit to the tomb, go to the cave and return home. Therefore, it is possible that the custodian also classifies someone who can perform prayer and intermediary ritual at another tomb as nu *ziarah* biasa when they do not understand the particular sequence for Pamijahan. The pilgrims usually believe that each place has its own sequence and set of rules or tali paranti. In this case, pilgrims actually recognise the local custom and the custodian's authority. The custodian calls them nu *ziarah* biasa as long as they do not carry out other specific rituals and only perform the standard ritual that he suggests. Also slassified as ordinary visitors are *nu awam* who are unable to perform rituals and need guidance.

Second categories of pilgrim are those who mastered visitation to sacred tombs. Belonging to this category, are the specialists such as Muslim leaders (*ajengan*), pupil at pesantre schools (*santri*), teacher and klerik (*kiai*), and expert in Islam (*akhli hikmah*), as well asp people who want to obtain particular knowledge (*ngelmu*) and those seeking solutions for their problems (*nu gaduh pamaksadan*). Like ordinary visitors, they also report to the custodian and give some money.

This is not in return for guidance but out of charity, which is relied on to regularly maintain the shrine. After registration, they visit tomb alone or with their followers. Such visitors claim that they have often come to Pamijahan before. They perform their own *tawassul* and other additional rituals. Belonging to this type, for example, is Haji Hassan from Bekasi. For Haji Hassan such a pilgrimage is his and good deed. He carries out *tawassul* by himself and for his followers. He has a boarding school (pesantren) and a travel company, which assists anyone who wants to go (ngumbra) on the lesser pilgrimage to Mecca. According to him, he and his followers regularly come to Pamijahan at least once a year. When I met him on 21 July 1996, he had brought with him 60 followers. His followers were charged for transport and accommodation. They usually spend only one hour or a night at the shrine but the custodian believes that pilgrims like this can communicate with the wali effectively. Staff (kuncen) said that one ajengan from Manonjaya Tasikmalaya had met Kangjeng Shaykh face to face in the cave. This ajengan only made a short visit but he was able to communicate with Kangjeng Shaykh.

Some ordinary pilgrims perform an additional ritual such as fasting (tirakat) or practice austerity (tapa). I found about twenty pilgrims who spent forty days doing tirakat near the tomb during the period of Safar and Mulud in 1996. An example of this type is Karjo, 27, from Cirebon. When I found him at the corner of the shrine, he had been staying for 25 days. Karjo is a santri. According to him, he came to Pamijahan for tabaruk is gain blessing. Tabaruk is well known in Sufi rituals (see Chapter 8). His guru suggested that he stay at the shrine for 41 days. During this period he had to fast and only eat rice and drink water when he broke his fast. Mostly he spent his time doing *tawassul* and dhikir at the shrine. Such individuals will leave after they obtain some sign from Kangjeng Shaykh. Mostly they stay in a corner of the shrine. They only go outside to take a bath or find some food. Some of them were able to make personal connections with the villagers. When villagers performed *salametan*, they were often invited.

The sacred cave is the second most popular site after the Shaykh's tomb among visitors who want to seek spiritual power by tapa and tirakat. An example of this type of pilgrim (Satrio) is a man who has been staying and doing, tapa, there for almost two years. He will complete his visitation in 2000. He has made his own hut (saung) near the sacred cave.

The reasons for which pilgrims come are varied. It is difficult to identify their intentions without detailed interviews with them. In Pamijahan, pilgrims tend to describe their intentions in general terms; that is, as bade *ziarah*. Of course, there are some pilgrims who state their intentions in detail, but it is often a particular request to the custodian, which is made personally by visitors at the tomb when the ritual is about to start. In other places, such as in Tembayat or in Cirebon, it is common to answer the custodian more explicitly in the ritual jawab during the first stage.

Based on my interviews with pilgrims, I found that their motivations and intentions (*pamaksadan*) usually concerned personal wellbeing. Such an intentions are also common at other sacred sites in Java. One shrimp farmer (Munir, 39) from Lampung Sumatra is an example of this type of pilgrim. When I met him, he had already spent eleven days at the shrines. According to his guru, he had to stay there for at least fourteen days. It is common among the specialists to consult their guru first before going to sacred sites. Munir had a problem with his shrimp ponds (udang). Almost twice a season he had been unable to harvest his shrimps. The shrimps either died before harvesting or were swept away by the waves. He stated that until a couple of years ago he regularly came to Pamijahan before he put the shrimp into the pond. According to him, he always got a good harvest (panen). After that, he stopped coming to Pamijahan. Thereafter, predators easily attacked his shrimp. So he decided to *ziarah*. After he had spent fourteen days, he returned to Lampung with holy water, which he sprinkled onto his ponds.

Pamijahan is indeed popular among farmers like Munir. It is not surprising that Pamijahan is often associated with fertilisation, as suggested by the name for the village. Pamijahan means a "hatching place" where something always doubles, triples, and so on. Visitors who seek fertility for their paddy fields or sawah include paddy farmers from Indramayu who frequently make visitations to the shrine and bring gifts to the custodian and his family after they harvest their paddy.

E. The sequence of rituals

Travelling to the sacred sites has a grammar. Pilgrims as "the reader" should have a certain competence in syntax in order to obtain blessings. In the previous chapter, I have mentioned that the space in Pamijahan is imagined to have four sides or *pongpok*. The ideology of closeness, which is derived from the structure of the genealogy, is applied to the notion of space. The closer to the holy men, the more privilege people may have. The privilege and the blessing of the locals have been attached to their land since the Shaykh made his first shelter in the village. If the villagers have privilege attached instantly to their land and of course to their village culture, the pilgrims outside these linkages and outsiders should performed special rituals in order to grasp such privilege from their holly men (wali). Privilege should be achieved through a structured process. On the other hand, the villagers have the obligation to help the pilgrims. Thus, they try to translate what their ancestors prescribed and what they did not. One of their obligations is to make a sign. For instance, locals designate locations to make boundaries between outer and inner space for both villagers and pilgrims. Furthermore, they codify a sacred protocol and its sequences in their village.

Sequence is crucial in ritual. A ritual should be started and finished within a certain period. Pilgrimage in Pamijahan is also structured in conventional ways. It is slightly different to anti-structure (Turner 1984) The space and place in Pamijahan are to some extent similar to other parts in the hilly areas of West Java. Turner argues that unusual sites are the characteristic of pilgrimage. In fact, Pamijahan is not special from the perspective of oddness. It has a cave; but there are lots of the caves in Tasikmalaya. In an anomalous city like Jakarta, we can go to a pilgrimage site known as Batang. Indeed, the most important locus is the erected sign. In Pamijahan created signs should be connected to Shaykh Abdul Muhyi. One of the displayed signs in Pamijahan is the gate.

Turner (Turner 1968) argues that pilgrimage forms a series of structure-communitas (anti-structure)-communitas. Pilgrims move from structured environments to anti-structure environments and back again to the structured one. Meaning is acquired by passage through the liminal.

From Pamijahan we learn that the terms of 'communitas' (Turner 1968) are experienced differently due to fact that pilgrims consist of various categories and each category may have different practices on the site. For the weekender, the sense of communitas in the Turnerian view may not always be achieved. They often come with a large group and bring with them their own master (guru) and ulama, and even their village headman (Ketua RT). When they come to the sites, such structured environments to some extent still closely adhere to the group. It is different for the specialist pilgrims who stay for a long time in the shrine, interact with other specialists, and create a sense of similarity without being influenced by previous lived structures.

The most apparent aspect in pilgrimage is the demarcation between profane and sacred space. The sacredness starts at the gate (Kaca-kaca). Kaca-kaca is a Sundanese term for gate. The gate is built on the most eastern side of the village. It is a sign with reference to tradition. Pilgrims have to learn about this tradition. Prohibitions called tali paranti are written on the gate wall. According to texts written on that wall, pilgrims should wear appropriate clothes. Woman must use their veils. Neither villagers nor visitors are allowed to use their vehicles in the sacred village (kampung Pamijahan). The gate regiments pilgrims to act in certain ways. The regimentation is acquired through the structured affect of the gate. The gate physically points to the sacredness. Villagers find the gate as the starting point for the sacred journey. It is like the front door of the sacred village. Based on tali paranti, the gate should be erected and maintained by the all the families of Muhyi or ka*pongpok*an who stay inside as well as outside of Pamijahan.

However, according to the custodian, the current gate was build by the prominent family of Abdul Muhyi who became a famous Islamic scholar (ulama) in Cianjur (200 km to the West) a long time ago. Thus, in Jakobsonian terms, the gate is a message. It is also a code providing pilgrims with information and referential function. The code of pilgrimage (*adab jarroh*) as stated on the wall also expresses the presence of the addresser in Jakobsonian terms.

Approaching Pamijahan from the main gate, visitors enter a non-smoking area. According to local narratives, Shaykh Abdul Muhyi ordered his family and his followers not to smoke in the area close to his residence (and now his tomb). Pamijahan recognises such prohibitions as part of the tali paranti, which should be obeyed by both villagers and visitors.

For instance, villagers do not hesitate to warn pilgrims (nu*ziarah*) who break custom (tali paranti) by shouting at them not to smoke on the way to the shrine: "Please put out your cigarette." They believe that a person who disobeys tradition (tali paranti) will receive punishment. The custodian told the story that some visitors who break this custom have problems with their cars or even become sick on their way home. The custodian said, "Everywhere, as a guest, they have to respect the host" (*Di mana bae tamu mah kedah ngahargaan kana tali paranti atawa kabiasaan satempat tuan rumah.*) He stressed the word host, which not only refers to the villagers but, most importantly, also to Kangjeng Shaykh. So breaking tradition (tali paranti) means not respecting Kangjeng Shaykh.

Passing the gate and the bridge and walking for about ten minutes along the concrete path, visitors find the custodian's office. Between the gate and the custodian's headquarters some residents sell fried fish and handicrafts made in Tasikmalaya. The sacredness of this place exists side by side with its worldliness. I found some pilgrims from Jakarta who were surprised when they found that the village (kampung) Pamijahan is unlike other remote areas. After visitors walk down to the valley where Kampung Pamijahan is situated they find a mosque renovated at a cost of five hundred billion rupiah, soaring from the valley up to the hills. The house of the custodian and his staff member are designed as in cities (kota.) Parabolic antennas have been erected on the roofs. In the background, the green hills characterise Pamijahan as a country area. Even Rinkes, on his first 'pilgrimage' to this site found "a first class hotel in the country." (1910)

Visitors should write down their names at the custodian's office. This stage establishes the relation between visitors, the custodian, and his staff. The visitor approaches the custodian, his staff, shakes hands with them and they sit crossed-legged (*sila*). The custodian opens his registration book and his staff offer a cup of tea and some sweets. When I was there, I noted the transaction as follows

> The kuncen asked the pilgrims: Do you want to do Pilgrimage? How many people?
>
> Visitor: Yes, I am coming with four friends; they are outside.

The kuncen then checked the date in his book and gave the guest book to the visitors. Each visitor was asked to write down his identity and his intention and the number of people who accompanied him.

Kuncen: Have you brought your own ajengan, Ustad, or Kiai for tawassul?

Visitor: No, we have not.

Kuncen: You will be accompanied by nu ngajarohkeun (The Kuncen then appoints a member of his staff who is sitting close to him)

Visitor: This is hatur lumayan (He gives an envelope to the Kuncen and the Kuncen then puts it under the guest book)

The Kuncen: Haturnuhun.

Next, the custodian offers ritual accessories such as perfume, incense, isim, and the book, which describes the history of Kangjeng Shaykh. These packages cost five thousand to ten thousand rupiah. The custodian realises that not all visitors can afford these packages so he suggests that they only buy a particular item such as perfume or a book. After that, the custodian assigns a caretaker to accompany the visitors. Visitors can perform their own ritual after reporting (ngadaftar), but the majority ask the custodian for guidance.

The visitors proceed From the custodian's office to the Shrine; after the ten minute walk along the village path, visitors make ablution. The manual *Risalah Adab al-jairin* suggests that pilgrims should first purify their body and clothe; after that they should make ablution. Ablution (*wudu*) in fiqh is to purify the body from minor najis. The *Risalah Adab al-jairin* does not explain when or where *wudu* should be made. Mostly pilgrims purify themselves before they step on to the hill where the shrine is located. There are three washing areas, which can be used for ablution. This stage makes clear to visitors that they are entering the most sacred place in Pamijahan.

After performing *wudu*, visitors should consider their intention. According to the custodian, there is no ibadah without intention (*niat*). He says, "All conduct will be rewarded based on its intention (*sagala oge tergantung kana niat*)." According to him, the first intension (*niat* berangkat) is recited at home and the second, *niat* ngalaksanakeun, before approaching the sites. The manual makes clear that pilgrims should not hesitate to come to the tomb site since they believe that pilgrimage is recommended by their faith.[17] After that, visitors take off their shoes and put them on a shelf. Before they trek up the hill, some are offered the accessories of the rituals (kelengkapan). Afterward, visitors climb the steps to the hill where Kangjeng Shaykh's Makom is situated.

The manual advises that visitors should step with the right foot first when entering the shrine and greeting the wali (*kedah sampean tengah anu tipayun bari maos assalamualaikum*). By that time, the custodian has approached the gate of the shrine. He then leads visitors on to take their places in a cross-legged position. The manual also suggests that one should perform this stage with respect. Furthermore, one should also imagine that one will meet the saint as one will meet the leader pangagung.[18] The next stage is to deliver the ritual greeting: the first greeting is delivered to the Prophet Muhammad, then to his companions; the second greeting is to Kangjeng Shaykh Haji Abdul Muhyi.[19] For the third greeting, the custodian recites a set of Quranic verses ten times.

These stages are designed to introduce another stage; that of delivering the gift or *hadiyah*. The *hadiyah* is a recitation of fatiha or the opening verses of Quran. However, before the kuncen delivers the *hadiyah* he has to do a greeting ritual. The greeting says:

> Ya Allah salam atas bagimu wahai kekasih Allah, salam bagimu wahai kekasih Rasulullah Sayyidina Muhammad SAW. Engkau di tempat yang mulia dengan kekasih Tuhan semesta alam. Salam bagimu wahai kangjeng Shaykh Haji Abdul Muhyi dan siapa saja disekitarnya dan akhli kubur mukmin engkau semua telah mendahului kami dan kami insyallah akan menyusul kemudian... (Risalah Adab al-jairin p. 5)

> May God grant His blessing to you, His beloved, His blessings upon you, beloved Prophet of God, our lord Muhammad (peace be upon you). You reside in exaltation in the love of God for all of the world. And blessings upon you, honoured Shaykh Haji Abdul Muhyi, and those close to you and all the faithful departed. You have gone before us and with God's grace we will follow... (Risalah Adab al-jairin, 5.)

The benefit of the recitation is addressed to the dead. In popular practice, *hadiyah* is an additional daily ritual which is performed after, for instance, the five prayer times. The ritual *hadiyah* consists in reciting the formulaic chants, for instance,

> "To the elect prophet Muhammad, peace and prayers of Allah be upon him and upon his house and all of this companions. Let us recit al-Fatiha for them!

The *hadiyah* or the 'gift' can be sent to figures other than the Prophet depending on the intention made and the context in which *hadiyah* is recited. In the context of individual Muslims, at home, the *hadiyah* is delivered to one's dead parents or neighbours or their teachers. In the context of *ziarah*, *hadiyah* is addressed to the people who are 'historically' connected to the holy men buried in the shrines, or to other people who are believed to have a relationhips with the dead in the shrine, or to the people who have been connected by Sufi silsilah. So, the first, the ritual *hadiyah*, is to address the Prophet and, the second is to address the martyrs and the masters of the Sufimaster, Abd al-Qadir al-Jailani. The third is to address the master of the particular tarekat, Shaykh Abdul Muhyi. The fourth is to address the holy men visited at the shrines. The fifth is to address the murid of Shaykh Abdul Muhyi and all prominent families buried around the Shrine and neighbouring areas. The sixth is to contemporary figures that are important from the point of view of nu *ziarah*. The gift is the *Al-Fatiha* recitation.

Radical scripturalist groups such as Muhammadiyyah and Persis reject this practice. The rejection is based on their beliefs that the dead can not do anything expect wait for judgment. Only pious children are believed to have the opportunity to send *hadiyah* for their dead mothers and fathers. The meaning of *hadiyah* in their interpretation is also limited to praying to God to enhance their parents' status on God's side.

In contrast to Muhammadiyyah and Persis, the popular practice, which is in the majority came from Nahdatul Ulama, provides further meaning for the ritual *hadiyah*. It is not only presented to one's parents but also to the wali, the master of the tariqa, even to the local dead in the village. Such believers perceive the reciprocal values between the dead and pilgrims could emerge in ritual *hadiyah*, as stated in the manual of pilgrimages such as *Risalah Adab al-jairin* of Pamijahan. This ritual is close to the ideology of *tawassul*.

The *hadiyah* is also seen as part of the preliminary set of rituals. *Risalah Adab al-jairin* states *hadiyah* as part of the greeting to the wali, "ari ieu risalah sakadar hajat paranti hadiyhana uluk salam…" The manual was written to provide pilgrims with the ritual guidance. One important section in ritual pilgrimage is making *hadiyah* or the greeting ritual. In the case of Pamijahan, after sending the gift to the Prophet, the same gift is also directed to the *sahabat* and *Karabat*. Sayidinia Abubakar, Sayyidina Umar, and Sayyidina Ali, also receive *hadiyat* from pilgrims. Next, the gift is also given to the *mujtahid, ulama, amilin, fuqaha, ahlul Sufi* and *tabi'in*. Then, the gift is sent to the *wali* from Magrib until Masyrik. After that, one should send the gift to Shaykh Abdulqadir Jailani. Special holy men are addressed here. They are particularly people who have been linked with the Order or the founder of the Order and his companions. The gift is initially addressed to the Kangjeng Shaykh Haji Abdul Muhyi and his familiy and friends such as Sembah Khatib Muwahid, Sembah Kudrat, Sembah Dalem Sacaparana, and Sembah Dalem Yudanagara.

The *hadiyah* is a important preliminary protocol permitting entry into a symbolic transaction, and reciprocally between the dead and nu *ziarah*. After delivering *hadiyah*, visitors recite a set of verses, personal prayers such as *salawat*, istigfar, tahlil and doa *tawassul*.[20] The *doa tawassul* contains *salawat* to the Prophet and also address Shayh Abdul Muhyi in the following terms:

> Ya Allah dengan Karamah Kangjeng Shaykh Haji Abdul Muhyi, aku memohon agar Engkau tetapkan iman kami dan engkau sampaikan maksud dan tujuan kami agar Engkau sampaikan maksud dan tujuan

> kami agar Engkau angkat duka lara kami dan melunasi hutang-hutang kami
>
> Almighty God, under the grace of our honoured Shaykh Haji Abdul Muhyi, I beg You to strengthen our faith and convey our hopes and our desires, we ask you to convey our hopes and our desires, so that you release us from our burdens and lighten all our worldly obligations

Finally, the custodian recites the *hadiyah* ritual again, followed by doa.

> Tiada Tuhan kecuali Allah. Apa apa yang telah kami sampaikan dari shalawat atas Nabi baginda nabi Muhammad SAW di majlis ini sebagai hadiah yang kami sampaikan dari kami, kami hadiahkan dan kami haturkan kepada hadrat sayidina wa maulana tuan dan penolong kami Shaykh Haji Abdul Muhyi dan kepada asa muasal nenek moyang serta cabang-cabangnya, istrinya dan kaum keluarga serta karib kerabatnya. Dan kepada seluruh arwah, seluruh yang hadir di kuburan ini, sebagai hadiyah…dan baginya nikmat yang berlimpah dan tinggi mulia. Ya Allah berilah dia pertolongan dan diri kami dan pertolongan bagi seluruh yang hadir dan seluruh pada penziarah. (Adabuljairin, p. 8)
>
> There is no God but God. May what we have offered in our greetings upon Your Prophet Muhammad (peace be upon him) in this assembly be a gift from us, we present it and we offer it to our lord, our teacher and our master and our help, Shaykh Haji Abdul Muhyi. And to his ancestors and their kin, to his wives and family, and to his kinfolk. And to all the departed souls, all those whose dwelling is this resting place here, we offer this gift… and to them may exalted blessings flow. Oh, Almighty give them and give us help, and Your help to all those present now and to all pilgrims. (Adabuljairin, p.8)

The custodian prays for the visitors, their families and friends. In the prayer, the custodian mediates the visitors' wishes.[21] The custodian's palms are raised and the pilgrims follow his gestures by saying "Amen…Amen…Amen…". If a visitor explicitly asks the custodian to deliver his wishes, then the custodian recites a particular doa. The custodian also recites "an additional" doa without the visitors,' explicit request. For example, if the custodian knows the occupation of the visitors, he then recites a doa to strengthen their position in office or to develop their business. He also recites a doa for researchers like me.

> Kangjeng Shaykh…. ieu seuweu putu Kangjeng Shaykh anu nuju mayunan studi. Anjeunna hoyong terang sagala rupi perkawis Ajaran Kangjeng Shaykh sapuratina. Mugi ajeunna tiasa ngamalkeun elmuna, mangfaat di dunya rawuh diakherat. Amin.
>
> Honoured Shaykh… this grandchild of yours, Kangjeng Shaykh is engaged in research. He desires to learn your teaching in its entirety.

May he make good use of his knowledge, may it be of benefit here in the world and in the hereafter. Amen.

Finally, the custodian turns to face his visitors and shakes hands with them. The custodian delivers salam to them and returns to his office for the next assignment. At the final stage, visitors probably give the kuncen who accompanied them to the shrine, or the nu *ngaziarahkeun*, a consideration for his personal service.

After the custodian returns to his office, the *nu biasa ziarah* will stay at the tomb to recite their personal doa and find appropriate shelter in a corner of the shrine while women visitors enter a special room (*rohangan kanggo istri*). However other visitors will continue to other sacred sites.

Unlike other pilgrimage sites in Java, at Kangjeng Shaykh Abdul Muhyi's shrine, there is no burning of incense or scattering of flowers. According to the villagers, this unwritten procedure is a response to the critics who condemn such practice as heresy. However, when the Dutch orientalist, A.D. Rinkes visited to this site in 1909 (Rinkes 1910), he found visitors burning incense.

A specialist pilgrim will stay for the length of time, that has been suggested by his guru or the tradition in his school, while other nu *ziarah* biasa will continue their pilgrimage to the Safarwadi cave, Guha Safarwadi—which is also often called Guha Pamijahan. At the gate to the shrine, a cave guide, or *nu nganteur kag guha*, will offer guidance to visitors. One to five visitors make use of one of them. So, if the visitors belong to groups, which may consist of one to five buses, four-nunganteur ka guha are needed to serve the passengers from each bus. In peak season such as Maulid and Rajab, a *nu nganteur kag guha* earns about twenty thousand rupiah a day. Sometimes, they are lucky because pilgrims give them tips as well.

The cave guides are important in maintaining traditions. On the way to the cave, they often make conversation with their clients. On the way to the cave, they are 'broadcasting' the story (cf. Fox 2002) at the site, answering questions, suggesting the route, shelter, or even restaurants. On these occasions, for example, they will describe what the miracle, kaghaiban, in the cave is. Visitors often ask many questions about the cave.

Visitors need ten minutes to walk from the tomb to the cave. They have to climb the path. This journey is not easy for older visitors. During my fieldwork, I found a visitor had died on the way to the cave because he was too old and probably had a heart attack. The p*akuncen*an, like an insurance office, had the responsibility of calling for an ambulance and sending him back to his village in Semarang. The difficult path for the pilgrims may enhance the potency of the site.

Before entering the cave, visitors should recite the call for prayer (*adzan*). *Nu nganteur kag guha* say that *adzan* gives visitors a sense of calm, '*katenangan*'.

Someone who has never entered a cave (*guha*) probably feel scared because he may think that inside there are snakes and other poisonous animals. One *Nu nganteur kag guha* said that a lot of visitors feel extremely close to God when they approach the cave because they realise that only God can help them if something happens inside. Therefore, besides reciting azan, other visitors voluntarily recite verses from the Quran and *salawat* when they are inside the cave. Adzan is a standard chant in Islam. However, according to the text, *adzan* should be performed before prayer five times each day and not at times other than that. It is common for the Sundanese and probably the Javanese, to extend the use of such formulaic chants to different settings and for different purposes.

Villagers believe that the Guha Pamijahan called the cave of Safarwadi in manuscripts, is sacred. The cave was an important place for Kangjeng Shaykh Abdul Muhyi after he returned from Mecca. As discussed previously 6, there is convincing evidence that Shaykh Abdul Muhyi obtained the Shatariyah *silsilah* from Abd al-Rauf al-Singkel, the prominent Sumateran Sufi of the 17th century (Christomy 2001; Krauss 1995; Rinkes 1909). However, in the oral tradition of Panyalahan and Pamijahan, Shyakh Abdul Muhyi is reported to have found the cave at Abd al-Rauf's suggestion made when Muhyi and Abd al-Rauf were in Mecca.

Oral traditions regarding regarding Shaykh Abdul Muhyi, some of which have become available in printed form (see Khaerusalam 1997), provide an emphasis different from that of the *Babad Pamijahan*. The 'manager of the sacred site", to borrow Fox's phrases, a 'broadcaster', uses oral traditions of the kind given below fo fill a gap in 'the sign of history'. To illustrate how a custodian gives an oral account of their *Wali* I will present here verbatim one such narrative written down by Zainal Musfofa bin Muhammad Jabidi, a custodian, 1978. In 1970 researchers from Padjadjaran University in Bandung, West Java, witnessed a custodian reciting the same narrative as that written down by Zainal Mustof. (Kossim 1974). When the Padjadjaran University team came to Pamijahan, a custodian was still designated by an older title, *panembahan*. The present oral narrative was evidently copied by the *panembahan*'s successor. Zainal Mustofa, an older brother of the current custodian.

To give more comprehensive perception of how villagers recognise the past I will describe this oral account in terms similar to those I employed in my discussion of the *Babad Pamijahan*. The *Babad Pamijahan* provided a genealogical framework for the reconciliation of mystical narratives relating to the realms of Sunda and Java. It also connects Shaykh Abdul Muhyi to the Nine Saints of Java (see Rinkes 1911). Tin the oral account, the contemporariness of Muhyi is given more attention. For this purpose, I describe the journey of Shaykh Abdul Muhyi and compare it with this journey as given in the *Babad Pamijahan*. The comparison produces a clear result: the Babad and the oral account fulfil different functions in the telling of the past. The oral text is segmented according to the main place referred in each unit of the narrative.

THE LIFE OF KANGJENG SYEKH

He is born in Mataram [A] around 814 H./1394 A.D. and is immediately taken to Geresik, his mother's home.

His Education: While still young he studies Qur'an in Geresik and Ampel, East Jawa. At the age of 19 he goes to the Pesantren Kuala in Aceh. He remains there for 8 years (833-841 H./1413-1421 A.D.). His teacher in Kuala is Syekh Abd Rauf Bin Abdul Jabbar bin Syekh Abdul Qadir Jaelani of Baghdad.

Travels to Baghdad and makes the Pilgrimage. At the age of 27 (841 H./1421 A.D.) he and his fellow students are taken by their teacher to visit Baghdad. There he visits the grave of Syekh Abdul Qadir and reads Qur'an with a Baghdadi ulama. From Baghdad he is taken to make the Pligrimage in Mecca . As they approach the House of God, his teacher receives inspiration, or dreams that among his santris there is one who will show the signs of Sainthood (kawalian). 'When you see/recognise this sign, the santri must be ordered to retreat from the world, and the place of his retreat must be sought out. It is a cave situated on the island of Java, in its western part and the very cave in which Syekh Abd Qadir Jaelani was initiated by his teacher, the Imam Sanusi. And it happened that at one time, about the time of the Asar prayers, Syekh Abd Muhyi and his fellow students were sitting together in the Masjidil Haram. His teacher saw sparks of light falling on his face and thought to himself that this surely was the sign promised him in the dream. The teacher did not however reveal this to his students.

Returns from Mecca. Having witnessed the sign, Syekh Abd Rauf and his students returned immediately to Kuala. On their arrival there, Syekh Abd Rauf instructed Syekh Abdul Muhyi to return straightway to Geresik and to withdraw to a cave in which Syekh Haji Abdul Qadir had been initiated by his teacher, Imam Sanusi. The cave was in the western part of the island of Java. There, his teacher ordered, Syekh H. Abdul Muhyi was to dwell, to perform his religious duties steadfastly (istiqomah ibadah) and to preach religion.

Returns to Geresik. After receiving his teacher's instructions, he went back to Geresik. Upon his arrival, he informed his parents and asked their blessing on his departure, because he was going in search of a place/cave to make his retreat, following his teacher's instructions. He then set out from Geresik, travelling in a westerly direction. He traversed the countryside until he reached Kampung Darma/Kadu Gede Lengkong in the district of Kuningan.

He Stays in Darma. In Kampung Darma he rested and got to know the local people, who, it happened, were already Muslims. Presented with his friendliness towards them and his piety, which rested on a high degree of learning, vision and accomplishments, the people became so attached to him that they pressed him to remain in Darma and to teach them religion. He complied with their wishes and remained in Darma for seven years. The news of his sojourn in Darma was sent back to his parents in Geresik. They immediately went to Darma and stayed with him there.

He Leaves Darma/Kuningan. After seven years' stay in Darma he took his leave from the people to search for the place that his teacher had told him about. He continued his journey, turning southward. He arrived in Pameungpeuk (South Garut) where he remained, teaching religion for two years. It was while he was in Pameungpeuk that his father was called back to God, and was buried there.

His Sojourn in Lebaksiuh. After residing for two years in Pameungpeuk, he resumed his travels, and came to Batuwangi. There he was welcomed and stayed to teach religion. We do not know how long he was there. It was while he was in Batuwangi that his mother died and was buried there. From Batuwangi he set out again on his journey and came to Lebaksiuh, remaining there for 4 years to propagate religion. In Lebaksiuh he suffered all kinds of harassment and opposition from the adherents of the pre-Islamic religion (Agama Budha). Yet he remained steadfast in the holy task of preaching the faith of Islam there, until it became widspread.

His Sojourn in Saparwadi (Pamijahan). After four years in Lebaksiuh, he continued his journeying in search of the place/cave where he was to practise meditation. He did not cease from praying to the Almighty that he might be shown the place he was seeking. It is then told that one day he lighted upon a valley. There he discovered a cave, whose appearance matched the description given by his teacher. Surely this was the cave that he was seeking (and now it is called the Cave of Pamijahan). He named the cave mujarrod (the place of purifying the mind). East of the cave he founded a settlement in which to reside and to propagate Islam. He named the settlement, or Kampung Saparwadi, which is now known as Pamijahan. The length of his stay in Saparwadi was 40 years. He passed away in Saparwadi on 14 Mulud 894 H./1474 A.D. and was buried in Saparwadi (Pamijahan). He came to us on 12 Mulud 854 H./ 1434 A.D.

The End. God Knows Best the Truth of This. If It Prove False, Return it to its Origin.

Pamijahan 13 Rewah 1390, Rebo Kaliwon

18 July 1978. Written by Z. Mustopa Bin M. Jabidi.

Unlike *Babad Pamijahan* oral tradition gives more lively narrative on the relation between the Sunda wali and his Sumateran Sufi Master, Abd al-Rauf. Acording to oral tradition, when Abdul Muhyi was studying Sufism in Mecca, before he established a settlement in the valley of Safarwadi, his master Abd al-Rual al-Singkili order him to meditate in the Safarwadi café. There are a popular recitations about this episode, and the role of custodians is quite important in preserving and transmitting them. A. A. Khaerusalam, a graduatet of Unswagati University in Cirebon and a custodian ath Abdul Muhyi's tobm wrote down and published what had originallu been a local oral history of the saint under the title *Sejarah Perjuangan* Shyakh Abdul Muhyi Waliyullah. As summary of the story indicates, the cave is internationalized' in it, and connected to a wider tradition of Islam.

> At the age of 27 he and his fellow students at the pasantren were taken by their Teacher to Bagdad. There they made a pilgrimage to the tomb of Syekh Abdul Qodir Jaelani Qoddasallahu Sirrohu. They stayed there for two years in order to take their licence in Islam.
>
> After the two years' sojourn in Bagdad, their Teacher took them straight away to the holy city of Mecca to perform the duty of the great pilgrimage.
>
> When they had all assembled at the House of God, their Teacher, Abdul Rauf received a sudden revelation that among his students there was one destined to sainthood.
>
> Within the revelation it was also conveyed that once the signs (of sainthood) became apparent, then he, Syekh Abdul Rauf must immediately order the person to return home and to seek out a cave on the western part of the island of Java to dwell there. That cave was actually the place where Syekh Abdul Qodir Jaelani had performed meditation, or tawajuh, and had received the teachings of Islam from his Teacher, the Imam Sanusi. About the hour of the mid-afternoon prayers, Syekh Abduh Muhyi and his friends had gathered at the Great Mosque of Mecca, when suddenly a light shone upon the face of Syekh Abdul Muhyi and this was perceived by the Teacher, Syekh Abdul Ra'uf. Witnessing this, Syekh Abdul Rauf was greatly amazed and remembered the revelation that he had received. Having considered the mater carefully, he was conviinced that his indeed was the sign of sainthood

which he had been expecting. And yet he kept all of tihis in his heart, mot revealling it even to his students. (Khaerusalam 1992).

There is nothing unsulua about custodians of sacred places preserving and transmitting histories in this way. Fox (Fox 2002), in his account of the role of custodian in the graveyard of Brawijaya in Trowulan and The Tombs of Senopati in Mataram Central Java, mentions the important part of juru kunci in broadcasting 'the history' of the dead. When the manuscripts, the Babad, are silent about a particular episode, then, the juru kunci fills the gap. He also states that "tombs in Java function as popular 'broadcast centres' for the historical traditions of Java, then it is the juru kunci who keep these traditions alive and relevant to contemporary Javanese" (2002: 172).

The custodian in Pamijahan narrates that in the cave of Safarwdi or Guha Pamijahan, Shaykh Abd al-Qadir al-Jailani obtained ijazah from his master Shaykh Sanusi. Abd al-Qadir al-Jailani (d.1077) is the founder of Qadiriyya born in Jilan. In Sunda the figure is still popular; people always pray for him. His name can not be detached from the majority of Sundanese Muslim practices. In West Java he is known as the Sufi founder who was able to perform miracles even after his is death. Adabuljairin clearly mentions the importance of the influence of Abd al-Qadir,

> "Dalam manaqib Shaykh dari segala Shaykh Abd Qadir Jailani, sesungguhnya arwah arwah para nabi dan wali Allah membentuk jasad sebagaimana terbentuknya jasad (p. 3).
>
> According to the book of Manaqib of Shaykh Abd al-Qadir Jailini, indeed, the spirits of the prophets, the friends of Allah are able to reappear as physically (p. 3)

The cave is also recognised as the place for meditation, or tempat tawajjuh, which connects the cave 'mystically' with the great tradition of Sufism. In the golden age of Syattariyah in Sunda, a new novice should perform two days meditation in the cave before he was initiated and took the oath of Syattariyah. This place is also recognised as a meeting place where Kangjeng Shaykh met other saints. This cave, which is 284 metres long and 24.5 wide, has several rooms, which are regarded as "doors." These doors connect the cave to the centre of pilgrimage in Mecca and to the tombs of other great wali such as Sunan Gunung Jati of Cirebon, Sunan Giri of Surabaya, and Shaykh Maulana Mansur of Banten.

Besides the doors, the cave also has a place for meditation, a place for the holy water, a small natural chamber that is a 'mosque' for men and one for women, and the hill of "the *haji* hat" or *Jabal kupiah*, the boarding school, or *pesantren*, kitchen, or *dapur*, and altars. The cave has a complete room for staying more than a week or even months for devotees who want to perform *tawajjuh*. According to oral tradition, when Shaykh Yusuf al-Makassri[22] was sought by the Dutch troops, he fled to the cave and consolidated and launched guerilla operation from this place. Oral tradition states that on Friday from 11 am--2 pm when the cave is closed, villagers believe that Kangjeng Shaykh performs Friday prayer or *jumaahan* there.

In the cave, visitors first take holy water, or *cai zam-zam* believed to come from Mecca, and put it in their cans, or *jariken*. After that, they climb to the masjid. This place is believed to be another *masjid karamat* where Kangjeng Shaykh Haji Abdul Muhyi used to *shalat* when he was doing meditation. Visitors often chant azan in the quba. For older visitors, it is difficult to stay in Masjid for long during the peak season because the oxygen is reduced by the hundreds of pilgrims and the nu jajap kaguha who bring push kerosene lamps, or patromak.. However, in the low season, in the month of Ramadhan, this place is very quiet and some visitors prefer to perform tirakat or tapa. For *nu ziarah biasa*, they stay here for ten minutes. They recite their own doa.

From the mosque, guides take visitors to *cai kahuripan* and *cai kajayaan*. These are rivers, which flow in the lowest part of the cave. Pamijahanese believe that anyone who takes a bath in *cai kahuripan* will be free from disease, and those who take bath in *cai kajayaan* will succeed in business.

After this, visitors exit from the opposite gate which leads them to Kampung Panyalahan, the second most popular sacred site in Pamijahan. In this village is buried Shaykh Khatib Muwahid. He is not a wali but is a pious man with the title of Shaykh. Shaykh Khatib Muwahid married Kangjeng Shaykh Abdul Muhyi's sister. *Nu nganteur kag guha* have an important role since they can suggest whether pilgrims visit Shaykh Khatib Muwahid's tomb or not. In the peak season *nu nganteur kag guha* are very busy. Sometimes they do not suggest that people continue their sacred journey to Panyalahan but rather that they return to Pamijahan so that *nu nganteur kag guha* will have more opportunity to guide other visitors.

The caretaker of Shaykh Khatib Muwahid's tomb in Panyalahan states that only 15 percent of all pilgrims who come to Pamijahan continue their sacred journey to Panyalahan. Realising this problem, the custodian Panyalahan has provided incentives for *nu nganteur kag guha* to encourage their clients to continue their visitation by going on to Panyalahan.

The custodian at Panyalahan applies the same system as Pamijahan. The custodian identifies visitors and assigns a staff member to accompany them and perform *tawassul* at the tomb of Khatib Muwahid. Unlike in Pamijahan, the custodian of Panyalahan is present in his office the full day. They do not need to share with other families as in Pamijahan. He is the sole single care taker.

F. The Prescribed Sequences

Ritual consists of symbolic and social signs (Turner 1966; Parmentier 1996). Between symbolic and social signs there is a medium, as Catherine Bell has pointed, out called discourse. Bell (Bell 1992) tries to elaborate further what has been stated by Geertz (1976: 355) about the cultural and social dimension of ritual by proposing discourse, the third category, which frames individually practised particular rituals or a discourse. The model developed by Geertz (1976) and Bell (1992), to some extent, resembles the Peircean (Peirce 1997; Parmentier 1994) idea whereby there are three elements of a sign: *representamen, reference,* and *interpretant*. *Representamen* is a form or structure. Reference is an individual meaning, and interpretant is a public interpretation, or, using Bell's terms, a discourse.

Pilgrimage, like the plot of a story, is constructed by various events. Pilgrims choose their own succession of times and places. Different sequences often indicate the pilgrims' different objective and spiritual levels. Furthermore, the sequence also indicates a negotiating process related to signification. In Pamijahan, *ziarah* represents a sacred sequence as the main text as indicated by the official narrative found in the manual of pilgrimage or in the book written by the family of the custodians. However, pilgrimage in Pamijahan also represents the subtext, which is open to individual interpretation: a text, which appears within the main text. Furthermore, based on sequential analyses, pilgrimage is connected to other systems of meaning (intertextuality) where the more public and shared meaning can 'regiment' our interpretation of the sequence (cf Parminter 1994).

[A] passing the gate or kaca-kaca

[B] reporting to the custodian and submitting an amount of money

[C] accompaniment by the staff of the custodian to the Shrine

[D] performance of ritual tawassul led by the custodian,

[E] return with the custodian back to his office, or

[F] continuation to the cave, [F1] accompanied by the lantern man

[G] going to the Panyalahan Custodian and Shrine

[H] back to Pamijahan passing the custodian office

[I] return home

Figure 28 The Sequence of Ziarah

This chain of events is taken from the manual given by the custodians. The string can be read in terms of various strategies. As is evident the main text consists of a standard order as stated by the custodian and the book of pilgrimage: it is the syntax, which is accepted by most Pamijahanese. The logical concept is tightly dependent on the point of view of the 'storyteller' (e.g. Danesi and Parron, 1999:249). From the list of possibilities of prescribed sequences, we can identify that the most important point is visiting the shrine [D] whether accompanied by the staff or not. Furthermore, the pattern also sugested that passing the gate and reporting to the custodian office is important. After that, going to the cave and Panyalahan is the next prescribed route.

The linear aspects described above can be abstracted as follows.

#									
1.	A	B	C	D	E	F		H	I
2.	A	B	C	D	E			H	I
3.	A	B	C	D	E			H	I
4.	A	B		D		F		H	I
5.	A	B		D				H	I
6.				D	E	F	G	H	I
7.	G			D		F	G	H	I
9.	(G)			(F)		(D)		H	I
10.	(g)			(F)					I

Figure 29 The possible strategies in the pilgrimage 'narrative'

However, if we look carefully, there is a contrast between the sequence of no. 1, 2, 3, 4, 5 with no. 6, 7, and 8. Instead of passing the gate [A] and the custodian office of Pamijahan [B], some pilgrims go, first, to the custodian of Panyalahan [G] (see the sequence no. 6—8). From the point of view of the book of pilgrimage written by the Pamijahanese, such a journey is not proper. For them, pilgrimage should started from the gate, or *kaca-kaca* and pass the custodian's office located between the gate (*kaca-kaca*) and the shrine of Shaykh Abdul Muhyi. For the villagers the proper journey should follow proper sequences as stated by the manual. Finally, the sequence of no. 9 is not a preferred succession because according to them, pilgrims do not pay respect to the Shaykh.

There are several reasons why pilgrims choose this route (sequence no. 6--8). The first may be simple ignorance, they do not know what should be done first. Some pilgrims said that when they arrived at the car park outside the sacred village, some one offered guidance and led them directly to Panyalahan [G→D→F→G→H→I] or [G→F→D→H→I] instead to Pamijahan first [A] →[B]→[C].... However, they may have come once before and used the Panyalahan route [G] and so they consider it the appropriate method because it was suggested by the custodian of Panyalahan [G]. Another reason for the use of this route may be a special purpose suggested by their local teacher.

If the syntagmatic axis was applied here, then we have to find an underlaying system that puts events in an acceptable string of pilgrimage. It is clear that, from the point of view of Pamijahanese, *ziarah* to the shrine of Muhyi has two 'minimal unit' (1) **reporting** to the custodian [B] of Pamijahan and (2) **visiting** the tomb of Muhyi or {[B]→[D]}. Reporting (*ngalapor*), in fact, is the crucial event in Pamijahan. There is a proverb among the villagers that "if you come I can see your face, if you return I can see your back." Visiting the tomb is the core of *ziarah*. Of course, people can create their own combination. However, such a combination will influence the quality of the *ziarah*. In this regard, the custodian states that there are three kinds of sequence: (1) perfect, or *sampurna*, (2) good , or *sae*, and (3) in appropriate or *henteu dipikahoyong*.

In the view of the custodians the perfect sequence (sae pisan) should consisted of the full series of [A, B, C, D, E, F, G, H, I]. The *sae* or good sequence should consist of [B, F] or [A, B, C, D, E, F]. The inappropriate sequence is the sequence without the elements of reporting [B] and visiting [F].

It is a fact that the structure of the pilgrimage, from a sequential analysis, consists of two compulsory elements: **reporting to key bearer** and **visiting the shrine**. Pilgrims, of course, have to visit to decide their preferred progression. There are some possibilities to be inserted between [B] and [F]. However, the choice is limited.

The custodian office and the shrine are located at the centre while other sacred sites including Panyalahan are at the periphery (see Chapter 5). The non-smoking area is the most sacred territory where the compulsory sequences take place.

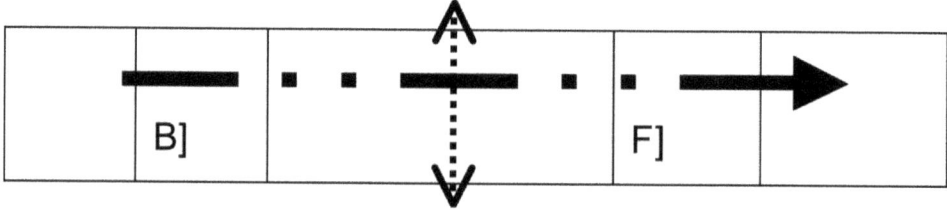

Figure 30 Syntagmatic and Paradigmatic Axis

Ritual is a structure; but as the result of alternative interpretations and contestation the rigidity of the structure as both a sensible and intlleligible order is not stable. On the other hand, in Pamijahan, the custodian states that all pilgrims are guests of the wali. To be a pilgrim is to follow the prescription stated by the book or custodian directly. It is easy for the custodian to differentiate between the sacred and the profane.[23] If a peddler comes to the sites to sell something to the villagers or pilgrims, then he should not be categorised as pilgrim. Similarly, if a peddler came to the kuncen and went to the shrine to perform *tawassul* and then sold his goods, he would be considered a pilgrim. For the custodian of Pamijahan, as long as the people report to his office and carry out the intermediary ritual, then they should be considered pilgrims. The custodian even says that if peddlers achieve good fortune in the market after visitation to the tomb then they are indeed blessed. In other words, it may be difficult for the custodian to identify all true *niat* but it is easier for him to identify whether visitors have followed the prescribed sequence or not.

In Islam, there is a compulsory precondition for performing *ibadah*: these are first true intention, and the second is true action or *amalan*, and the third is knowledge. Thus, the proper pilgrimage should meet such prerequisites. However, intention is an intelligble aspect for the custodian. In the ritual *ngadaftar* or subsequently the custodian often asks the visitor's intention. Most of the visitors, according to the custodian, state general motives such as solving their problems and seeking *barokah* from the process. Often, more specific motives will be retained in their hears and delivered to God personally in the front of the Muhyi tomb. Some times, *nu ziarah* also tell the custodian in detail and ask his help. Based on my interviews, I found some visitors have huge debts and come to Pamijahan for help. Some of them have even run away from their wives and families because their cannot support their family life.

The custodian says that all *niat* should be translated into *amalan* or action. He states that if you have a good *niat*, then God will grant you a reward. If you have a good *niat* and you are able to actualise it, God will grant you multiple rewards; but if you are unable to actualise it, God will grants you only one reward. Action is the second stage in the ritual. The kuncen explains that *amalan*, good deeds, without knowledge will reduce the rewards. Knowledge, or *ilmu*, is basic to perform in the ritual. In the case of pilgrimage, the custodians feel responsible for help people in this third area.

Knowledge of the ritual can be learned from various sources. For instance, a group of the pilgrims often brings their own *ulama* to the sites in order to get lessons and guidance so that their *niat* and action are performed in harmony. In reality, the custodians are still perceived many visitors as the main source of knowledge in the village. This is due to the belief that ritual pilgrimage is connected to the local codes for which the kuncen is the key bearer. For instance, the kuncen will allow visitors to perform their own *niat* and amalan with some precautions. Ideally, pilgrims are not expected to stay in the sacred site for more than a week. In fact, there some specialists who spent more that 41 days in the shrine. For this reason, the kuncen will give special permission. The custodian also will allow specialists who ask special permission to enter the main room in the shrine. In normal circumstances, such an area is a forbidden place.

The specialists and 'ordinary pilgrims' may perform different sequences. The minimal structure, however, should be tightly connected to what the custodian calls "proper conduct", that is, reporting to his office and visiting the shrine. However, if we carefully examine the table of sequences, the space for negotiation is apparent. While the power of the kuncen regulates the prescribed sequence by limiting the accepted choice of 'paths', others still have space for negotiation as seen in what the kuncen often calls *sae pisan, kirang sae,* or *teu dipikahoyong*.

Ziarah practice in Pamijahan is not only influenced by outsiders but also by the contestation among the groups who claim to have the same ancestral sources. As seen in the table above structural variation coincides with the two different sequences prescribed by the two different custodian offices: Pamijahan and Panyalahan. And indeed in practice, the custodian of Pamijahan's account may be contested by the custodian of Panyalahan who also shares the same lineage.

ENDNOTES

[1] How the Five Pillars help us to remember the basic obligation of being Islam.

[2] See A. Yusuf Ali (translator), The Holy Quran: Text, Translation and Commentary.

[3] "Nu *Jaroh* daratang teu diondang ku urang, maranehna datang sorangan ku sabab di dieu aya Wali."

[4] Makom meaning 'tomb'. The word originates from Arabic meaning 'station'.

[5] This is a manual of pilgrimage which is sold in the custodian office or in the gateway to the shrine of Shaykh Abd a-Muhyi.

[6] Ibn Taimiyah (1976) Ibn Taimiya's Struggle against Popular Religion: with an Annotated Translation of his Kitab iqtida as-sirat al-mustaqima mukhalafat ashab al-jahim, Mouton The Hague.

[7] Pamijahanaese translate the word *wasillah* to mean (al-Maidah: 35) *lantaran*. *Lantaran* can also be translated as '*a cause*'.

[8] salihin

[9] '*Eta teh disebat* **tawassul**'. Tawassul from Arabic al -wasillah meaning ' means' or 'a way' as seen in Quran Al-Maidah: 35 and Al-Isra: 57 " Tawassul meaning to find a way. *The tawassul* ritual is the most important sequence in pilgrimage at the *maqom* of Kangjeng Shaykh Haji Abdul Muhyi.

[10] In Sundanese, *nyantelkeun* originates from the word *cantel* meaning 'to hook'. Attaching the affixes ny- and –keun produces the meaning of 'to put something on', so *nyantelkeun* is 'to entrust something to someone', or in this case 'to attach our wishes to the holiness of the wali'.

[11] Baqing is the graveyard in Mecca where martyrs are buried.

[12] The nominal construction pa+noun+an in Sundanese means 'a means for x' or 'a place of x'. In this case, pa + *kuncen* + an can be translated as 'a place for/of caretakers'.

[13] (see also Jamhari, p. 130).

[14] Sajarah Sukapura

[15] At that time there was a tension between those who made a contact with the Dutch administrator and the Moslem movements. The result of this conflict was that the Bupati Wiradadaha was exiled to Ceylon and his successors were divided. Oral narratives recite that before Wiradadha was exiled, he ordered Kangjeng Shaykh to send a rosary to him in Batavia (Jakarta).

[16] *Saha bae anu nyisikudi kana katangtuan anu parantos diserenkeun ti luhur... aya basa kaluhur aja sirungan ongsor aja oyodan* (The Kuncen)

[17] "Ulah aya deui manah ka sisi ka gigir sarta pangdumeuheus teh ka pakuburkan Wali karana sidiq mahabbah sara peracaya (iman) kana karamatna anu di paparinkeun ku Allah ka para Wali" (Adabuljairin, p. 6)

[18] Dimana dongkap kana panto maqam anu dilebetkeun (ngalengkah) kedah sampean tengah anu tipayun ...lajeng linggih sila sing rekep sakumaha tatakrama adak kapangagung anu aya oayuneun urang lajeng uluk salam kawaliyullah (p. 6)

[19] "Assalamaualaikum ya Kangjeng Shaykh Haji Abdul Muhyi wa man haulahu min amwatin al mursalina antumu as-sabiquna wa nahnu insya alllahu bikum la hiquna" (p. 7)

[20] 1) *qulhu* eleven times, 2) *falak bi nas* one time, 3) *fatiha* one time, 4) the first *ayat* of *albaqarah* one time, (and surah?) 5) *ayat kursi* one time, (followed by *al-baqarah*; [Surah 284] 6) the last ayah of *surah al-Baqarah* one time, 7) wa fu anna wagfirlana (al-B aqarah), sakawasana, 8) some personal *dua*, 9) *Shalawat* 10) *istigfar* 11) *tahlil* 12) *zikir* and finally 13) *dua tawassull*.

[21] "Nitipkeun jisim abdi kana awal jisim abdu sareng ka pun Bapa sareng ka pun Biang sareng ka pun Bojo sareng ka pun Anak, Incu, jisim abdi sareng ka sadayana dulur-dulur jisim abdi sareng ka sadayana ahli-ahli jisim abdi sareng kasobat-sobat jisim abdi ti kawit dinten ieu dugi kayaumil qiyamat nitipkeun ka dampal gamparan nyuhunkeun ulah lepat tina kalimah asyhadu ana la ilaha ila allahu wa asyadu anna Muhammada ar-rasulullah."

[22] For the Dutch accounts on Shaykh Yusuf activities and his relation with the Hajj from Carrang or Shaykh Abdul Muhyi see F. Dehan, De Prianger.

[23] In his account on pilgrimage at The Shrine of Mu'in al-din Chishti in Ajmer, Currie (1992) states that there are four motives behind the practices. The first is a practical motives such finding the help from the saints. The second is material motives where people come to the site in order to find material benefit directly. Curry reports that pilgrims come to the shrine only for performing special ritual..."they were at the shrine for purposes linked with life-cycle rituals." (Currie 1992:133). This third motive, according to Curry is of declining. The fourth motive is the relation between the Creator and the created such as in mystical terms, which is called by Curry as spiritual motive (p. 133).

Chapter 10: Conclusion

Throughout the discussion presented in this volume I have attempted to demonstrate the nature and function of narrative in the context of the sacred site of Pamijahan.

I found that even though within the faculty of our minds there resides the possibility to produce an unending chain of 'semiosis', in fact a 'limit to interpretation' is present in 'the signifying order'. Culture regiments our interpretation of particular signs. To see this in the context of Pamijahan means to reveal the 'signs', the 'references' and the 'interpretant' or the possibilities of interpretation and negotiation related to the ancestral narratives performed by the villagers. A careful examination of various interrelated representations of the signs of the *wali* reveals that the pragmatics around these signs are dense in the society of Pamijahan.

It is evident that in Pamijahan the 'past' is towed into the present through *tali paranti*, the modalities of narrative. These are the 'signs of the past' containing the sayings of the ancestors, *saur sepuh*. Most written sacred narratives in the village, namely the historical *Babad Pamijahan*, the manual of pilgrimages, or *Adab Al-Jairin*, the guidances of Sufism, or the *Kitab Wali* and even some recent pamphlets and publications, all rely upon the key word of the *karuhun*, the ancestors' testimony and teaching. By inviting the testimony of the *karuhun* into the narratives, the past is 'broadcast'.

However, the narration of the past always leaves space for negotiation or contestation. Narrative is an open text which invites readers to execute their own signification. This reading process takes place in the contestation for precedence that is expressed in different narratives and symbolic acts within the village. Accordingly, the 'grand narrative' of Shaykh Abdul Muhyi is in fact fragmented into various smaller narratives or metaphors. Within a structuralist Saussurean or Levi-Straussean paradigm these metaphors of the past could be seen as a rather rigid structure of the *langue*. Such unconscious phenomena, however, are balanced by the pragmatic, conscious narratives produced when the villagers deliberately bring into play various symbolic signs within their narratives: more than one door of metaphor can be opened to tap the signs of the *wali*.

The narratives of the ancestors, then, are not only retold but also translated into metaphors of space in which the four main lines of Abdul Muhyi's descent occupy the four sides, the *pongpok*, of the village.

There is also evidence enough to support the argument that the villagers assume that the *wali's* blessing, *barakah*, inheres in Pamijahan. Thus their main responsibility is to make sure that the blessing stays in their hamlets through ritualized language and behaviour, as may be seen in the Sufi practice of the *khataman*, through the mediation, or *tawassul* of the *kuncen* on behalf of visiting pilgrims and through other kinds of service rendered to them. The management of this sacred 'business' is then institutionalised and distributed among the main families. Within the *pakuncenan*, all members of the descendants of Shaykh Abdul Muhyi enjoy a very fruitful access to the blessings that flow side by side with the coming of pilgrims, or *tamu*, from outside.

Glossary

Abangan	A variant of Islam perceived to be not of the 'pure' tradition which blends Muslim practice with local beliefs in Java
Adzan	To recite the call to prayer; this ritual is also used by the villagers on entering the caves at Pamijahan
Ajengan	Religious scholar in the Sunda region
Amalan	Formulaic chants given to pilgrims by the custodian and the ajengan
Apuputra	Genealogical term, "begat", thus "he/she has offspring"
barakah	Divine favour, blessing received by any good Muslim. In the local context of Pamijahan, this could be a blessing given to the place, to the wali.
Babad	A chronicle, sometimes also indicates "a manual" for making something, i.e. *Babad Kawung, see below*.
Babad Pamijahan	The chronicle of Pamijahan
Babad Kawung	'Instructions on the cultivation and use of the sugar palm'.
Babad Tanah Jawi	The Chronicle of Java
bedog	Sundanese machete
Buku Sajarah	A book of history
Buruh	Unskilled labourer in Pamijahan
Cai zam-zam	Water from the spring in the cave of Pamijahan, the name is taken from a famous sacred spring in Mecca
Cai kajayaan	Holy water from another spring in the cave, believed to give invulnerability
Cai kahuripan	Water from another spring in the cave, believed to heal any physical ailment
Darul Islam	"Home of believers", the Islamic state
Desa	Village
Desa pamijahan	The village of Pamijahan
Eyang	Grand-grand father/mother, also used for 'the ancestors"

fatwâ	Interpretation or advice given by religious experts regarding theological and juridical cases
Fuqaha	Expert in Islamic jurisprudence
Guha Karamat	The "Sacred Cave", the most revered site in Pamijahan
Hadith	Traditions based on the actions and sayings of the Prophet Muhammad
Hadiyah	"Gift", the act of reciting holy texts as a gift for the souls of the dead
Hajj	Pilgrimage to Mecca
Hajj from Carang	Deprecatory name given by Dutch colonial officers to refer to the "rebel" from Karang
Hikayat	Traditional story, account, history
Ibadah	Pious activity
Ijazah	Local inauguration given to a person who has completed a certain stage of Sufi learning
Ilmu karang	Magical knowledge associated with the karang area, both pre-dating Islam and after
Imam	Muslim leader
Isnad	Intellectual chain of transmission in Sufism
Jabal kupiah	The "rock of the hat", a formation in the wall inside the sacred cave
Jubah	Long robe of Arabic style
Jumaah	Friday prayers
Kabupaten,	Regency
Kabuyutan	The term for a sacred space believed to have been inhabited and used for ritual purposes by the ancestors for centuries, yet still evident
Kebatinan	Batin, the inner aspects of the human being, hence Kebatinan, a set of practices among Javanese mystics
Kacamatan	Subdistrict
Kaca-kaca	The main gate to the Pamijahan area
kâfir billah	Unbeliever
Kampung	Village

Kampung naga	A traditional village located in the Tasikmalaya regency believed to have connections with the old Sundanese Kingdoms
Kakantun	Heritage
Karamat	Sacred
Kapamijahanan	Spatial concept referring to the Pamijahan entity
Kapongpokan	Spatial concept associated metaphorically with the tomb
Karang	Limestone, name of a place close to Pamijahan
Karangnunggal	"Single limestone formation, name of a place close to Pamijahan believed to have spiritual power derived from the pre-Islamic period
Karuhun	Ancestors
karuhun urang	Our ancestors
Karya sastra	Literary works
Kasauran karuhun	Ancestors' words or sayings
Kebatinan	Inner knowledge, Javanese mysticism
Kejaksaan	District attorney
Kelurahan	Village administration
Kemusnahan naskah	The disappearance of manuscripts
Ketua pongpok	Leader of the four lines of family of the wali
Kepala desa	Village head
Kesusastraan lama	Old or traditional literature
Khatib	Leader of the Friday prayers as imam who may also give sermons
Kitab Papakem Kuning	"Book of the Yellow Guide", oldest manual of guidance on Sufism in Pamijahan
Kitab Patorekan Shaykh Abdu	The Catechism of Shaykh Abdul Muhyi
kitab tarekat	Book of Sufi orders
kolot urang	Our ancestors, cf. karuhun
kokocoran	The "flowing of rivers", genealogy, lineage

Kitab Istiqal Tarekat Qadiriyyah-Naqhsabandiyyah	Book on the Qadiryyah and Naqshabandiyyah orders
Kris	Dagger
Kulambu	Bed canopy, the silk covering of the sacred tomb
kuncen	Key bearers, custodians of the Pamijahan areas
Imu laduni	Special knowledge believed to endow the adept with a capacity for quick learning; in the local context, the ability to be in two places at once
Lauk mijah	"Fish hatchlings", metaphor given to the Pamijahan area as a place for developing spirituality
Maghrib	Sunset prayers
Makom	1. An advanced station in Sufism, 2. a grave yard
Makom Bengkok	The grave of Bengkok
Makom Panyalahan	The grave of Panyalahan
Makom Yudanagara	The grave of Yudanagara
Makom Kangjeng Shaykh	The grave of Kangjeng Shyakh
Martabat tujuh	The seven grades of being, the mystical doctrine of the Shattariyah order
Maung	Tiger
Masjid	Mosque
Masjid Karamat	Sacred mosque
Menyan	Incense
Mutih	"White diet", a program of fasting for one conducting mystical practice, consuming only rice and water.
Muhammadiyah	The chief revivalist institution promoting a return to the Quran and the Sunnah
Naskah kuno	Old manuscripts, handwritten texts
Neangan tarekah	Finding a path, way
Niatt	Intention
Nu nganteur	A guide to the cave or graveyard
Orang Jawa Barat	The people of West Java
paesan	Tomb

Paimaran	A place in the mosque from where the imam leads ritual
Pakuncenan	Custodianship
Pamujaan	Place for worship
Pakuat-pakait	Interconnected/ness
Pamasalahan	The place for solving problems
Panyalahan	Village of those accused of the wrong siting of their village
Perdikan	Villages free of taxes under the time of Mataram's influence
Pasantren	Traditional Islamic boarding school
Penghulu	A person in charge in religious affairs; traditional intermediary between the village and state
Pitutur	Narration, words of the ancestors
Pongpok	The four "sides" around Abdul Muhyi's tomb, used to indicate the lines of descent from the Saint's wives; a metaphor of social division
Punduh	Government apparatus in the village dealing with local administrative matters
Pancuran	Spring water from a bamboo pipe
Pangeran Seda Lautan	The "king who died at sea"
paranti	Customary tool, place regularly used for an activity, hence custom, tradition
Paririmbon	Various texts important to the villagers, associated with local knowledge and Sufism, containing instructions and prohibitions
Patilasan	Place which has been used by ancestors, hence, grave
Pegon	Javanese and Sundanese written in Arabic characters
Petunjuk	Guidance
Perjuangan	Mission (of Abdul Muhyi)
Pitutur karuhun	Sayings of the ancestors
Pucuk	Green leaves, new sprouts, associated with hope for the future
Priyayi	Aristocracy

Qaraba	Relatives, close linkages
Rabiulawwal (Maulid)	Third month of the Islamic calendar, in which the birth of the Prophet is celebrated
Rajab	Seventh month of the Islamic calendar, in which the Night Journey of the Prophet is celebrated
Saur Sepuh	Narratives of the ancestors
Santri	Pupil in a pesantren
Shalat	Daily prayers
Shalat wajib	The five daily formal obligatory prayers
Sharî'ah	Islamic law
Shattariyyah	The Shattariyah Sufi order
Sastra	Literature
Sastra lama	Old literature
Sastra modern	Modern literature
Sejarah	History
Sejarah Babad Kuna	Genre of narrative of pre- and early Islamic propagation in a region
Sastra tradisional	Traditional literature
Sepuh urang	Our ancestors
Syahadat	Statement of Islamic doctrine, recited during the obligatory prayers, and on conversion
Surutu	Cigar, often used by the locals in traditional Sundanese villages as an offering
Silsilah	Genealogy
Surat wasiat	Testaments
Tajallî	Illumination
Tali paranti	The strings of custom
Talqin	Instructions given to the *murid* (pupils) of a Sufi order; also instructions to the soul around the moment of death to prepare it for the hereafter
Tanam paksa	Forced agriculture, the enforced cultivation of plantation crops
Tanah pasidkah, 97, 116	Charity lands, once free from land tax, but today under government imposed taxes

Tarekah	The Way, Sufi order; also Sundanese word for any method or way to achieve an end
Tarekat	Sufi Order
Tasawwuf	Sufism
Tatar Sunda,	The Sundanese region
Tawassul	Mediation
Tempat nu ziarah	Pilgrimage place
Tempat penziarahan pertama	The first stage of visitation in Pamijahan
Tempat cai zam-zam	Place of sacred water
Tempat cai kahuripan	Place of healing water
Tempat tapa,	Place for meditation
Tempat tawajjuh	Place for coming "face to face with God", place for contemplation or concentration
Tentara Islam Indonesia	Indonesian Islamic soldiers of the Islamic separatist rebellion in West Java
Tetengger	Tombstone
Tirakat	Vigilance
Torikoh Shattariyyah	Shattariyah order, Sundanese rendering
Tukang batik	Batik trader
Turunan	Successors
Turuq	Arabic plural form of tarekah
Tutuik	Words or sayings of the ancestors, meaning close to tuturan in Sundanese
Tuturan	Sayings
Ujian sarjana	Examination for achieving a degree
Ulama,	Islamic scholars
Urang Jawa,	The Javanese people
Urang gunung	People from the mountain
Urang wetan	People from the east, hence, the Javanese
Urang Karang	People of the Karang area
Urang hindu	Hindus

Wujud makhlûq	The realities of mankind
Wahdat al-wujûd	The Unity of Being, mystical philosophy
Wali	Saint
Wali Sanga,	The Nine Saints of Java
Warisan kebudayaan	Cultural heritage
Wudu	Ablutions performed before the formal prayers
Wujud Haq Ta'la,	The Reality, Essence of the Most High
Yayasan Kakaramatan	The non-profit Institution of the sacred places of Pamijahan
Ziarah	Pilgrimage

Figure 31 The custodian of Pamijahan

Figure 32 Heading towards the cave at 2.15 AM

Figure 33 Peak season

Figure 34 Pilgrims from Tasikmalaya

Figure 35 Pilgrims from East Java (about 800 km from Pamijahan) hired deluxe buses to reach Pamijahan (1997)

Figure 36 Pilgrims in the cave of Pamijahan (1997)

Figure 37 Pilgrims queue at the gate of the cave of Pamijahan at midnight (1996)

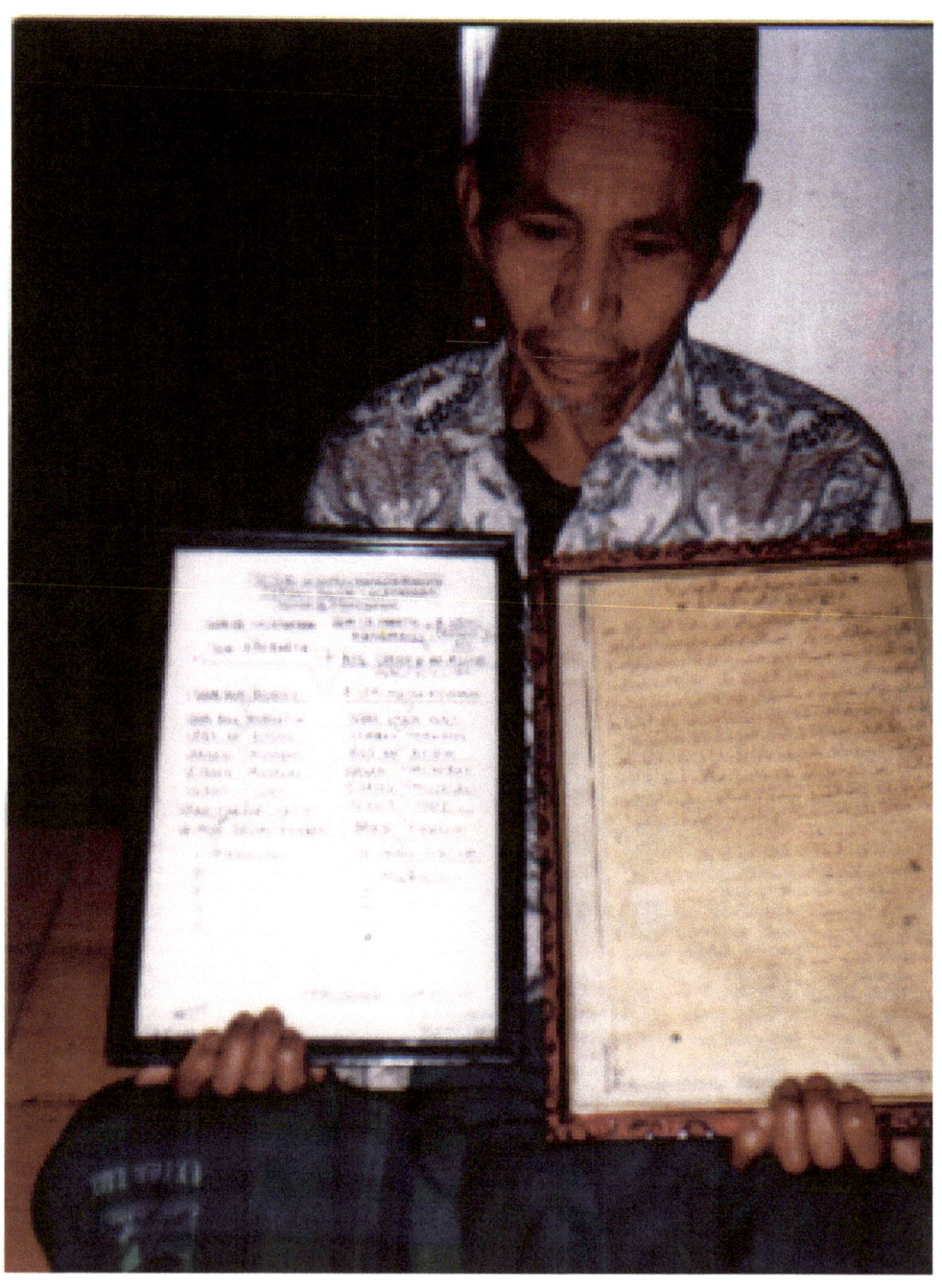

Figure 38 The Custodian of Bengkok with his genealogy (*silsilah*)

Figure 39 The custodian of Pandawa

Figure 40 The custodian of Panyalahan in his office

Figure 41 The grand mosque of Pamijahan in 1996

Figure 42 The grand mosque of Pamijahan in 1910 (Rinkes 1910)

Bibliography

Alfian, Teuku Ibrahim. 1987. *Perang di Jalan Allah: Perang Aceh 1873--1912*. Jakarta: Pustaka Sinar Harapan.

Alisjahbana, S. Takdir. 1961. *Puisi Lama*. 5 ed. Jakarta: PT PUSTAKA RAKJAT.

Atja. 1968. Tjarita Parahijangan: naskah titilar karuhun urang Sunda abad ka-16 Masehi. Bandung: Jajasan Kebudjaan Nusalarang.

Atja, Ayatrohaedi. 1984/1985. Nagarakertabhumi. Yogyakarta: Departemen Pendidikan dan Kebudayaan Direktorat Jenderal Kebudayaan Proyek Penelitian dan Pengkajian Kebudayaan Nusantara (Javanologi).

Atja, Drs. 1968. *Tjarita Parahijangan*. Bandung: Jajasan Nusalarang.

Atja, Saleh Danasasmita. 1981. Amanat dari Galunggung (kropak 632 dari Kabuyutan Ciburuy, Bayongbong-Garut). Jawa Barat: Proyek Pengembangan Permuseuman Jawa Barat.

Azra, Azyumardi. 2001. Networks of the Ulama in the Haraymayn: Connections in the Indian Ocean Region. *Studia Islamika: Indonesian Journal For Islamic Studies* 8 (2).

Bachtiar, H.W. 1992. The Religion of Java: A commentary. *Madjalah Ilmu-Ilmu Sastra* V (1).

Becker, Alton L A. 1995. *Beyond Translation: essays towards a modern philology*. Ann Arbor: University of Michigan Press.

Bell, Cathrine. 1992. *Ritual Theory: Ritual Practice*.

Bellwod, Peter. 1996. Hierarchy, Founder Ideology and Austronesian Expansion. In *Origins, Ancestry and Alliance*. Canberra: The Comparative Austronesian Project Research School of Pacific and Asian Studies The Australian national University.

Brakel, L.F. 1977. *The Hikyat Muhammad Hanafiyyah: A Medieval Moslem-Malay Romance*. The Hague: Martinus Nijhoff Bibliotheca Indonesia 12.

Bruinessen, Martin van. 1994. Origins and Development of the Sufi Orders. *Studia Islamika: Indonesian Journal For Islamic Studies* I (1):1-23.

Christomy, Tommy. 2001. Shattariyah Tradition in West Java: The Case of Pamijahan. *Studia Islamika: Indonesian Journal For Islamic Studies* 8 (2):55-82.

Culler, Jonathan. 1975. *The Pursuit of Signs: Semiotics, Literature, Deconstruction*. Itacha: Cornell University Press.

———. 1975. *Structuralist Poetics: Structuralism, Linguistics, and the Study of Literature*. Itacha: Cornell University Press.

Dhofier, Z. 1980. *Tradisi Pesantren: Studi tentang Pandangan Hidup Kyai*. Jakarta: Lembaga Penelitian, Pendidikan dan Penerangan Ekonomi dan Sosial. Jakarta: Lembaga Penelitian, Pendidikan dan Penerangan Ekonomi dan Sosial.

Djajadiningrat, Hoesein. 1913. *Critische beschouwing van de Sadjarah Banten: bijdrage ter kenschetsing van de javaansche geschiedschrijving*. Haarlem: Joh. Enschede en Zonem.

———. 1965. Local Traditions and the Study of Indonesian History. In *An Introduction to Indonesian Historiography*. New York: Cornell University Press.

E Kossim, Ahmad Mansur, Rosad Amidjaja, E Suhardi Ekadjati. 1974. Sejarah Masuk dan Berkembangnya Agama Islam di Jawa Barat Khususnya di Cirebon dan Pamijahan. Bandung: Fakultas Sastra Universitas Padjadjaran.

Eco, Umberto. 1979. *A Theory of Semiotics*. Bloomington: Indiana University Press.

———. 1999. *Kant and the Platypus: Essays on Language and Cognition*. Translated by A. McEwen. London.

Edi S, Ekadjati. 2000. *Direktori Edisi Naskah Nusantara*. Jakarta: Yayasan Obor Indonesia.

Eickelman, Dale F. 1990. *Muslim travellers: Pilgrimage, Migration, and the Religious Imagination*. London: Routledge.

Eickelman, Dale F. 1976. *Moroccan Islam tradition and society in a pilgrimage center*. Austin and London: University of Texas Press.

Ekadjati, E. Suhardi. 1982. *Ceritera Dipati Ukur Karya Sastra Sejarah Sunda*. Jakarta: Pustaka Jaya.

Ekadjati, Edi S. 1983. Naskah Sunda Lama di Daerah Kotamadya dan Kabupaten Bandung. Bandung: Proyek Penelitian Bahasa dan Sastra Indonesia dan Daerah Jawa Barat, Departemen Pendidikan dan Kebudayaan.

———. 1995. *Kebudayaan Sunda: Suatu Pendekatan Sejarah*. Pustaka Jaya: Jakarta.

Elizabeth Mertz, Richard J. Parmentier, ed. 1985. *Semiotic Mediation: Sociocultural and Psychological Perspectives*. Orlando: Academic Press.

———, ed. 1985. *Semiotic Mediation: Sociocultural and Psychological Perspectives*. New York, Toronto, Sydney, Tokyo, Orlando, London, San Diego: Academic Press, Inc.

Fathurhman, Oman. 1999. *Menyoal Wahdatul Wujud*. Jakarta: Penerbit Mizan.

Fox, James J. 1986. *Bahasa, Sastra, dan Sejarah: Kumpulan Karangan Mengenai Masyarakat Pulau Roti*. Translated by S. Djokodamono, *Indonesian Linguistics Development Project*. Jakarta: Djambatan.

———. 1991. Ziarah Visits to the tombs of the wali, the founders of Islam on Java. In *Islam in the Indonesian Social Context*, edited by M. C. Ricklefs. Clayton: Monash University.

———. 1996. The Transofrmation of Progenitor Lines of Origin: Patterns of Precedence in Eastern Indonesia. In *Origins, Ancestry and Alliance*, edited by C. S. James J Fox. Canberra: The Comparative Austronesian Project Research School of Pacific and Asian Studies The Australian national University.

———. 1997. Place and Landscape in Comparative Austronesian Perspective. In *The Poetic Power of Place*, edited by J. J. Fox. Canberra: The Comparative Austronesian Project Research School of Pacific and Asian Studies The Australian national University.

———. 2002. Ancestors, Saints and Heroes in Contemporary Indonesia. In *The Potent Dead*, edited by A. R. Henri Chamber-Loir. Honolulu: Allen & Unwin and University of Hawai'i Press.

Frye, Northrop, ed. 1969. *Anatomy of Criticism: four essays*. Edited by C. ed. N.Y.: Atheneum.

Geertz, Clifford. 1973. *The Interpretation of Cultures*. New York: Basic Books.

Geertz, Cliford. 1976. *The Religion of Java*. Phoenix Edition ed. Chicago: University of Chicago Press.

Gellner, Ernest. 1969. *Saints of the Atlas*. London: Weidenfeld and Nicolson.

Haan, F.D. 1910-12. *de Preanger-Regenschappen onder het Nederlandsch bestuur tot 1811*. Batavia: Bataviaasch Genootschap van Kunsten en Wetenschappen [gedrukt ter Boekdrukerij G. Kolff].

Harari, Josue V., ed. 1979. *Textual Strategies Perspectives in Post-Strucrualist Criticism*. Itacha, New York: Cornell University Press.

Heffner, Robert W. 1985. *Hindu Javanese: Tengger Tradition and Islam*. Princeton, New Jersey: Princeton University Press.

Hermansoemantri, Emuch. 1979. *Sajarah Sukapura: sebuah telaah filologis*. Jakarta: Universitas Indonesia.

Hooker, Virginia Matheson, ed. 1991. *Tuhfat al-Nafis: sejarah Melayu-Islam*. Kuala Lumpur: Dewan Bahasa dan Pustaka, Kementerian Pendidikan Malaysia.

Jackson, Benard S. 1990. Narrative in Legal Practices. In *Narrative in Culture*, edited by C. Nash. London and New York: Routledge.

Jackson, Karl D. 1980. *Traditional Authority, Islam, and Rebelion: A Study of Indonesian Political Behaviour*. London, England: Univesity of California Press.

Johns, A.H. 1965. *The Gift Addressed to The Spirit of The Prophet*. 1965: The Australian national University.

Khaerussalam, A.A. 1992. *Sejarah Perjuangan Syekh Haji Abdul Muhyi Waliyullah Pamijahan*: Grafiana Offset.

Krauss, W. 1995. An Enigmatic Saint: Sheykh Abdulmuhyi of Pamijahan (1640-1715). *Indonesian Circle*.

Levi-Strauss, Claude. 1968-1977. *Structural anthropology / Claude Levi-Strauss*. London: Allen Lane.

Lombard, Denys. 1996. *Nusa Jawa: Silang Budaya*. Jakarta: Gramedia.

Makruf, Jamhari. 2000. Popular Voices of Islam: discourse on Muslim orientations in south central Java, Australian National University, Canberra.

Marcel-Danesi, Paul Perron and. 1999. *Analyzing Cultures*. Bloomington: Indiana University Press.

McCloskey, Donald N. 1990. Storytelling in Economics. In *Narrative in Culture*, edited by C. Nash. London and New York: Routledge.

Miller, J. Hillis. 1990. Narrative. In *Critical Terms for Literary Study*, edited by T. M. Frank Lentricchia. Chicago and London: The University of Chicago Press.

Muhaimin, Abdul Ghoffur. 1995. The Islamic Traditions of Cirebon: Ibadat and Adat Among Javanese Muslims, Department of Anthropology Division of Society and Environment Research Scholl of Pacific and Asian Studies, The Australian National University, Canberra.

———. 2001. *Islam dalam Bingkai Budaya Lokal Potret dari Cirebon*. Jakarta: Logos.

Mulyadi, Sri Wulan Rujiati. 1994. *Kodikologi Melayu di Indonesia*. Jakarta: Universitas Indonesia.

Noth, Winfried. 1990. *Handbook of Semiotics*. Bloomington: University Press.

Pannell, Sandra. 1997. From the Poetics of Place to the Politics of Space: Redefining Cultural Landscapes on Damer, Maluku Utara. In *The Poetic of Power*, edited by J. J. Fox. Canberra: The Comparative Austronesian Project Research School of Pacific and Asian Studies The Australian national University.

Parmentier, R. J. 1997. Semiotic of Anthropology. *Semiotica* 166-1:1-91.

Parmentier, Richard J. 1987. *The Sacred Remains: myth, history, and polity in Belau*. Chicago: University of Chicago Press.

———. 1994. *Signs in society: studies in semiotic anthropology*. Bloomington: Indiana University Press.

Pemberton, John. 1994. *On the subject of 'Java'*. Ithaca: Cornell University Press.

———. 1994. *On the Subject of "Java"*. Ithaca and London: Cornell University Press.

Pleyte, Cornelis Marinus. 1910. *Lutung Kasarung De legende van den Loetoeng Kasaroeng: een gewijde sage uit Tji-rebon*. Batavia: Albrecht & C.

Prickett, Stephen. 2002. *Narrative, Religion and Science*. Cambridge: Cambridge Univesity Press.

Quinn, George. 2002. The Role of Javanese Burial ground in local government, edited by H. C.-L. a. A. Reid. Honolulu: Allen&Unwin.

Ricklefs, M.C. 1998. *The Seen and Unseen Worlds in Java 1726-1749: History, Literature and Islam in the Court of Pakubuwana II*. Edited by A. Miller, *ASAA Southeast Asia Publications*. St. Leonards NSW, Honolulu: Allen & Unwin and univesity of Hawaii Press.

Riddell, Peter G. 1984. Abd al-Rauf al-Singkili's Tarjuman al-Mustafid: a critical study of his treatment of Juz 16. Ph.D, Australian National University, Canberra.

Rinkes, A.D. 1910. De Heiligen van Java. *Tijdscrift voor Indische Tall, Land-, en Volkenkunde* 53:431--581.

Rinkes, D.A. 1909. *Abdoerraoef van Singkel*. Leiden: Leiden University.

Rizvi, S.A.A. 1983. *History of Sufism in India*. India: Muhishram Manoharial.

Robson, Stuart. 1988. *Principles of Indonesian Philology*. Dodrecht-Holland / Providence-USA.

Rochberg-Halton, Eugene. 1986. *Meaning and Modernity Social Theory in the Pragmatic Attitude*. Chicago & London: The University of Chicago Press.

———. 1986. *Meaning and Modernity: Social Theory in the Pragmatic Attitude*. Chicago: University of Chicago Press.

Sakai, Minako. 1997. Rembering Origins: Ancestors and Places in the Gumai Society of South Sumatra. In *The Poetic Power of Place*, edited by J. J. Fox. Canberra: The Comparative Austronesian Project Research School of Pacific and Asian Studies The Australian national University.

Schimmel, Annemarie. 1986. *Dimensi Mistik Dalam Islam*. Jakarta: Pustaka Firdaus.

———. 1994. *Deciphering The Signs of God: A Phenomenological Approach to Islam*. Albany: State University of New York Press.

Scholes, Robert E. 1974. *Title Structuralism in literature: an introduction*. Yale University Press: Published New Haven.

Simuh. 1987. *Mistik Islam Kejawen Radeng Ngabehi Ranggawarsita:suatu studi terhadap serat wirid Hidayat Jati*. Jakarta: Universitas Indonesia.

Sperber, Dan. 1990. The Epidemiology of Beliefs. In *The Social Psychological Study of Widespread Beliefs*, edited by C. F. a. G. Gaskell. Oxford: Clarendon Press.

Stibbe, van D.G. 1929. *Nederlands Indie: land en volk, geschiedenis en bestuur, bedrijf en samenleving, door tal van deskundigen*. Amsterdam: H. Colijn.

Taylor, Christopher S. 1999. *In the Vicinity of The Righteous*. Leiden, Boston, Koln: Brill.

Tilley, Christoper. 1994. *A Phenomenology of Landscape*. Oxford/Providence, USA: Berg.

Trimingham, J. Spencer. 1998. *The Sufi Orders in Islam*. Oxford: Oxford University Press.

Turner, Victor. 1968. *The Ritual Process*. Chicago: Aldine.

———. 1984. Liminality and the Performative Genres. In *Rite, Drama, Festival, Spectacle*, edited by J. J. McAloon. Philadelphia: Institute for the Study of Human Issues.

Turner, Vitor. 1967. *The Forest of Symbols*. Ithaca, New York: Cornell University Press.

Vincent M. Colapietro, Thomas M. Olshewsky. 1996. *Peirce's Doctrine of Signs: Theory, Applications, and Connections*. Berlin, New York: Mouton de Gruyter.

Voll, John O. 1980. Hadith Scholars and tariqahs: An Ulama Group in the 18th Century Haramayn and their Impact in the Islamic World. *JAAS* XV (3-4):246-73.

Wellek, Rene. 1955-1992. *A History of Modern Criticism: 1750-1950*. New Haven: Yale University Pres.

Wessing, Robert. 1978. *Cosmology and Social Behavior in a West Javanese Settlement*. Ohio: Ohio University Center for International Studies.

Whtie, Hayden. 1981. The value of narrativity in the representation of reality. In *On Narrative*, edited by M. W.J.T. Chicago: Chicago Press.

Wilkinson. 1959. *A Malay-English Dictionary*. Singapore: Macmillan.

Winsted, Richard. 1969. *A History of Classical Malay Literature*. Reprint from second edition (1969) ed. New York London Melbourne: Oxford University Press.

Worsley, P. J A, ed. 1972. *Babad Buleleng: a Balinese dynastic genealogy*. The Hague: Nijhoff.

Zoetmulder, P.J. 1985. *Kalangwan Sastra Jawa Kuno Selayang Pandang*. Jakarta: Penerbit Djambatan.

Zulkifli. 1994. *Sufism in Java: The Role of the Pesantren in the Maintenance of Sufism in Java*. Master of Arts, The Australian National University, Canberra.

Zulkifli 2002. Sufism in Java: The Role of the Pesantren in The Maintenance of Sufism in Java. Leiden-Jakarta: INIS.

Original Acknowledgments for the Thesis

I am grateful to the Government of the Commonwealth of Australia for its funding through a scholarship awarded by AIDAB, the Australian International Development Assistance Bureau. AIDAB and AUSAID officers of the ACT Regional Office in Canberra, Mrs Alicia Curtis and Mrs Lynn Tohey gave me full support during my bridging programmes, courses and fieldwork.

The Australian National University in Canberra is a foremost institution for Southeast Asian Studies. It has a strong appreciation of the cultures of the region, an excellent collection of materials, a collegial atmosphere and the largest number of scholars working on the area.

Professor Virginia Hooker of the Southeast Asia Centre, Faculty of Asian Studies, ANU provided me with invaluable support throughout my studies. This thesis is due to her initiative and her encouragement. She responded enthusiastically to the rare prospect of research in Sundanese, sparing no effort to make me welcome. Her knowledge of manuscripts in many regions of Nusantara was soon to shape my perception of the written materials of rural Java.

On her recommendation, my study was transferred from the degree of Master by research to PhD in 1997. Professor Hooker, or Ibu Nia as Indonesian students now call her, provided me with facilities beyond the norm for students in course work. She gave me access to her personal library. She also wrote me a letter, a *surat cap* of recommendation which allowed me to carry out research in the library of the Rijksuniversiteit in Leiden in 1996. When in the middle of 2002 she reminded me to finalise my thesis, again a *surat cap* from her enabled me to obtain a travel grant from the Yayasan Naskah Nusantara and permission for leave from the administrator in the Faculty of Humanities, University of Indonesia. Her *surat cap* was also useful when I arrived in Sydney Airport on the day after the tragic and barbaric Bali bombing. It was her letter that permitted me to make an easy re-entry to Australia at a moment when this might have been difficult for an Indonesian studying rural Islam.

Professor Dr James J. Fox, Director of the Research School of Pacific and Asian Studies, ANU and Dr George Quinn, Head of the Southeast Asia Centre, Faculty of Asian Studies, ANU tirelessly helped me bring my research to a conclusion. In this respect, Jim Fox opened perspectives on the concept of 'living manuscripts' before I went to the field. His knowledge and expertise in Indonesian-Austronesian culture has been recognised by Indonesian students and researchers with another 'professional title', Pak Jim. Close to the deadline of my studies, Pak Jim gave invaluable support in commenting on my thesis drafts and allowing me to use his personal office and library in the 'labyrinth' of the Coombs building. Before I realised it, I had one foot in cultural anthropology. Before I came to The Faculty of Asian Studies, ANU, I had been trained in literary theory and philology, but after undertaking a reading course in the Anthropology of Islam, in his office, I entered a delicate area in the study of culture.

Dr George Quinn is another prominent scholar at the Australian National University, also given the title of 'Pak' by Indonesian students. He has shared his strong insights into the sociology of Indonesian traditional literatures and culture in general. His work on Javanese literature is well known in the Faculty of Letters of the University of Indonesia. He was willing to make a 'pilgrimage' to my field site in Pamijahan, West Java. During his visit we had many valuable on-site discussions. His careful supervision and reading of my drafts brought my thesis to finalisation. He even convinced me that I would submit it on time! I also learned much about diligence and optimism from Pak George. His deep knowledge of sacred sites in Javanese culture was stimulating and inspiring.

I have especially appreciated the companionship of Indonesian colleagues also studying at ANU: Dr. Philipus Tule, Dr. A.G. Muhaimin, Dr. Jamhari Makruf, Dr. Dedi Adhuri, Mr. Hidayat al-Hamid and Mr. Yudhi Latif. They were the best sparring partners in discussing culture and Islam in Canberra. I am also indebted to Dr Minako Sakai of the University of New South Wales at the Australian Defence Force Academy who involved me in her Indonesian Teaching Project when I needed financial support for daily expenses.

It should be noted that I was also supported financially by The Ford Foundation, Jakarta in my library research at the Rijksuniversiteit Leiden in 1996. Dr Mary Zurburchen and Dr Jennifer Lindsay, respectively Director and Officer of the Ford Foundation, gave significant help. The travel grant given by the Ford Foundation Jakarta was made possible through the recommendation of Prof. Dr. Achadiati Ikram and Dr. Tety MPSS of Masyarakat Naskah Nusantara and Asosiasi Tradisi Lisan. Finally, in 2002, Prof. Dr. Achadiati Ikram, my *guru* in philology, through her NGO, Yayasan Naskah Nusantara provided me with another travel grant to finalise my thesis in Canberra.

My closest friends in Australia, Dr. Wendy Mukherjee and Dr. Christine Campbell of the Southeast Asia Centre gave their best efforts to correct my English style. In my early communications with ANU Wendy encouraged me with information on Sundanese holdings in the libraries in Canberra. Her work on Sundanese literature gave me the perspective to think of the importance of Sunda as a cultural category. Sunda was already for her a 'pilgrimage destination', and in 2000 she too visited my field site in Pamijahan.

The people of Pamijahan, Panyalahan and Karangnunggal at large, deserve my sincere expression of thanks. I owe particular debt of gratitude to Pak Kuncen, Ajengan Endang, Pak Beben, and Pak Undang, who willingly devoted so much time to talk with me.

Finally, to thanks Suherti and Nabeela, the two most beautiful women in my life, who realise that a PhD thesis does not just need 'stamina' but also 'imagination'. They were there all the time.

Above all, HE says "All signs are placed in the world for those who understand" (Al-Qur'an).

www.ingramcontent.com/pod-product-compliance
Lightning Source LLC
Chambersburg PA
CBHW060929170426
43192CB00031B/2884